CONTENTS

INTRODUCTION

Want to follow a ketogenic diet but not sure where to start? Struggling with finding delicious and tummy-filling recipes when going "against the grains"? Do not worry! This book will not only give you amazing keto recipes that will get you started in a jiffy, but it will also teach you the greatest tricks for adopting a keto lifestyle forever.

Mouth-watering delights for any occasion and any eater, you will not believe that these recipes will help you restore your health and slim down your body. Ditching carbs do not mean ditching yummy treats, and with these ingenious recipes, you will see that for yourself.

Successfully practiced for more than nine decades, the ketogenic diet has proven to be the ultimate long-term diet for any person. The restriction list may frighten many, but the truth is, this diet is super adaptable, and the food combinations and tasty meals are pretty endless.

Ketogenic Diet — The New Lifestyle

It is common knowledge that our body is designed to run on carbohydrates. We use them to provide our body with the energy that is required for normal functioning. However, what many people are clueless about, is that carbs are not the only source of fuel that our bodies can use. Just like they can run on carbs, our bodies can also use fats as an energy source. When we ditch the carbs and focus on providing our bodies with more fat, then we are embarking on the ketogenic train.

Despite what many people think, the ketogenic diet is not just another fad diet. It has been around since 1920 and has resulted in outstanding results and amazingly successful stories. If you are new to the keto world and have no idea what I am talking about, let me simplify this for you.

For you to truly understand what the ketogenic diet is all about and why you should choose to follow it, let me first explain what happens to your body after consuming a carb-loaded meal.

Imagine you have just swallowed a giant bowl of spaghetti. Your tummy is full, your taste buds are satisfied, and your body is provided with much more carbs than necessary. After consumption, your body immediately starts the process of digestion, during which your body will break down the consumed carbs into glucose, which is a source of energy that your body depends on. So one might ask," what is wrong with carbs?". There are some things. For starters, they raise the blood sugar, they make us fat, and in short, they hurt our overall health. So, how can ketogenic diet help?

A ketogenic diet skips this process by lowering the carbohydrate intake and providing high fat and moderate protein levels. Now, since there is no adequate amount of carbs to use as energy, your liver is forced to find the fuel elsewhere. And since your body is packed with lots of fat, the liver starts using these extra levels of fat as an energy source.

The Benefits Of The Keto Diet

Despite the fact that it is still considered to be 'controversial,' the keto diet is the best dietary choice that one can make. From weight loss to longevity, here are the benefits that following a ketogenic diet can bring to your life:

<u>Loss of Appetite</u>

Cannot tame your cravings? Do not worry. This diet will neither leave you exhausted nor with a rumbling gut. The ketogenic diet will help you say no to that second piece of cake. Once you train your body to run on fat and not on carbs, you will experience a drop in your appetite that will work magic for your figure.

<u>Weight Loss</u>
Since the body is forced to produce only a small amount of glucose, it will also be forced to lower the insulin production. When that happens, your kidneys will start getting rid of the extra sodium, which will lead to weight loss.

<u>HDL Cholesterol Increase</u>
While consuming a diet high in fat and staying clear of the harmful glucose, your body will experience a rise in the good HDL cholesterol levels, which will, in turn, reduce the risk for many cardiovascular problems.

<u>Drop in Blood Pressure</u>
Cutting back on carbs will also bring your blood pressure in check. The drop in the blood pressure can prevent many health problems such as strokes or heart diseases.

<u>Lower Risk of Diabetes</u>
Although this probably goes without saying, it is important to mention this one. When you ditch the carbs, your body is forced to lower the glucose productivity significantly, which naturally leads to a lower risk of diabetes.

<u>Improved Brain Function</u>
Many studies have shown that replacing carbohydrates with fat as an energy source leads to mental clarity and improved brain function. This is yet another reason why you should go keto.

<u>Longevity</u>
I am not saying that this diet will turn you into a 120-hundred-year-old monk; however, it has been scientifically proven that once the oxidative stress levels are lowered, the lifespan gets extended. And since this diet can result in a significant drop in the oxidative stress levels, the corresponding effect it could have on a person's lifespan is clear.

The Keto Plate
First, just because it is called a 'diet' doesn't mean that you are about to spend your days in starvation. The ketogenic diet will neither tell you not to eat five times a day if you want to nor will it leave your bellies empty.

The only rule that the keto diet has is to eat fewer carbohydrates, more foods that are high in fat, and consume a moderate protein intake. But how much is too much and what is the right amount? The general rule of a thumb is that your daily nutrition should consist of: **70-75% Fat; 20-25% Protein; 5-10% Carbohydrates**

To be more precise, it is not recommended that you consume more than 20 grams of carbs when on a ketogenic diet. This macronutrient percentage, however, can be achieved in whichever way you and your belly are comfortable with. For instance, if you crave a carb meal now, and want to eat, for example, 16 grams of carbs at once, you can do so, as long as your other meals do not contain more than 4 grams of carbs combined.

Some recipes in this book offer 0 grams of carbs, while others are packed with a few grams. By making a proper meal plan that works for you, you can easily skip the inconvenience cloaked around this diet, and start receiving the fantastic benefits.

Keto Flu
The term Keto flu describes a very common experience for new ketoers, but it often goes away in the first week. When starting with keto, you may have some slight discomfort or feel fatigue, headache, nausea, cramps, etc.

The reasons Keto flu occurs are two:

1.Keto diet is diuretic; therefore you visit the bathroom quite often, which leads to the loss of electrolytes and water. The solution is either drinking more water or bouillon cube, to replenish electrolytes reserves. I suggest that you also increase the consumption of potassium, magnesium. calcium, and phosphorus.

2.Shifting to Keto is at first a big shock for the body. The reason is that it's designed to process carbs and now there are almost none. You may feel increased fatigue, nausea, etc. The solution is to decrease carbs intake gradually.

What To Eat

Certain foods will help you up your fat intake and provide you with more longer-lasting energy: Meats, Eggs, Fish and Seafood, Bacon, Sausage, Cacao and sugar-free chocolate, Avocado and berries, Leafy Greens - all of them, Vegetables: cucumber, zucchini, asparagus, broccoli, onion, Brussel sprout, cabbage, tomato, eggplants, seaweed, peppers, squash, Full-Fat Dairy (heavy cream, yogurt, sour cream, cheese, etc.); Nuts — nuts are packed with healthy fats, chestnuts, and cashews, as they contain more carbs than the rest of the nuts. Macadamia nuts, walnuts pecans, and almonds are the best for the Keto diet.; Seeds - chia, flaxseeds, sunflower seeds; Sweeteners - stevia, erythritol, xylitol, monk fruit sugar. I use mostly stevia and erythritol. The latter is a sugar alcohol, but it doesn't spike blood sugar thanks to its zero glycemic indexes; Milk - consume full-fat coconut milk or almond milk; Flour - coconut or almond flour and almond meal; Oils - olive oil, avocado oil; Fats - butter or ghee;

What To Avoid

For you to stay on track with your Keto diet, there are certain foods that you need to say farewell to:

Sugar, honey, agave, soda and sugary drinks, and fruit juices. Starchy vegetables such as potatoes, beans, legumes, peas, yams, and corn are usually packed with tons of carbs, so they must be avoided. However, sneaking some starch when your daily carb limit allows, is not exactly a sin. Flours - all-purpose, wheat, and rice. Dried fruits and fruit in general, except for berries. Grains — rice, wheat, and everything made from grains such as pasta or traditional breads are not allowed. No margarine, milk, refined oils and fats such as corn oil, canola oil, vegetable oil, etc.

Keto Swaps

Just because you are not allowed to eat rice or pasta, doesn't mean that you have to sacrifice eating risotto or spaghetti. Well, sort of. For every forbidden item on the keto diet, there is a healthier replacement that will not contradict your dietary goal and will still taste amazing.

Here are the last keto swaps that you need to know to overcome the cravings quicker, and become a Keto chef:

Bread and Buns Bread made from nut flour, mushroom caps, cucumber slices
Wraps and Tortillas Wraps and tortillas made from nut flour, lettuce leaves, kale leaves
Pasta and Spaghetti Spiralized veggies such as zoodles, spaghetti squash, etc.
Lasagna Noodles Zucchini or eggplant slices
Rice Cauliflower rice (ground in a food processor)
Mashed Potatoes Mashed Cauliflower or other veggies
Hash Browns Cauliflower or Spaghetti squash
Flour Coconut flour, Hazelnut flour, Almond Flour
Breadcrumbs Almond flour

Pizza Crust Crust made with almond flour or cauliflower crust
French Fries Carrot sticks, Turnip fries, Zucchini fries
Potato Chips Zucchini chips, Kale chips
Croutons Bacon bits, nuts, sunflower seeds, flax crackers

Traditional High Carb Comfort Foods Made Keto
Bagel 1 plain 50g net carbs **Low-Carb or FatHead Bagel** 1 plain 4.7g net carbs
Bread 1 slice 12g net carbs **Keto Bread** - 1 slice 1.6g net carbs
Risotto 1 cup 40g net carbs **Cauliflower Risotto** 1 cup 4.2g net carbs
Mashed Potatoes 1 cup 30g net carbs **Mashed Cauliflower** 1 cup 5.3g net carbs
Roasted Potatoes 1 cup 20g net carbs **Roasted Radishes** 1 cup 4.4g net carbs
Pasta 1 cup 40g net carbs **Zoodles/Shirataki Noodles** 1 cup 3.6g/1.3g net carbs
Pepperoni Pizza 1 slice 23g net carbs **Cheesy Bell Pepper Pizza** 3.5g net carbs
Waffle 1 waffle 17g **Keto Waffle** 1 waffle 4.6g net carbs

Getting Started In 5 Easy Steps
1.Time to Revise The Pantry - get rid of all pasta, rice, bread, potatoes, corn, wraps, sugary foods, drinks, legumes, fruits, etc. The less you see those foods, the less you will be tempted to drop on the Keto diet.
2.Get the Basics - now that you've cleaned out your pantry it's time to restock. Your journey toward a healthy and energetic lifestyle has started!
3.Set Up Your Kitchen- cooking delicious food requires additional help from some kitchen appliances. They will make your life easier and the cooking quick and efficient.
My kitchen always has food scales, a blender/food processor, hand mixer, cast iron pans, baking dish, heatproof bowls, and a spiralizer. You will need most of these for the recipes in this cookbook, so I strongly suggest you acquire them to maximize results.
4.Create a Meal Plan - having a meal plan is a great start on the Keto diet. It improves your chances of success, and it's essential for beginners on a diet. That's why my team and I developed a complete 21-Day Meal Plan, which, if followed strictly, would make the transition to Keto diet smooth and delicious.
5.Try to Exercise - your body is designed to be in a constant move. Being on Keto diet isn't going to change that. Yeah, I know that it's difficult and you feel tired. You also have to think constantly about the macros and the food you are eating, but I guarantee you that the more you exercise, the easier you will stick to the diet. Any anaerobic activity would suffice - jogging, running, bicycling, even walking for at least 30 minutes a day will activate your body for optimal performance. I would also suggest some strength exercises but always consult previously on how to train, being on a diet, with your fitness instructor.

BREAKFAST & BRUNCH

No-Bread Avocado Sandwich

Ingredients for 2 servings
1 avocado, sliced
1 large red tomato, sliced
2 oz little gem lettuce
½ oz vegan butter, softened
1 oz tofu, sliced
Chopped parsley to garnish
Directions and Total Time: approx. 10 minutes
Arrange the lettuce on a flat serving plate. Smear each leave with vegan butter, and arrange tofu slices in the leaves. Then, share the avocado and tomato slices on each cheese. Garnish the sandwiches with parsley and serve.
Per serving: Cal 385; Net Carbs 4g; Fat 32g; Protein 12g

Blueberry Chia Pudding

Ingredients for 2 servings
¾ cup coconut milk
½ tsp vanilla extract
½ cup blueberries
2 tbsp chia seeds
Chopped walnuts to garnish
Directions and Total Time: approx. 10 min + chilling time
In a blender, pour coconut milk, vanilla extract, and half of the blueberries. Process the ingredients in high speed until the blueberries have incorporated into the liquid. Mix in chia seeds. Share the mixture into 2 breakfast jars, cover, and refrigerate for 4 hours to allow it to gel. Garnish with the remaining blueberries and walnuts. Serve.
Per serving: Cal 301; Net Carbs 6g; Fat 23g; Protein 9g

Creamy Sesame Bread

Ingredients for 6 servings
4 tbsp flax seed powder
1 cup dairy-free cream cheese
5 tbsp sesame oil
1 cup coconut flour
2 tbsp psyllium husk powder
1 tsp salt
1 tsp baking powder
1 tbsp sesame seeds
Directions and Total Time: approx. 40 minutes
In a bowl, mix flax seed powder with 1 ½ cups water until smoothly combined and set aside to soak for 5 minutes. Preheat oven to 400 F. When the flax egg is ready, beat in cream cheese and 4 tbsp sesame oil until mixed. Whisk in coconut flour, psyllium husk powder, salt, and baking powder until adequately blended. Spread the dough in a greased baking tray. Allow to stand for 5 minutes and then brush with remaining sesame oil. Sprinkle with sesame seeds and bake the dough for 30 minutes. Slice and serve.
Per serving: Cal 285; Net Carbs 1g; Fat 26g; Protein 8g

Bulletproof Coffee

Ingredients for 2 servings
2 ½ heaping tbsp ground bulletproof coffee beans
1 tbsp coconut oil
2 tbsp unsalted vegan butter
Directions and Total Time: approx. 3 minutes
Using a coffee maker, brew one cup of coffee with the ground coffee beans and 1 cup of water. Transfer the coffee to a blender and add the coconut oil and vegan butter. Blend the mixture until frothy and smooth.
Per serving: Cal 336; Net Carbs 0g; Fat 36g; Protein 2g

Breakfast Naan Bread

Ingredients for 6 servings
¾ cup almond flour
2 tbsp psyllium husk powder
1 tsp salt + extra for sprinkling
½ tsp baking powder
¼ cup olive oil
2 cups boiling water
8 oz vegan butter
2 garlic cloves, minced
Directions and Total Time: approx. 25 minutes

In a bowl, mix almond flour, psyllium husk powder, ½ teaspoon of salt, and baking powder. Mix in olive oil and boiling water to combine the ingredients, like a thick porridge. Stir and allow the dough rise for 5 minutes. Divide the dough into 6 to 8 pieces and mold into balls. Place the balls on a parchment paper and flatten. Melt half of the vegan butter in a frying pan and fry the naan on both sides to have a golden color. Transfer to a plate and keep warm. Add the remaining vegan butter to the pan and sauté garlic until fragrant, about 2 minutes. Pour the garlic butter into a bowl and serve a_s a dip along with the naan.

Per serving: Cal 224; Net Carbs 3g; Fat 19g; Protein 4g

Seeds Breakfast Loaf

Ingredients for 6 servings
¾ cup coconut flour
1 cup almond flour
3 tbsp baking powder
2 tbsp psyllium husk powder
2 tbsp desiccated coconut
5 tbsp sesame seeds
¼ cup flaxseed
¼ cup hemp seeds
1 tsp ground caraway seeds
1 tbsp poppy seeds
1 tsp salt
1 tsp mixed spice
6 eggs
1 cup cream cheese, softened
¾ cup heavy cream
4 tbsp sesame oil

Directions and Total Time: approx. 55 minutes
Preheat oven to 350 F. In a bowl, mix coconut and almond flours, baking powder, psyllium husk, desiccated coconut, sesame seeds, flaxseed, hemp seeds, ground caraway, poppy seeds, salt, and mixed spice. In another bowl, whisk eggs, cream cheese, heavy cream, and sesame oil. Pour the mixture into the dry ingredients and combine both into a smooth dough. Pour the dough in a greased loaf pan. Bake for 45 minutes. Remove onto a rack, and let cool.

Per serving: Cal 584; Net Carbs 7.4g; Fat 50g; Protein 23g

Blackberry Chia Pudding

Ingredients for 4 servings
1 ½ cups coconut milk
½ cup Greek yogurt
4 tsp sugar-free maple syrup
1 tsp vanilla extract
7 tbsp chia seeds
1 cup fresh blackberries
Chopped almonds to garnish
Mint leaves to garnish

Directions and Total Time: approx. 45 minutes
In a bowl, combine coconut milk, Greek yogurt, sugar-free maple syrup, and vanilla extract until evenly combined. Mix in the chia seeds. Puree half of blackberries in a bowl using a fork and stir in the yogurt mixture. Share the mixture into medium mason jars, cover the lids and refrigerate for 30 minutes to thicken the pudding. Remove the jars, take off the lid, and stir the mixture. Garnish with remaining blackberries, almonds, and some mint leaves.

Per serving: Cal 309; Net Carbs 6.8g; Fat 26g; Protein 7g

Blueberry Soufflé

Ingredients for 4 servings
1 cup frozen blueberries
5 tbsp erythritol
4 egg yolks
3 egg whites
1 tsp olive oil
½ lemon, zested to garnish

Directions and Total Time: approx. 35 minutes
Pour blueberries, 2 tbsp erythritol and 1 tbsp water in a saucepan. Cook until the berries soften and become syrupy, 8-10 minutes. Stir in vanilla and set aside. Preheat oven to 350 F. In a bowl, beat egg yolks and 1 tbsp of erythritol until thick and pale. In another bowl, whisk egg whites until foamy. Add in remaining erythritol and whisk until soft peak forms, 3-4 minutes. Fold egg white mixture into egg yolk mix. Heat olive oil in a pan over low heat. Add in olive oil and pour in the egg mixture; swirl to spread. Cook for 3 minutes and transfer to the oven; bake for 2-3 minutes or until puffed and set. Plate

omelet and spoon blueberry sauce all over. Garnish with lemon zest.
Per serving: Cal 99; Net Carbs 2.8g; Fat 5.9g; Protein 5.5g

Cheddar Biscuits

Ingredients for 4 servings
2 ½ cups almond flour
2 tsp baking powder
2 eggs beaten
3 tbsp melted butter
¾ cup grated cheddar cheese
Directions and Total Time: approx. 30 minutes
Preheat oven to 350 F; line a baking sheet with parchment paper. In a bowl, mix flour, baking powder, and eggs until smooth. Whisk in the melted butter and cheddar cheese until well combined. Mold 12 balls out of the mixture and arrange on the sheet at 2-inch intervals. Bake for 25 minutes until golden brown. Remove, let cool and serve.
Per serving: Cal 355; Net Carbs 1.4g, Fat 28g, Protein 21g

Vanilla Buttermilk Pancakes

Ingredients for 4 servings
½ cup almond flour
½ tsp baking powder
1 tbsp swerve sugar
½ cup buttermilk
1 lemon, juiced
3 eggs
1 vanilla pod
2 tbsp unsalted butter
2 tbsp olive oil
3 tbsp sugar-free maple syrup
Greek yogurt to serve
Blueberries to serve
Directions and Total Time: approx. 25 minutes
Into a bowl, sift almond flour and baking powder and stir in swerve sugar. In a small bowl, whisk buttermilk, lemon juice, and eggs. Combine the mixture with the flour mix until smooth. Cut the vanilla pod open and scrape the beans into the flour mixture. Stir to incorporate evenly. In a skillet, melt a quarter each of the butter and olive oil and spoon in 1 ½ tablespoons of the pancake mixture into the pan. Cook for 4 minutes or until small bubbles appear. Flip and cook for 2 minutes

or until set and golden. Repeat cooking until the batter finishes using the remaining butter and olive oil in the same proportions. Plate the pancakes, drizzle with maple syrup, top with a generous dollop of yogurt, and scatter some blueberries on top.
Per serving: Cal 168; Net Carbs 1.6g; Fat 11g; Protein 7g

Berry & Mascarpone Bowl

Ingredients for 4 servings
1 ½ cups blueberries and raspberries
4 cups Greek yogurt
liquid stevia to taste
1 ½ cups mascarpone cheese
1 cup raw pistachios
Directions and Total Time: approx. 10 minutes
Mix the yogurt, stevia, and mascarpone in a bowl until evenly combined. Divide the mixture into 4 bowls, share the berries and pistachios on top of the cream. Serve.
Per serving: Cal 480, Net Carbs 5g, Fat 40g, Protein 20g

Avocado Halloumi Scones

Ingredients for 4 servings
1 cup crumbled halloumi cheese
2 cups almond flour
3 tsp baking powder
½ cup butter, cold
1 avocado, pitted and mashed
1 large egg
1/3 cup buttermilk
Directions and Total Time: approx. 35 minutes
Preheat oven to 350 F and line a baking sheet with parchment paper. In a bowl, combine flour and baking powder. Add butter and mix. Top with halloumi cheese, avocado, and combine again. Whisk the egg with buttermilk and stir in the halloumi mix. Mold 8-10 scones out to the batter. Place on the baking sheet and bake for 25 minutes or until the scones turn a golden color. Let cool.
Per serving: Cal 432; Net Carbs 2.3g; Fat 42g; Protein 10g

Almond-Berry Pancakes with Sweet Syrup

Ingredients for 4 servings

1 handful of strawberries and raspberries, mashed
1 handful fresh strawberries and raspberries for topping
½ cup almond flour
1 tsp baking soda
A pinch of salt
1 tbsp swerve sugar
A pinch of cinnamon powder
1 egg
½ cup almond milk
2 tsp butter
1 cup Greek yogurt
Stevia for serving
Directions and Total Time: approx. 25 minutes
In a bowl, combine almond flour, baking soda, salt, swerve, and cinnamon. Whisk in mashed berries, and egg, and mix in the milk until smooth. Melt ½ tsp of butter in a skillet and pour in 1 tbsp of the mixture into the pan. Cook until small bubbles appear, flip, and cook until golden. Transfer to a plate and proceed using up the remaining batter for pancakes. Top pancakes with yogurt, berries, and stevia.
Per serving: Cal 234; Net Carbs 7.6g; Fat 17g; Protein 9g

Toast Sticks with Yogurt Berry Bowls

Ingredients for 2 servings
2 cups Greek yogurt
2 tbsp sugar-free maple syrup
½ cup strawberries, halved
½ cup blueberries
½ cup raspberries
2 eggs
¼ tsp cinnamon powder
¼ tsp nutmeg powder
2 tbsp almond milk
Salt and black pepper to taste
4 slices zero carb bread
1 ½ tbsp butter
1 tbsp olive oil
Directions and Total Time: approx. 15 minutes
In a bowl, mix yogurt, maple syrup, and berries. Chill the salad for about 1 hour. In another bowl, whisk eggs, cinnamon, nutmeg, milk, salt, and pepper. Set aside. Cut each slice into four strips. Heat butter and olive oil in a skillet. Dip each bread strip into the egg

mixture and fry in the olive oil, flipping once until golden brown on both sides. Transfer to a serving plate and serve with the salad.
Per serving: Cal 207; Net Carbs 7.3g; Fat 14g; Protein 7.7g

Quick Protein Bars

Ingredients for 4 servings
1 cup almond butter
4 tbsp coconut oil
2 scoops vanilla protein
½ cup sugar-free maple syrup
4 tbsp unsweetened chocolate chips + extra for topping
1 tsp cinnamon powder
1 tbsp chopped toasted peanuts
Directions and Total Time: approx. 5 min + chilling time
Line a baking sheet with parchment paper. In a bowl, mix almond butter, coconut oil, vanilla protein, maple syrup, salt, chocolate chips, and cinnamon. Spread the mixture onto the sheet and scatter chocolate and peanuts on top. Refrigerate until firm, at least 1 hour. Cut into bars.
Per serving: Cal 326; Net Carbs 0.4g, Fat 29g, Protein 0.5g

Breakfast Ratatouille with Eggs & Avocado

Ingredients for 2 servings
1 tbsp olive oil
1 zucchini, sliced
1 medium red onion, sliced
1 red bell pepper, sliced
1 yellow bell pepper, sliced
2 medium tomatoes, diced
1 cup vegetable broth
4 eggs
1 avocado, chopped
2 tbsp chopped parsley
Directions and Total Time: approx. 50 minutes
Heat olive oil in a skillet and sauté the zucchini, onion, and bell peppers for 10 minutes. Pour in tomatoes, vegetable broth, and season with salt and pepper. Bring to a boil and then simmer until the sauce thickens slightly. Create four holes in the sauce and break an egg into each hole. Allow the eggs to cook through and turn the heat off. Plate the

sauce, top with the avocado, and garnish with parsley.
Per serving: Cal 450; Net Carbs 5.6g; Fat 32g; Protein 18g

Ultra Flaxy Cookies

Ingredients for 4 servings
¼ cup golden flaxseed meal finely ground
1 ½ cups butter, melted
2 eggs
2 cups sour cream
3 tbsp water
2 tbsp apple cider vinegar
2 tsp cream of tartar
3 cups almond flour
2 tsp xanthan gum
1 tbsp whey protein powder
4 tsp baking powder
2 tsp baking soda
½ tsp salt
3 tbsp coconut flour
Directions and Total Time: approx. 30 minutes
Preheat oven to 350 F; line a baking sheet with parchment paper. Using a food processor, mix butter, eggs, sour cream, water, vinegar, and cream of tartar until smooth. In a bowl, mix flours, xanthan gum, protein, baking powder, baking soda, salt, and flaxseed. Gradually, pour the mixture into the food processor and mix until smooth batter forms. Mold 12 balls out of the mixture and arrange on the baking sheet at 2-inch intervals. Bake for 25 minutes or until golden brown. Remove, let cool and serve.
Per serving: Cal 335; Net Carbs 5.2g, Fat 38g, Protein 5g

Shakshuka

Ingredients for 2 servings
1 tsp olive oil
1 garlic clove, minced
1 small white onion, chopped
1 red bell pepper, chopped
1 small green chili, minced
1 cup diced tomatoes
½ cup tomato sauce
Salt and black pepper to taste
1 tsp cumin powder
1/3 cup baby kale, chopped
½ tsp dried basil
4 large eggs
¼ cup yogurt
½ lemon, juiced
Directions and Total Time: approx. 40 minutes
Heat olive oil in a deep skillet and sauté garlic, onion, bell pepper, and green chili until softened, 5 minutes. Stir in tomatoes, tomato sauce, salt, pepper, and cumin.
Cover and cook for 10 minutes. Add kale to wilt and stir in basil. Create four holes in the sauce with a wooden spoon, crack an egg into each hole, and sprinkle with parsley. Cover with a lid and cook until the eggs are firm, 8-10 minutes. In a bowl, mix yogurt with lemon juice and set aside. Plate shakshuka, top with a dollop of yogurt mixture, and serve.
Per serving: Cal 320; Net Carbs 8g; Fat 16.9g; Protein 17g

Gruyere Breakfast Soufflés

Ingredients for 4 servings
2 ½ cup Gruyere cheese, grated + a little extra for topping
2 egg whites, beaten until stiff
2 ½ tbsp butter, softened
2 ½ tbsp almond flour
1 ½ tsp mustard powder
½ cup almond milk
4 yolks, beaten
Directions and Total Time: approx. 20 minutes
Preheat oven to 370 F and brush the inner parts of 4 ramekins with butter. Melt the remaining butter in a pan over low heat and stir in flour for 1 minute. Remove from the heat, mix in mustard powder until evenly combined and slowly whisk in milk until no lumps form. Return to medium heat, while stirring until the sauce comes to a rolling boil. Stir in Gruyere cheese until melted. Into the egg yolks whisk ¼ cup of the warmed milk mixture, then combine with the remaining milk sauce. Fold in egg whites gradually until evenly combined. Spoon the mixture into the ramekins and top with the remaining cheese. Bake for 8 minutes, until the soufflés have a slight wobble, but soft at the center. Let cool and serve.
Per serving: Cal 488; Net Carbs 3.8g; Fat 39g; Protein 26g

Pumpkin Donuts

Ingredients for 4 servings

½ cup heavy cream

1 egg

2 egg yolks

½ tsp vanilla extract

2 tsp pumpkin pie spice

½ cup pumpkin puree

¼ cup sugar-free maple syrup

1 cup almond flour

¼ cup coconut flour

1 tsp baking powder

A pinch of salt

For the glaze:

2 cups swerve confectioner's sugar

4 tbsp water

Directions and Total Time: approx. 25 minutes

Preheat oven to 350 F. In a bowl, mix heavy cream, egg, egg yolks, vanilla extract, pie spice, pumpkin pie puree, and maple syrup. One after another, smoothly mix in almond and coconut flours, baking powder, and salt. Pour the batter into greased donut cups and bake for 18 minutes or until set. Remove, flip onto a wire rack and let cool. In a bowl, whisk the swerve and water until smooth. Swirl the glaze over the donut and enjoy immediately.

Per serving: Cal 189; Net Carbs 4.3g, Fat 16g, Protein 7.7g

Chorizo, Goat Cheese & Eggs

Ingredients for 4 servings

2 green onions, thinly sliced diagonally

1 tsp olive oil

1 tsp smoked paprika

3 oz chorizo, diced

4 eggs

½ cup crumbled goat cheese

2 tbsp fresh parsley, chopped

Directions and Total Time: approx. 15 minutes

Preheat oven to 350 F. In a pan, heat olive oil along with paprika for 30 seconds. Add the chorizo and cook until lightly browned; set aside. Crack the eggs into the pan, cook for 2 minutes, and then sprinkle with chorizo and crumble goat cheese all around the egg white, but not on the yolks. Transfer the pan to oven and bake for 2 more minutes, until the yolks are quite set, but still runny within. Garnish with green onions and parsley. Serve.

Per serving: Cal 257; Net Carbs 5.6g; Fat 18g; Protein 17g

Berries & Cream Bowl with Nuts

Ingredients for 6 servings

5 tbsp flax seed powder

1 cup dark chocolate

1 cup butter

1 pinch salt

1 tsp vanilla extract

2 cups fresh blueberries

4 tbsp lemon juice

1 tsp vanilla extract

2 cups coconut cream

4 oz walnuts, chopped

½ cup roasted coconut chips

Directions and Total Time: approx. 10 minutes

Preheat oven to 320 F. Line a springform pan with parchment paper. In a bowl, mix the flax seed powder with 2/3 cup water and allow thickening for 5 minutes. Break chocolate and butter into a bowl and microwave for 2 minutes. Share the flax egg into 2 bowls; whisk the salt into one portion and then, 1 tsp of vanilla into the other. Pour the chocolate mixture into the vanilla mixture and combine well. Fold into the other flax egg mixture. Pour the batter into the springform pan and bake for 20 minutes. When ready, slice the cake into squares and share into serving bowls. Pour blueberries, lemon juice, and remaining vanilla into a small bowl. Break the blueberries and let sit for a few minutes. Whip coconut cream with a whisk until a soft peak forms. To serve, spoon the cream on the cakes, top with blueberry mixture, and sprinkle with walnuts and coconut flakes.

Per serving: Cal 345; Fat 31g; Net Carbs 7g; Protein 6g

Coffee-Flavored Muffins

Ingredients for 4 servings

For the batter:

2 tbsp butter, softened
2 oz cream cheese, softened
1/3 cup sugar-free maple syrup
4 eggs
2 tsp vanilla extract
½ cup vanilla almond milk
1 cup almond flour
2 tsp instant coffee powder
½ cup coconut flour
1 tsp baking powder

For the topping:

1 cup almond flour
2 tbsp coconut flour
¼ cup swerve sugar
¼ cup butter softened
1 tsp cinnamon powder
½ tsp sugar-free maple syrup

Directions and Total Time: approx. 35 minutes

Preheat oven to 350 F and line a 12-cup muffin pan with paper liners. In a bowl, whisk butter, cream cheese, maple syrup, eggs, vanilla, and almond milk until smooth. In another bowl, mix almond flour, coffee powder, coconut flour, baking powder, and a pinch of salt. Combine both mixtures and fill the muffin cups two-thirds way up. In a bowl, mix flours, swerve, butter, cinnamon powder, and maple syrup. Spoon the mixture onto the muffin batter and bake for 25 minutes or until a toothpick inserted comes out clean. Remove from the oven, and let cool to serve.
Per serving: Cal 294; Net Carbs 5g, Fat 23g, Protein 17g

Pecan Cookies

Ingredients for 8 servings
1 egg
2 cups ground pecans
¼ cup sweetener
½ tsp baking soda
1 tbsp butter
20 pecan halves

Directions and Total Time: approx. 25 minutes

Preheat oven to 350 F. Mix the ingredients, except for the pecan halves, until combined. Make 20 balls out of the mixture and press them with your thumb onto a lined cookie sheet. Top each cookie with a pecan half. Bake for about 12 minutes. Serve warm or chilled.
Per serving: Cal 101; Net Carbs 0.6g; Fat 11g; Protein 2g

Cinnamon Faux Rice Pudding

Ingredients for 6 servings
1 ¼ cups coconut cream
1 tsp vanilla extract
1 tsp cinnamon powder
1 cup mashed tofu
2 oz fresh strawberries

Directions and Total Time: approx. 17 minutes

Pour coconut cream into a bowl and whisk until a soft peak forms. Mix in vanilla and cinnamon. Lightly fold in tofu and refrigerate for 10-15 minutes to set. Spoon into serving glasses, top with the strawberries and serve.
Per serving: Cal 225; Fat 20g; Net Carbs 3g; Protein 6g

Zucchini Muffins

Ingredients for 6 servings
½ cup almond flour
1 tsp baking powder
½ tsp baking soda
1 ½ tsp mustard powder
Salt and black pepper to taste
1/3 cup almond milk
1 large egg
5 tbsp olive oil
½ cup grated cheddar cheese
2 zucchinis, grated
6 green olives, sliced
1 spring onion, chopped
1 red bell pepper, chopped
1 tbsp freshly chopped thyme

Directions and Total Time: approx. 10 minutes

Preheat oven to 325 F. In a bowl, combine flour, baking powder, baking soda, mustard powder, salt, pepper. In a smaller bowl, whisk milk, egg, and olive oil. Mix the wet ingredients into dry ingredients and add cheese, zucchini, olives, spring onion, bell pepper, and thyme; mix well. Spoon the batter into greased muffin cups, and bake for 30 minutes or until golden brown. Let the muffins to cool.

Per serving: Cal 172; Net Carbs 1.6g; Fat 16g; Protein 4g

Chia Pudding with Blackberries

Ingredients for 2 servings
1 cup full-fat natural yogurt
2 tsp swerve
2 tbsp chia seeds
1 cup fresh blackberries
1 tbsp lemon zest
Mint leaves, to serve

Directions and Total Time: approx. 35 minutes
Mix together the yogurt and swerve. Stir in chia seeds. Reserve 4 blackberries for garnish and mash the remaining with a fork until pureed. Stir in the yogurt mixture. Refrigerate for 30 minutes. Divide the mixture into 2 glasses. Serve topped with raspberries and mint leaves.

Per serving: Cal 169, Net Carbs 1.7g, Fat 10g, Protein 7g

Lemon Muffins

Ingredients for 4 servings
For the muffins:
½ cup butter, softened
¾ cup swerve sugar
3 large eggs
1 lemon, zested and juiced
1 ½ cups almond flour
½ cup coconut flour
2 tsp baking powder
¼ tsp arrowroot starch
½ tsp vanilla extract
1 cup sour cream
A pinch of salt

For the topping:
3 tbsp butter, melted
¾ cup almond flour
3 Tbsp swerve sugar
1 tsp lemon zest
1 tbsp coconut flour

For the lemon glaze:
½ cup swerve confectioner's sugar
3 tbsp lemon juice

Directions and Total Time: approx. 35 minutes
For the muffins:
Preheat oven to 350 F and line a 12-cup muffin pan with paper liners. In a bowl, mix butter, swerve, eggs, lemon zest, and lemon juice until smooth. In another bowl, combine flours, baking powder, and arrowroot. Combine both mixtures and mix in vanilla, sour cream, and salt until smooth. Fill the cups two-thirds way up; set aside.

For the topping:
In a bowl, mix butter, almond flour, swerve, lemon zest, and coconut flour until well combined.

Spoon the mixture onto the muffin batter and bake for 25 minutes or until a toothpick inserted comes out clean. Remove the muffins from the oven and cool while you prepare the glaze.

For the glaze:
In a bowl, whisk confectioner's sugar and lemon juice until smooth and semi-thick. Drizzle over the muffins.

Per serving: Cal 439; Net Carbs 7.6g; Fat 42g; Protein 8g

Yogurt Strawberry Pie with Basil

Ingredients for 4 servings
For the crust:
2 eggs
1 tsp vanilla extract
¼ cup erythritol
¼ tsp salt
1 cup almond flour
½ cup cold butter, cubed
5 tbsp cold water

1 tbsp olive oil

For the filling:

1 cup unsweetened strawberry jam

¼ cup heavy cream

1/3 cup erythritol

1 cup Greek yogurt

1 tbsp chopped basil leaves

Directions and Total Time: approx. 90 min + chilling time

For the piecrust:

In a bowl, whisk eggs, olive oil, and vanilla until well combined. In another bowl, mix erythritol, salt, and flour. Combine both mixtures into a stand mixer and blend until smooth dough forms. Add butter and mix until breadcrumb-like mixture forms. Add one tbsp of water, mix further until the dough begins to come together. Keep adding water until it sticks together. Lightly flour a working surface, turn the dough onto it, knead a few times until formed into a ball, and comes together smoothly. Divide into half and flatten each piece into a disk. Wrap each dough in plastic and refrigerate for 1 hour.

Preheat oven to 375 F and grease a 9-inch pie pan with olive oil. Remove the dough from the fridge, let it stand at room temperature and roll one piece into 12-inch round. Fit this piece into the bottom and walls to the rim of the pie pan while shaping to take the pan's form. Roll out the other dough into an 11-inch round and set aside.

For the filling:

Whip the heavy cream and erythritol in a stand mixer until creamy and smooth. Mix in the Greek yogurt, strawberry jam, basil and mix on low speed until well combined. Fill the pie dough in the pie pan with the filling and level well. Brush the overhanging pastry with water and attach the top pastry on top of the filling. Press the edges to merge the dough ends and trim the overhanging ends to 1-inch. Fold the edge under itself and then, decoratively crimp. Cut 2 slits on the top crust. Bake the pie for 75 minutes until the bottom crust is golden and the filling bubbly.

Per serving: Cal 341; Net Carbs 6.1g; Fat 33g; Protein 5.6g

STARTERS & SALADS

Cherry Tomato Salad with Chorizo

Ingredients for 4 servings
2 ½ cups cherry tomatoes
2 ½ tbsp olive oil
4 chorizo sausages, chopped
2 tsp red wine vinegar
1 small red onion, chopped
2 tbsp chopped cilantro
Salt and black pepper to taste
Sliced Kalamata olives

Directions and Total Time: approx. 10 minutes
Heat 1 tbsp of olive oil in a skillet and fry chorizo until golden. Cut in half tomatoes. In a salad bowl, whisk the remaining olive oil with vinegar and add onion, tomatoes, cilantro, and chorizo. Mix to coat in the dressing; season with salt and pepper. Garnish with olives to serve.

Per serving: Cal 138; Net Carbs 5.2g; Fat 8.9g; Protein 7g

Broccoli Salad with Tempeh & Cranberries

Ingredients for 4 servings
3 oz vegan butter
¾ lb tempeh slices, cubed
1 lb broccoli florets
Salt and black pepper to taste
2 oz almonds
½ cup frozen cranberries

Directions and Total Time: approx. 10 minutes
In a deep skillet, melt vegan butter over medium heat and fry tempeh cubes until brown on all sides. Add in broccoli and stir-fry for 6 minutes. Season with salt and pepper. Turn the heat off. Stir in almonds and cranberries to warm through. Share the salad into bowls and serve.

Per serving: Cal 740; Net Carbs 7g; Fat 72g; Protein 12g

Tangy Nutty Brussel Sprout Salad

Ingredients for 4 servings
1 lb Brussels sprouts, grated
1 lemon, juice and zest
½ cup olive oil
Salt and black pepper to taste
1 tbsp vegan butter
1 tsp chili paste
2 oz pecans
1 oz pumpkin seeds
1 oz sunflower seeds
½ tsp cumin powder

Directions and Total Time: approx. 20 minutes
Place Brussels sprouts in a salad bowl. In a bowl, mix lemon juice, zest, olive oil, salt, and pepper, and drizzle the dressing over Brussels sprouts. Toss and let marinate for 10 minutes. Melt vegan butter in a pan. Stir in chili paste, pecans, pumpkin and sunflower seeds, cumin powder, and salt. Cook on low heat for 4 minutes just to heat up; let cool. Mix nuts and seeds with Brussel sprouts to serve.

Per serving: Cal 420; Net Carbs 8g; Fat 35g; Protein 12g

Pesto Caprese Salad Stacks with Anchovies

Ingredients for 4 servings
4 red tomato slices
4 yellow tomato slices
12 fresh mozzarella slices
1 cup basil pesto
4 anchovy fillets in oil

Directions and Total Time: approx. 10 minutes
On a serving platter, alternately stack a tomato slice, a mozzarella slice, an yellow tomato slice, another mozzarella slice, a red tomato slice, and then one a mozzarella slice. Repeat making 3 more stacks in the same way. Spoon pesto all over. Arrange anchovies on top to serve.

Per serving: Cal 178; Net Carbs 3.5g; Fat 6.1g; Protein 17g

Antipasti Skewers

Ingredients for 4 servings
4 zucchini lengthwise slices
8 cubes cheddar cheese
4 mini bamboo skewers
8 cherry tomatoes
8 fresh mint leaves

Directions and Total Time: approx. 45 minutes

Lay zucchini slices on a flat surface and place 2 cheddar cubes on one end of each slice. Wrap zucchini around the cheese cubes and insert a skewer each to secure. Alternately, thread the tomatoes and mint leaves onto the skewers and season with salt. Place the skewers on a plate, cover with plastic wrap, and chill for 30 minutes. Serve.
Per serving: Cal 93; Net Carbs 1.8g; Fat 3.9g; Protein 7g

Greek Salad

Ingredients for 2 servings
½ yellow bell pepper, sliced
3 tomatoes, sliced
½ cucumber, sliced
½ red onion, sliced thinly
½ cup tofu cheese, cubed
10 Kalamata olives, pitted
½ tbsp red wine vinegar
4 tbsp olive oil
Salt and ground black pepper
2 tsp dried oregano
Directions and Total Time: approx. 10 minutes
Pour bell pepper, tomatoes, cucumber, red onion, and tofu cheese in a bowl. Drizzle red wine vinegar and olive oil all over and season with salt, pepper, and oregano; toss to coat. Transfer to a salad platter, top with olives, and serve.
Per serving: Cal 580; Net Carbs 13g; Fat 49g; Protein 15g

Buttered Greens with Almonds & Tofu Salad

Ingredients for 4 servings
2 tbsp olive oil
1 (7 oz) block tofu, cubed
2 tbsp butter
1 cup green beans, trimmed
1 cup asparagus, halved
Salt and black pepper to taste
½ lemon, juiced
4 tbsp chopped almonds
Directions and Total Time: approx. 25 minutes
Heat olive oil in a skillet and fry the tofu until golden, 10 minutes; set aside. Add butter to the skillet and pour in green beans and asparagus; season with salt and pepper, toss and cook until softened. Mix in tofu and stir-

fry further for 5 minutes. Drizzle with lemon juice and scatter almonds on top. Serve warm.
Per serving: Cal 237; Net Carbs 3.9g; Fat 15g; Protein 13g

Zucchini & Dill Bowls with Goat-Feta Cheese

Ingredients for 4 servings
4 zucchinis, spiralized
Salt and black pepper to taste
½ lemon, zested and juiced
1 tbsp olive oil
¼ tsp Dijon mustard
1 tbsp chopped dill leaves
½ cup baby kale
1/3 cup crumbled goat cheese
1/3 cup crumbled feta cheese
2 tbsp toasted pine nuts
Directions and Total Time: approx. 35 minutes
Put the zucchinis in a bowl and season with salt and pepper. In a small bowl, mix the lemon juice, olive oil, and mustard. Pour the mixture over the zucchini and toss evenly. Add the dill, kale, goat cheese, feta cheese, and pine nuts. Toss to combine and serve.
Per serving: Cal 457; Net Carbs 9.5g; Fat 36g; Protein 26g

Roasted Bell Pepper Salad with Olives

Ingredients for 4 servings
8 large red bell peppers, deseeded and cut in wedges
½ tsp swerve sugar
2 ½ tbsp olive oil
1/3 cup arugula
1/3 cup pitted Kalamata olives
1 tbsp mint leaves
3 tbsp toasted chopped walnuts
½ tbsp balsamic vinegar
Crumbled goat cheese
Toasted pine nuts for topping
Salt and black pepper to taste
Directions and Total Time: approx. 30 minutes
Preheat oven to 400 F. Pour bell peppers on a roasting pan; season with swerve sugar and drizzle with half of the olive oil. Roast for 20 minutes or until slightly charred; set aside to cool. Put arugula in a salad bowl and scatter

with roasted bell peppers, olives, mint, walnuts, and drizzle with vinegar and olive oil. Season with salt and pepper. Toss, top with goat cheese and pine nuts and serve.
Per serving: Cal 163; Net Carbs 4.3g; Fat 13g; Protein 3.3g

Grandma's Cauliflower Salad with Peanuts

Ingredients for 4 servings
1 small head cauliflower, cut into florets
12 green olives, chopped
8 sun-dried tomatoes, drained
3 tbsp chopped scallions
1 lemon, zested and juiced
2 tbsp sesame oil
A handful of toasted peanuts
3 tbsp chopped parsley
½ cup watercress
Salt and black pepper to taste
Lemon wedges to garnish
Directions and Total Time: approx. 20 minutes
Bring water to a boil in a pot. Pour cauliflower into a steamer basket and soften over the boiling water, 10 minutes. Transfer cauliflower to a salad bowl. Add in olives, tomatoes, scallions, lemon zest and juice, sesame oil, peanuts, parsley, and watercress. Season with salt, pepper, and mix using a spoon. Serve with lemon wedges.
Per serving: Cal 203; Net Carbs 6.4g; Fat 15g; Protein 6.6g

Bruschetta with Tomato & Basil

Ingredients for 4 servings
3 ripe tomatoes, chopped
6 fresh basil leaves
5 tbsp olive oil
Salt to taste
4 slices zero carb bread, halved
1 garlic clove, halved
Directions and Total Time: approx. 1 hour 15 minutes
In a bowl, mix tomatoes and basil until combined. Drizzle with 2 tbsp olive oil and salt; do not stir. Set aside.
Brush bread slices with the remaining olive oil, arrange on a baking sheet, and place under the broiler. Cook for 2 minutes per side or until lightly browned. Transfer to a plate and rub garlic on both sides. Cover with

tomato topping. Drizzle a little more of olive oil on top and serve.
Per serving: Cal 212; Net Carbs 2.7g; Fat 19g; Protein 8g

Speedy Beef Carpaccio

Ingredients for 4 servings
1 tbsp olive oil
½ lemon, juiced
Salt and black pepper to taste
¼ lb rare roast beef, sliced
1 ½ cups baby arugula
¼ cup grated Parmesan cheese
Directions and Total Time: approx. 10 minutes
In a bowl, whisk olive oil, lemon juice, salt, and pepper until well combined. Spread the beef on a large serving plate, top with arugula and drizzle the olive oil mixture on top. Sprinkle with grated Parmesan cheese and serve.
Per serving: Cal 106; Net Carbs 4.1g; Fat 5g; Protein 10g

Roasted Asparagus with Goat Cheese

Ingredients for 4 servings
1 lb asparagus, halved
2 tbsp olive oil
½ tsp dried tarragon
½ tsp dried oregano
½ tsp sesame seeds
1 tbsp sugar-free maple syrup
½ cup arugula
4 tbsp crumbled goat cheese
2 tbsp hazelnuts
1 lemon, cut into wedges
Directions and Total Time: approx. 30 minutes
Preheat oven to 350 F. Pour asparagus on a baking tray, drizzle with olive oil, tarragon, oregano, salt, pepper, and sesame seeds. Toss and roast for 15 minutes; remove and drizzle the maple syrup, and continue cooking for 5 minutes or until slightly charred. Spread arugula in a salad bowl and spoon the asparagus on top. Scatter with the goat cheese, hazelnuts, and serve with the lemon wedges.
Per serving: Cal 146; Net Carbs 3.4g; Fat 13g; Protein 4.4g

Savory Gruyere & Bacon Cake

Ingredients for 4 servings
½ cup shredded Gruyere cheese
4 eggs, eggs yolks and whites separated
2 tbsp butter
2 tbsp almond flour
1 cup heavy cream
6 slices bacon, chopped
Directions and Total Time: approx. 50 minutes
Melt butter in a pan over medium heat and mix in 1 tbsp of almond flour until well combined. Whisk in heavy cream, bring to a boil and while stirring, mix in the remaining almond flour until smooth. Turn the heat off. Cool the mixture for 3 minutes and slowly mix the batter into the egg yolks until well combined without cooking. Stir in Gruyere cheese until evenly distributed. Beat the egg whites in a mixer until stiff peak forms. Fold the egg whites into the egg yolk mixture until well combined. Divide the mixture between 4 ramekins, top with bacon and bake in the oven for 35 minutes at 320 F.
Per serving: Cal 495; Net Carbs 2g, Fat 46g, Protein 17.3g

Warm Mushroom & Yellow Pepper Salad

Ingredients for 4 servings
1 cup mixed mushrooms, chopped
2 tbsp sesame oil
2 yellow bell peppers, sliced
1 garlic clove, minced
2 tbsp tamarind sauce
½ tsp hot sauce
1 tsp sugar-free maple syrup
½ tsp ginger paste
Salt and black pepper to taste
Chopped toasted pecans
Sesame seeds to garnish
Directions and Total Time: approx. 20 minutes
Heat half of the sesame oil in a skillet, sauté bell peppers and mushrooms for 8-10 minutes; season with salt and pepper. In a bowl, mix garlic, tamarind sauce, hot sauce, maple syrup, and ginger paste. Stir the mix into the vegetables and stir-fry for 2-3 minutes. Divide salad between 4 plates; drizzle with the remaining sesame oil and garnish with pecans and sesame seeds. Serve.

Per serving: Cal 289; Net Carbs 5.2g; Fat 27g; Protein 4.2g

Broccoli, Spinach & Feta Salad

Ingredients for 4 servings
2 tbsp olive oil
1 tbsp white wine vinegar
2 tbsp poppy seeds
Salt and black pepper to taste
2 cups broccoli slaw
2 cups chopped spinach
1/3 cup chopped walnuts
1/3 cup sunflower seeds
1/3 cup blueberries
2/3 cup chopped feta cheese
Directions and Total Time: approx. 15 minutes
In a bowl, whisk olive oil, vinegar, poppy seeds, salt, and pepper; set aside. In a salad bowl, combine the broccoli slaw, spinach, walnuts, sunflower seeds, blueberries, and feta cheese. Drizzle the dressing on top, toss, and serve.
Per serving: Cal 397; Net Carbs 4.9g; Fat 3.8g; Protein 9g

Tofu Pops

Ingredients for 4 servings
1 (14 oz) block tofu, cubed
1 bunch of chives, chopped
1 lemon, zested and juiced
12 slices bacon
12 mini skewers
1 tsp butter
Directions and Total Time: approx. 1 hour 17 minutes
Mix chives, lemon zest, and juice in a bowl and toss the tofu cubes in the mixture. Marinate for 1 hour. Remove the zest and chives off the cubes and wrap each tofu in a bacon slice; insert each skewer and the end of the bacon. Melt butter in a skillet and fry tofu skewers until the bacon browns and crisps. Serve with mayo dipping sauce.
Per serving: Cal 392; Net Carbs 9g, Fat 22g, Protein 18g

Blackberry Camembert Puffs

Ingredients for 4 servings
For the pastry cups:
¼ cup butter, cold and crumbled
¼ cup almond flour

3 tbsp coconut flour
½ tsp xanthan gum
½ tsp salt
4 tbsp cream cheese, softened
1/4 teaspoon cream of tartar
3 whole eggs, unbeaten
3 tbsp erythritol
1 ½ tsp vanilla extract
1 whole egg, beaten

For the filling:
5 oz Camembert, sliced and cut into 16 cubes
1 tsp butter
1 yellow onion, chopped
3 tbsp red wine
1 tbsp balsamic vinegar
5 tbsp erythritol
½ cup fresh blackberries
Freshly parsley to garnish

Directions and Total Time: approx. 30 minutes

Preheat oven to 350 F, turn a muffin tray upside down and lightly grease with cooking spray. In a bowl, mix almond and coconut flours, xanthan gum, and salt. Add in cream cheese, cream of tartar, and butter; mix with an electric hand mixer until crumbly. Stir in erythritol and vanilla extract until mixed. Then, pour in three eggs, one after another while mixing until formed into a ball. Flatten the dough on a clean flat surface, cover in plastic wrap, and refrigerate for 1 hour. Dust a clean flat surface with almond flour, unwrap the dough, and roll out the dough into a large rectangle. Cut into 16 squares and press each onto each muffin mound on the tray to form a bowl shape. Brush with the remaining eggs and bake for 10 minutes. To make the filling, melt butter in a skillet and sauté onion for 3 minutes. Stir in red wine, balsamic vinegar, erythritol, and blackberries. Cook until the berries become jammy and wine reduces, 10 minutes. Set aside. Take out the tray and place a cheese cubes in each pastry. Return to oven and bake for 3 minutes. Spoon a tsp each of the blackberry sauce on top. Garnish with parsley to serve.
Per serving: Cal 372; Net Carbs 4.4g, Fat 32g, Protein 14g

Mini Ricotta Cakes

Ingredients for 4 servings

2 tbsp olive oil
2 tbsp butter
2 garlic cloves, minced
1 white onion, finely chopped
1 cup cauli rice
¼ cup white wine
¼ cup vegetable stock
2 scallions, chopped
Salt and black pepper to taste
¼ cup grated Parmesan
½ cup ricotta cheese
1 cup almond flour
½ cup golden flaxseed meal
2 eggs

Directions and Total Time: approx. 40 minutes

Heat butter in a saucepan over medium heat. Stir in garlic and onion and cook until fragrant and soft, 3 minutes. Mix in cauli rice for 30 seconds; add in wine, stir, allow reduction and absorption into cauli rice. Mix in stock, scallions, salt, pepper, remaining butter, Parmesan and ricotta cheeses. Cover the pot and cook until the liquid reduces and the rice thickens. Open the lid, stir well, and spoon the mixture into a bowl to cool. Mold the dough into mini patties, about 14 to 16 and set aside. Heat olive oil in a skillet over medium heat; meanwhile pour the almond flour onto a plate, the golden flaxseed meal in another, and beat the eggs in a medium bowl. Lightly dredge each patty in the flour, then in eggs, and then coated accurately in the flaxseed meal. Fry in the oil until compacted and golden brown, 2 minutes on each side. Transfer to a paper towel-lined plate, plate, and garnish with some scallions.
Per serving: Cal 362; Net Carbs 6.2g, Fat 29g, Protein 13g

Mediterranean Roasted Turnip Bites

Ingredients for 4 servings
1 lb turnips, sliced into rounds
½ cup olive oil
2 garlic cloves, minced
1 tbsp chopped fresh parsley
2 tbsp chopped fresh oregano
3 tbsp dried Italian seasoning
¼ cup marinara sauce
¼ cup grated mozzarella

Directions and Total Time: approx. 1 hour

Preheat oven to 400 F. Place turnip slices into a bowl and toss with olive oil. Add in garlic, parsley, oregano, and Italian seasoning and mix well. Arrange on a greased baking sheet and roast for 25 minutes, flipping halfway. Remove and brush the marinara sauce. Sprinkle with mozzarella cheese and bake in the oven until the cheese is golden, 15 minutes. Garnish with parsley and serve warm.

Per serving: Cal 326; Net Carbs 3.8g; Fat 28g; Protein 5g

Cream Cheese & Caramelized Onion Dip

Ingredients for 4 servings
2 tbsp butter
3 yellow onions, thinly sliced
1 tsp swerve sugar
Salt to taste
¼ cup white wine
2 cups sour cream
8 oz cream cheese, softened
½ tbsp Worcestershire sauce
Directions and Total Time: approx. 30 minutes
Melt butter in a skillet and add in onions, swerve sugar, and salt and cook with frequent stirring for 10-15 minutes. Add in white wine, stir and allow sizzling out, 10 minutes. In a serving bowl, mix sour cream and cream cheese until well combined. Add onions and Worcestershire sauce; stir well into the cream. Serve with celery sticks.

Per serving: Cal 383; Net Carbs 8.3g; Fat 34g; Protein 8g

Tofu Jalapeño Peppers

Ingredients for 4 servings
For the poppers:
1 tbsp olive oil
4 oz firm tofu, chopped in bits
1 garlic clove, minced
½ cup cream cheese
1 lemon, zested juiced
4 scallions, finely chopped
2 tbsp chopped cilantro
Salt and black pepper to taste
6 jalapeño peppers, halved
3 tbsp grated cheddar cheese
For the dip:
1 tsp lemon juice

1 cup sour cream
1 tbsp chopped cilantro
Directions and Total Time: approx. 30 minutes
Preheat oven to 370 F. Heat olive oil in a skillet and fry tofu until golden. Transfer to a bowl. Mix in garlic, cream cheese, lemon zest, juice, scallions, cilantro, salt, and pepper. Arrange jalapeño peppers on a greased baking dish. Fill tofu mixture and sprinkle with cheddar cheese. Bake for 15 minutes or until the cheese is golden brown. In a bowl, mix lemon juice, sour cream, cilantro, and season with salt and pepper. Serve the dip with the poppers.

Per serving: Cal 247; Net Carbs 6.9g, Fat 21g, Protein 9g

Avocado Pate with Flaxseed Toasts

Ingredients for 4 servings
1/2 cup flaxseed meal
1 pinch salt
For the Avocado pate:
3 ripe avocado, chopped
4 tbsp Greek yogurt
2 tbsp chopped green onions
1 lemon, zested and juiced
Black pepper to taste
Smoked paprika to garnish
Directions and Total Time: approx. 5 minutes
For the flaxseed toasts:
Preheat oven to 350 F. Place a skillet over medium heat. Mix in flaxseed meal, 1/4 cup water, and salt and mix continually to form the dough into a ball. Place the dough between 2 parchment papers, put on a flat surface, and flatten thinly with a rolling pin. Remove the papers and cut the pastry into tortilla chips. Place on a baking sheet and bake for 8-12 minutes or until crispy. In a bowl, mix avocado, yogurt, green onions, lemon zest, juice, and black pepper until evenly combined. Spread the pate on the toasts and garnish with paprika. Serve immediately.

Per serving: Cal 364; Net Carbs 4g, Fat 31g, Protein 7.4g

Sweet Tahini Twists

Ingredients for 4 servings
For the puff pastry:

¼ cup almond flour
3 tbsp coconut flour
½ tsp xanthan gum
½ tsp salt
4 tbsp cream cheese, softened
¼ teaspoon cream of tartar
¼ cup butter, cold
3 whole eggs
3 tbsp erythritol
1 ½ tsp vanilla extract
1 whole egg, beaten

For the filling:
2 tbsp sugar-free maple syrup
3 tbsp tahini
2 tbsp sesame seeds
1 egg, beaten
2 tbsp poppy seeds

Directions and Total Time: approx. 15 min + cooling time

Preheat oven to 350 F and line a baking tray with parchment paper. In a bowl, mix almond and coconut flours, xanthan gum, and salt. Add in cream cheese, cream of tartar, and butter; mix with an electric mixer until crumbly. Add erythritol and vanilla extract until mixed. Then, pour in 3 eggs one after another while mixing until formed into a ball. Flatten the dough on a clean flat surface, cover in plastic wrap, and refrigerate for 1 hour.

Dust a clean flat surface with almond flour, unwrap the dough, and roll out the dough into a large rectangle. In a bowl, mix sugar-free maple syrup with tahini and spread the mixture over the pastry. Sprinkle with half of the sesame seeds and cut the dough into 16 thin strips. Fold each strip in half. Brush the top with the remaining egg, sprinkle with the remaining seeds, and poppy seeds. Twist the pastry three to four times into straws and place on the baking sheet. Bake until golden brown, 15 minutes. Serve with chocolate sauce.

Per serving: Cal 348; Net Carbs 3.1g, Fat 31g, Protein 11g

Feta Cheese Choux Buns

Ingredients for 4 servings
2 sprigs rosemary
6 tbsp butter
2/3 cup almond flour
3 eggs, beaten
1 tbsp olive oil
2 white onions, thinly sliced
2 tbsp red wine vinegar
1 tsp swerve brown sugar
1 cup crumbled feta cheese
½ cup heavy whipping cream

Directions and Total Time: approx. 40 minutes

Preheat oven to 350 F and line a baking tray with parchment paper. In a saucepan, warm 1 cup of water, salt, and butter melts. Bring to a boil and sift in flour, beating vigorously until ball forms. Turn the heat off; keep beating while adding the eggs, one at a time, until the dough is smooth and slightly thickened. Scoop mounds of the dough onto the baking dish. Press a hole in the center of each mound. Bake for 20 minutes until risen and golden. Remove from oven and pierce the sides of the buns with a toothpick. Return to oven and bake for 2 minutes until crispy. Set aside to cool.

Tear out the middle part of the bun (keep the torn out part) to create a hole in the bun for the cream filling. Set aside. Heat olive oil in a saucepan and sauté onions and rosemary for 2 minutes. Stir in swerve, vinegar, and cook to bubble for 3 minutes or until caramelized. In a bowl, beat whipping cream and feta together. Spoon the mixture into a piping bag and press a spoonful of the mixture into the buns. Cover with the torn out portion of pastry and top with onion relish to serve.

Per serving: Cal 384; Net Carbs 2.5g, Fat 37g, Protein 10g

SOUPS & STEWS

Asparagus & Shrimp Curry Soup

Ingredients for 4 servings
2 tbsp ghee
1 lb jumbo shrimp, deveined
2 tsp ginger-garlic puree
2 tbsp red curry paste
6 oz coconut milk
1 bunch asparagus
Directions and Total Time: approx. 20 minutes
Melt ghee in a saucepan and add shrimp. Season with salt and chili pepper and cook for 3 minutes; remove to a plate. Add ginger-garlic puree and red curry paste to the ghee and sauté for 2 minutes. Stir in coconut milk; add shrimp, and asparagus. Cook for 4 minutes. Reduce the heat and simmer for 3 more minutes. Serve with cauli rice.
Per serving: Cal 375; Net Carbs 2g; Fat 35.4g, Protein 9g

Thyme Tomato Soup

Ingredients for 6 servings
2 tbsp butter
2 large red onions, diced
½ cup raw cashew nuts, diced
2 (28-oz) cans tomatoes
1 tsp thyme
1 ½ cups water
Salt and black pepper to taste
1 cup half-and-half
Directions and Total Time: approx. 20 minutes
Melt butter in a pot and sautéthe onion for 4 minutes. Stir in tomatoes, thyme, water, cashews, and season with salt and pepper. Simmer for 10 minutes. Puree the ingredients with an immersion blender. Adjust the taste and stir in half-and-half. Spoon into soup bowls and serve.
Per serving: Cal 310; Net Carbs 3g; Fat 27g, Protein 11g

Cauliflower Soup with Kielbasa

Ingredients for 4 servings
1 cauliflower head, chopped
1 rutabaga, chopped
3 tbsp ghee
1 kielbasa sausage, sliced

2 cups chicken broth
1 small onion, chopped
2 cups water
Salt and black pepper, to taste
Directions and Total Time: approx. 40 minutes
Melt 2 tbsp of the ghee in a pot and cook onion for 3 minutes. Add cauliflower and rutabaga, and cook for another 5 minutes. Pour broth, water, salt. and pepper over. Bring to a boil and cook for 20 minutes. Melt remaining butter in a skillet. Add in kielbasa sausage and cook for 5 minutes. Puree the soup until smooth. Serve with kielbasa.
Per serving: Cal 251; Net Carbs: 5.7g; Fat: 19g, Protein: 10g

Tomato Soup with Parmesan Croutons

Ingredients for 6 servings
Parmesan Croutons:
3 tbsp flax seed powder
1¼ cups almond flour
2 tsp baking powder
5 tbsp psyllium husk powder
1¼ cups boiling water
2 tsp plain vinegar
3 oz butter
2 oz grated Parmesan
Tomato Soup
2 lb fresh ripe tomatoes
4 cloves garlic, peeled only
1 small white onion, diced
1 red bell pepper, diced
3 tbsp olive oil
1 cup coconut cream
½ tsp dried rosemary
½ tsp dried oregano
2 tbsp chopped fresh basil
Salt and black pepper to taste
Directions and Total Time: approx. 1 hour 25 minutes
For the parmesan croutons:
In a bowl, mix the flax seed powder with 2/3 cup of water and set aside for 5 minutes. Preheat oven to 350 F and line a baking sheet with parchment paper. In another bowl, combine almond flour, baking powder, psyllium husk powder. Mix the flax egg in the boiling water and plain vinegar. Add in flour

mixture and whisk for 30 seconds until well combined but not overly mixed. Form 8 flat pieces out of the dough. Place on the baking sheet while leaving enough room between each to allow rising. Bake for 40 minutes. Remove croutons to cool and break into halves. Mix butter with Parmesan and spread the mixture in the inner parts of the croutons. Bake for 5 minutes.

For the tomato soup:

In a pan, add tomatoes, garlic, onion, bell pepper, and drizzle with olive oil. Roast vegetables in the oven for 25 minutes and after broil for 4 minutes. Transfer to a blender and add in coconut cream, rosemary, oregano, salt, and pepper. Puree until smooth. Serve, topped with croutons.

Per serving: Cal 434; Fat 38g; Net Carbs 6g; Protein 11g

Colby Cauliflower Soup with Pancetta Chips

Ingredients for 4 servings
2 heads cauliflower, cut into florets
2 tbsp ghee
1 onion, chopped
2 cups water
3 cups almond milk
1 cup Colby cheese, shredded
3 pancetta strips

Directions and Total Time: approx. 30 minutes

Melt ghee in a saucepan and sauté onion for 3 minutes. Include cauli florets, sauté for 3 minutes, add water, and season with salt and pepper. Bring to a boil, reduce the heat, and cook for 10 minutes. Puree cauliflower and stir in almond milk and cheese until the cheese melts. Adjust the taste. In a skillet, fry pancetta until crispy. Top the soup with crispy pancetta and serve.

Per serving: Cal 402; Net Carbs 6g; Fat 37g; Protein 8g

Coconut Turkey Chili

Ingredients for 4 servings
1 pound turkey breasts, cubed
1 cup broccoli, chopped
2 shallots, sliced
1 (14-ounce) can tomatoes
2 tbsp coconut oil
2 tbsp coconut cream

2 garlic cloves, minced
1 tbsp ground coriander
2 tbsp fresh ginger, grated
1 tbsp turmeric
1 tbsp cumin
2 tbsp chili powder

Directions and Total Time: approx. 30 minutes

Melt coconut oil in a pan over medium heat and stir-fry turkey, shallots, garlic, and ginger for 5 minutes. Stir in tomatoes, broccoli, turmeric, coriander, cumin, chili, salt and pepper. Pour in coconut cream and cook for 20-25 minutes. Transfer to a food processor to blend well. Serve.

Per serving: Cal 318; Net Carbs 6.6g; Fat 18.7g; Protein 27g

Effortless Chicken Chili

Ingredients for 4 servings
1 tbsp butter
1 tbsp sesame oil
¼ tsp ginger, ground
4 chicken tenders, cubed
1 onion, chopped
2 cups chicken broth
8 oz diced tomatoes
2 oz tomato paste
1 tbsp cumin
1 red chili pepper, minced
½ cup shredded cheddar
Salt and black pepper to taste

Directions and Total Time: approx. 30 minutes

Put a pan and add chicken. Cover with water and bring to a boil. Cook for 10 minutes. Transfer to a flat surface to shred with forks. In a pot, pour in butter and sesame oil and sauté onion and ginger for 5 minutes. Stir in chicken, tomatoes, cumin, red chili pepper, tomato paste, and broth. Bring the mixture to a boil. Reduce heat and simmer for 10 minutes. Top with the cheddar cheese to serve.

Per serving: Cal 396; Net Carbs 5.7g; Fat 22.9g; Protein 38g

Cauliflower Beef Curry

Ingredients for 4 servings
1 head cauliflower, cut into florets
2 tbsp olive oil
1 ½ pounds ground beef

1 tbsp ginger-garlic paste
½ tsp cumin
¼ tsp allspice
6 oz canned whole tomatoes
Salt and chili pepper to taste

Directions and Total Time: approx. 26 minutes

Cook beef in hot oil over medium heat for 5 minutes while breaking any lumps. Stir in cumin, allspice, salt, and chili pepper. Stir in tomatoes and cauliflower, and cook covered for 6 minutes. Add a ¼ cup of water and bring to a boil over medium heat for 10 minutes or until the water has reduced by half. Adjust the taste with salt. Serve warm.

Per serving: Cal 518; Net Carbs 3g; Fat 34.6g; Protein 44.6g

Chicken Stew with Spinach

Ingredients for 4 servings

28 oz chicken thighs, skinless, boneless
2 oz sun-dried tomatoes, chopped
2 carrots, chopped
2 tbsp olive oil
2 celery stalks, chopped
2 cups chicken stock
1 leek, chopped
3 garlic cloves, minced
½ tsp dried rosemary
1 cup spinach
¼ tsp dried thyme
½ cup heavy cream
Salt and black pepper to taste
A pinch of xanthan gum

Directions and Total Time: approx. 50 minutes

In a pot, heat olive oil and add garlic, carrots, celery, and leeek; season with salt and pepper and sauté for 5-6 minutes. Stir in chicken and cook for 5 minutes. Pour in stock, tomatoes, rosemary, and thyme and cook for 30 minutes covered. Add in xanthan gum, cream, and spinach; cook for 5 minutes. Serve.

Per serving: Cal 224, Net Carbs 6g, Fat 11g, Protein 23g

Bacon Stew with Cauliflower

Ingredients for 6 servings

1 head cauliflower, cut into florets
8 oz grated mozzarella
2 cups chicken broth
½ tsp garlic powder

½ tsp onion powder
Salt and black pepper, to taste
4 garlic cloves, minced
¼ cup heavy cream
3 cups bacon, chopped

Directions and Total Time: approx. 40 minutes

In a pot, combine the bacon with broth, cauliflower, salt, heavy cream, black pepper, garlic powder, cheese, onion powder, and garlic, and cook for 35 minutes. Serve.

Per serving: Cal 380; Net Carbs 6g; Fat 25g; Protein 33g

Scottish Beef Stew

Ingredients for 4 servings

12 oz sweet potatoes, cut into quarters
2 tbsp lard
1 ¼ lb beef chuck roast, cubed
1 parsnip, chopped
1 onion, chopped
1 clove garlic, minced
Salt and black pepper to taste
1 ½ cups beef stock
2 tsp rosemary, chopped

Directions and Total Time: approx. 60 minutes

Melt lard in a skillet over medium heat and cook onion and garlic for 4 minutes. Add in the beef, season with salt and pepper, and brown on all sides, for about 7-8 minutes. Add sweet potatoes, parsnip, rosemary, and beef stock. Stir and cook on low heat for 35-40 minutes, covered. Serve.

Per serving: Cal 445; Net Carbs 12.3g; Fat 18g; Protein 42g

Vegetable Stew

Ingredients for 4 servings

1 large head broccoli, cut into florets
2 tbsp ghee
1 tbsp onion-garlic puree
4 medium carrots, chopped
2 cups green beans, halved
1 cup water
1 ½ cups heavy cream

Directions and Total Time: approx. 35 minutes

Melt ghee in a saucepan and sauté onion-garlic puree for 2 minutes. Stir in carrots, broccoli, and green beans, salt, and pepper, add water, stir again, and cook for 25 minutes. Mix in heavy cream, turn the heat off and adjust the taste. Serve the stew with almond flour bread.

Per serving: Cal 310; Net Carbs 6g; Fat 26.4g, Protein 8g

Chili Beef Stew with Cauliflower Grits

Ingredients for 4 servings
2 tbsp olive oil
2 lb chuck roast, cubed
1 large yellow onion, chopped
3 garlic cloves, minced
2 large tomatoes, diced
1 tbsp rosemary
1 tbsp smoked paprika
2 tsp chili powder
2 cups beef broth
2 tbsp butter
½ cup walnuts, chopped
2 cups cauliflower rice
1 cup half and half
1 cup shredded cheddar

Directions and Total Time: approx. 55 minutes
Heat olive oil in a pot. Season beef with salt and pepper and cook for 3 minutes. Stir in onion, garlic, and tomatoes, for 5 minutes. Mix in rosemary, paprika, chili and cook for 2 minutes. Pour in broth and bring to a boil, then simmer for 25 minutes; set aside. Melt butter in a pot, and cook walnuts for 3 minutes. Transfer to a cutting board, chop and plate. Pour cauli rice and ½ cup water into the pot and cook for 5 minutes. Stir in half and half for 3 minutes. Mix in cheddar cheese, fold in walnuts. Top with stewed beef.

Per serving: Cal 736; Net Carbs 7.8g; Fat 48g, Protein 63g

Rustic Lamb Stew with Root Veggies

Ingredients for 4 servings
2 tbsp olive oil
1 pound lamb chops
1 garlic clove, minced
1 parsnip, chopped
1 onion, chopped
1 celery stalk, chopped
Salt and black pepper to taste
2 cups vegetable stock
2 carrots, chopped
½ tbsp rosemary, chopped
1 tbsp sweet paprika
1 leek, chopped
1 tbsp tomato paste
½ fennel bulb, chopped

Directions and Total Time: approx. 1 hour 45 minutes
Warm olive oil in a pot over medium heat and cook celery, onion, leek, and garlic for 5 minutes. Add in lamb chops, and cook for 4 minutes. Add in paprika, carrots, parsnip, fennel, stock, tomato paste; let simmer for 1 hour. Adjust the seasoning, sprinkle with rosemary, and serve.

Per serving: Cal 472; Net Carbs 6.3g; Fat 37g; Protein 20.5g

Beef & Veggie Stew

Ingredients for 4 servings
1 pound ground beef
2 tbsp olive oil
1 onion, chopped
2 garlic cloves, minced
14 oz canned diced tomatoes
1 tbsp dried sage
Salt and black pepper, to taste
2 carrots, sliced
2 celery stalks, chopped
1 cup vegetable broth

Directions and Total Time: approx. 30 minutes
Warm olive oil in a pan and sauté onion, celery, and garlic for 5 minutes. Add in beef and cook for 6 minutes. Pour in tomatoes, carrots, broth, pepper, salt, and sage, lower the heat and simmer for 15 minutes.

Per serving: Cal 253, Net Carbs 5.2g, Fat 13g, Protein 30g

Veal Stew

Ingredients for 6 servings
3 lb veal shoulder, cubed

2 tbsp olive oil
1 onion, chopped
1 garlic clove, minced
1 ½ cups red wine
12 oz canned tomato sauce
1 carrot, chopped
1 cup mushrooms, chopped
½ cup green beans
2 tsp dried oregano

Directions and Total Time: approx. 120 minutes

Warm olive oil in a pot and brown the veal for 5-6 minutes. Stir in onion and garlic and cook for 3 minutes. Place in wine, oregano, carrot, pepper, salt, tomato sauce, 1 cup water, and mushrooms and bring to a boil. Reduce the heat to low and cook for 1 hour and 45 minutes, then add in green beans and cook for 5 minutes. Serve.

Per serving: Cal 415, Net Carbs 5.2g, Fat 21g, Protein 44g

Turkey Stew with Tomatillo Salsa

Ingredients for 6 servings
4 cups leftover turkey meat, chopped
2 cups green beans
6 cups chicken stock
Salt and black pepper to taste
1 chipotle pepper, chopped
½ cup tomatillo salsa
1 tsp ground coriander
2 tsp cumin
¼ cup sour cream
1 tbsp fresh cilantro, chopped

Directions and Total Time: approx. 30 minutes

Set a pan over medium heat. Add in the stock and heat. Stir in green beans, and cook for 10 minutes. Place in turkey, ground coriander, salt, tomatillo salsa, chipotle pepper, cumin, and black pepper, and cook for 10 minutes. Stir in the sour cream, kill the heat, and separate into bowls. Top with chopped cilantro to serve.

Per serving: Cal 193, Net Carbs 2g, Fat 11g, Protein 27g

Pork & Pumpkin Stew with Peanuts

Ingredients for 6 servings
1 cup puree
2 lb pork shoulder, cubed
1 tbsp peanut butter
4 tbsp chopped peanuts
1 garlic clove, minced
½ cup chopped onion
½ cup white wine
1 tbsp olive oil
1 tsp lemon juice
¼ cup granulated sweetener
¼ tsp cardamom
¼ tsp allspice
3 cups chicken stock
Salt and black pepper to taste

Directions and Total Time: approx. 45 minutes

Heat olive oil in a pot. Add onions and garlic and sauté for 3 minutes. Add in pork and stir-fry for 5-6 minutes. Pour in wine and cook for 1 minute. Throw in the remaining ingredients, except lemon juice and peanuts. Bring the mixture to a boil, and cook for 5 minutes. Reduce the heat and let cook for 30 minutes. Adjust seasoning. Stir in lemon juice before serving. Serve topped with peanuts.

Per serving: Cal 451; Net Carbs 4g; Fat 33g, Protein 27.5g

Paprika Chicken & Bacon Stew

Ingredients for 3 servings
8 bacon strips, chopped
¼ cup Dijon mustard
Salt and black pepper to taste
1 onion, chopped
1 tbsp olive oil
1 ½ cups chicken stock
3 chicken breasts
¼ tsp sweet paprika

Directions and Total Time: approx. 40 minutes

In a bowl, combine salt, pepper, and mustard. Massage onto chicken breasts. Set a pan over medium heat, stir in the bacon, cook until it browns, and remove to a plate. Heat oil in the same pan, add the breasts, cook each side for 2 minutes, set aside. Place in the stock and bring to a simmer. Stir in pancetta and onions. Return the chicken to the pan as well, stir gently, and simmer for 20 minutes over medium heat, turning halfway through. Serve. **Per serving:** Cal 313; Net Carbs 3g; Fat 18g, Protein 26g

Parsley Sausage Stew

Ingredients for 6 servings
1 lb pork sausage, sliced
1 red bell pepper, chopped
1 onion, chopped
Salt and black pepper, to taste
1 cup fresh parsley, chopped
6 green onions, chopped
¼ cup avocado oil
1 cup chicken stock
2 garlic cloves, minced
24 ounces canned tomatoes
16 ounces okra, sliced
6 ounces tomato sauce
2 tbsp coconut aminos
1 tbsp hot sauce

Directions and Total Time: approx. 35 minutes
Set a pot over medium heat and warm oil. Place in sausages and cook for 2 minutes. Stir in onion, green onions, garlic, black pepper, bell pepper, and salt, and cook for 5 minutes. Add in hot sauce, stock, tomatoes, coconut aminos, okra, and tomato sauce, bring to a simmer and cook for 15 minutes. Sprinkle with fresh parsley to serve.
Per serving: Cal 314, Net Carbs 7g, Fat 25g, Protein 16g

Brazilian Moqueca (Shrimp Stew)

Ingredients for 6 servings
1 ½ pounds shrimp, peeled and deveined
1 cup coconut milk
2 tbsp lime juice
¼ cup diced roasted peppers
3 tbsp olive oil
1 garlic clove, minced
14 ounces diced tomatoes

2 tbsp harissa sauce
1 chopped onion
¼ cup chopped cilantro
Salt and black pepper to taste

Directions and Total Time: approx. 25 minutes
Warm olive oil in a pot and sauté onion and garlic for 3 minutes. Add in tomatoes and shrimp. Cook for 3-4 minutes. Stir in harissa sauce, roasted peppers, and coconut milk and cook for 2 minutes. Add in lime juice and season with salt and pepper. Top with cilantro to serve.
Per serving: Cal 324; Net Carbs 5g; Fats 21g; Protein 23g

Yellow Squash Duck Breast Stew

Ingredients for 2 servings
1 pound duck breast, skin on and sliced
2 yellow squash, sliced
1 tbsp coconut oil
1 green onion bunch, chopped
1 carrot, chopped
2 green bell peppers, chopped
Salt and black pepper, to taste

Directions and Total Time: approx. 20 minutes
Set a pan over high heat and warm oil, stir in the green onions, and cook for 2 minutes. Place in the yellow squash, bell peppers, pepper, salt, and carrot, and cook for 10 minutes. Set another pan over high heat, add in duck slices and cook each side for 3 minutes. Pour the mixture into the vegetable pan. Cook for 3 minutes. Serve.
Per serving: Cal 433; Net Carbs 8g; Fat 21g, Protein 53g

Herby Chicken Stew

Ingredients for 6 servings
2 tbsp butter
2 shallots, finely chopped
2 garlic cloves, minced
1 cup chicken broth
1 tsp dried rosemary
1 tsp dried thyme
1 lb chicken breasts, cubed

1 celery, chopped
1 carrot, chopped
1 bay leaf
1 chili pepper, chopped
2 tomatoes, chopped
Salt black pepper to taste
½ tsp paprika

Directions and Total Time: approx. 60 minutes

Melt butter in a pot over medium heat. Add in shallots, garlic, celery, carrot, salt, and pepper and sauté until tender, about 5 minutes. Pour in chicken broth, rosemary, thyme, chicken breasts, bay leaf, tomatoes, paprika, and chili pepper; bring to a boil. Reduce the heat to low. Simmer for 50 minutes. Discard the bay leaf and adjust the seasoning. Serve warm.

Per serving: Cal 240; Net Carbs 5g; Fat 9.6g, Protein 245

South-American Shrimp Stew

Ingredients for 6 servings
1 cup coconut milk
2 tbsp lime juice
¼ cup diced roasted peppers
1 ½ lb shrimp, deveined
¼ cup olive oil
1 garlic clove, minced
14 ounces diced tomatoes
2 tbsp sriracha sauce
¼ cup chopped onions
¼ cup chopped cilantro
Fresh dill, chopped to garnish
Salt and black pepper to taste

Directions and Total Time: approx. 25 minutes

Heat olive oil in a pot and add cook onions and garlic for 3 minutes. Add in tomatoes, shrimp, and cilantro. Cook for about 3-4 minutes. Stir in sriracha and coconut milk, and cook for 2 more minutes. Do not bring to a boil. Stir in lime juice and season with salt and pepper. Spoon the stew in bowls, garnish with fresh dill, and serve.

Per serving: Cal 324; Net Carbs 5g; Fat 21g, Protein 23g

LUNCH & DINNER

Margherita Pizza with Broccoli Crust

Ingredients for 2 servings
1 small head broccoli, riced
2 ½ oz cremini mushrooms, sliced
4 eggs
¼ cup shredded cheddar
¼ cup Parmesan cheese
Salt and black pepper to taste
½ tsp Italian seasoning mix
6 tbsp tomato sauce
1 small red onion, sliced
½ cup cottage cheese
½ tbsp olive oil
A handful of fresh basil

Directions and Total Time: approx. 40 minutes

Preheat oven 400 F and line a baking sheet with parchment paper. Microwave broccoli for 2 minutes; let cool. Crack in the eggs, add cheeses, salt, pepper, and Italian seasoning; whisk until evenly combined. Spread the mixture on the baking sheet and bake for 15 minutes. Allow cooling the crust for 2 minutes. Spread tomato sauce on the crust, scatter with mushrooms, onion, and cottage cheese; drizzle with olive oil. Place the pan in the oven to bake for 15 minutes. Scatter with basil leaves, slice, and serve.

Per serving: Cal 290; Net Carbs 0.8g; Fat 22g; Protein 13g

Herby Mushrooms Stroganoff

Ingredients for 4 servings
½ cup grated Pecorino Romano cheese
3 tbsp butter
1 white onion, chopped
4 cups mushrooms, chopped
½ cup heavy cream
1 ½ tbsp dried mixed herbs
Salt and black pepper to taste

Directions and Total Time: approx. 15 minutes

Melt butter in a saucepan and sauté onion for 3 minutes. Stir in mushrooms and cook for 3 minutes. Add 2 cups water and bring to boil for 4 minutes. Pour in heavy cream and Pecorino Romano cheese. Stir to melt the cheese. Also, mix in dried herbs. Season with salt and pepper. Ladle stroganoff over spaghetti squash and serve.

Per serving: Cal 284; Net Carbs 1.5g; Fat 28g; Protein 8g

Meatless Florentine Pizza

Ingredients for 2 servings
1 cup shredded provolone cheese
1 (7 oz) can sliced mushrooms, drained
10 eggs
1 tsp Italian seasoning
2/3 cup tomato sauce
2 cups chopped kale, wilted
½ cup grated mozzarella
4 eggs

Directions and Total Time: approx. 35 minutes

Preheat oven to 400 F and line a pizza-baking pan with parchment paper. Whisk 6 eggs with provolone cheese and Italian seasoning. Spread the mixture on a pizza-baking pan, bake for 15 minutes; let cool for 2 minutes. Increase the oven's temperature to 450 F. Spread tomato sauce on the crust, top with kale, mozzarella cheese, and mushrooms. Bake for 8 minutes. Crack remaining eggs on top and continue baking until the eggs are set, 3 minutes.

Per serving: Cal 646; Net Carbs 4.9g; Fat 39g; Protein 36g

Hazelnut & Cheese Stuffed Zucchinis

Ingredients for 4 servings
2 tbsp olive oil
1 cup cauliflower rice
¼ cup vegetable broth
1 ¼ cup diced tomatoes
1 medium red onion, chopped
¼ cup pine nuts
¼ cup hazelnuts
4 tbsp chopped cilantro
1 tbsp balsamic vinegar
1 tbsp smoked paprika
4 medium zucchinis, halved
1 cup grated Monterey Jack

Directions and Total Time: approx. 35 minutes

Preheat oven to 350 F. Pour cauli rice and broth in a pot and cook for 5 minutes. Fluff the cauli rice and allow cooling. Scoop the flesh out of the zucchini halves using a spoon and chop the pulp. Brush the inner parts of the vegetable with olive oil. In a bowl, mix cauli rice, tomatoes, red onion, pine nuts, hazelnuts, cilantro, vinegar, paprika, and zucchini pulp. Spoon the mixture into the zucchini halves, drizzle with more olive oil, and sprinkle the cheese on top. Bake for 20 minutes until the cheese melts. Serve.

Per serving: Cal 330; Net Carbs 5.2g; Fat 28g; Protein 12g

Smoked Tempeh with Broccoli Fritters

Ingredients for 4 servings
2 eggs
1 tbsp soy sauce
3 tbsp olive oil
1 tbsp grated ginger
3 tbsp fresh lime juice
Salt and cayenne pepper to taste
10 oz tempeh slices
1 head Broccoli, grated
8 oz halloumi cheese
3 tbsp almond flour
½ tsp onion powder
Salt and black pepper to taste
4¼ oz butter

Directions and Total Time: approx. 40 minutes
In a bowl, combine soy sauce, olive oil, grated ginger, lime juice, salt, and cayenne pepper. Brush the tempeh slices with the mixture. Heat a grill pan and grill tempeh on both sides until golden brown; remove to a plate. Put broccoli in a bowl and grate halloumi cheese on top. Add in eggs, almond flour, onion powder, salt, and pepper. Mix and form 12 patties out of the mixture. Melt butter in a skillet and fry the patties until golden brown. Plate the grilled tempeh with the broccoli fritters and serve.

Per serving: Cal 850; Net Carbs 7g; Fat 71g; Protein 35g

Sesame Cauliflower Dip

Ingredients for 4 servings
¾ lb cauliflower, cut into florets
¼ cup olive oil
Salt and black pepper, to taste
1 garlic clove, smashed
1 tbsp sesame paste

1 tbsp fresh lemon juice
½ tsp garam masala

Directions and Total Time: approx. 15 minutes
Steam cauliflower until tender for 7 minutes. Transfer to a blender and pulse until you attain a rice-like consistency. Place in garam masala, oil, black paper, fresh lemon juice, garlic, salt, and sesame paste. Blend the mixture until well combined. Decorate with some additional olive oil and serve. Otherwise, refrigerate until ready to use.

Per serving: Cal 103; Net Carbs: 4.7g; Fat: 8.2g; Protein: 4g

Spanish Paella "Keto-Style"

Ingredients for 4 servings
½ pound rabbit, cut into pieces
½ pound chicken drumsticks
1 white onion, chopped
2 garlic cloves, minced
1 red bell pepper, chopped
2 tbsp olive oil
½ cup thyme, chopped
1 tsp smoked paprika
2 tbsp tomato puree
½ cup white wine
1 cup chicken broth
2 cups cauli rice
1 cup green beans, chopped
A pinch of saffron

Directions and Total Time: approx. 70 minutes
Preheat oven to 350 F. Warm oil in a pan. Season chicken and rabbit with salt and pepper. Fry on all sides for 8 minutes; remove to a plate. Add in onion and garlic and sauté for 3 minutes. Include in tomato puree, bell pepper, and paprika, and let simmer for 2 minutes. Pour in broth, and bring to a boil for 6 minutes. Stir in cauli rice, white wine, green beans, saffron, and thyme, and lay the meat on top. Transfer the pan to the oven and cook for 20 minutes.

Per serving: Cal 378; Net Carbs 7.6g; Fat 21g; Protein 37.2g

Baked Spicy Cauliflower & Peppers

Ingredients for 4 servings
1 lb cauliflower, cut into florets
1 yellow bell pepper, halved
1 red bell pepper, halved

¼ cup olive oil
Salt and black pepper, to taste
½ tsp cayenne pepper
1 tsp curry powder

Directions and Total Time: approx. 35 minutes

Set oven to 425 F. Line a parchment paper to a large baking sheet. Sprinkle olive oil to the peppers and cauliflower alongside curry powder, pepper, salt, and cayenne pepper. Set the vegetables on the baking sheet. Roast for 30 minutes as you toss in intervals until they start to brown. Serve alongside mushroom pate or homemade tomato dip.

Per serving: Cal 166; Net Carbs: 7.4g; Fat: 14g; Protein: 3g

Salami Cauliflower Pizza

Ingredients for 4 servings

2 cups grated mozzarella
4 cups cauliflower rice
1 tbsp dried thyme
¼ cup tomato sauce
4 oz salami slices

Directions and Total Time: approx. 40 minutes

Preheat oven to 390 F. Microwave cauliflower rice mixed with 1 tbsp of water for 1 minute. Remove and mix in 1 cup of the mozzarella cheese and thyme. Pour the mixture into a greased baking dish, spread out and bake for 5 minutes. Remove the dish and spread the tomato sauce on top. Scatter remaining mozzarella cheese on the sauce and then arrange salami slices on top. Bake for 15 minutes.

Per serving: Cal 276; Net Carbs 1.7g; Fats 15g; Protein 20g

Tofu & Bok Choy Stir-Fry

Ingredients for 4 servings

2 ½ cups baby bok choy, quartered lengthwise
5 oz vegan butter
2 cups extra firm tofu, cubed
Salt and black pepper to taste
1 tsp garlic powder
1 tsp onion powder
1 tbsp plain vinegar
2 garlic cloves, minced
1 tsp chili flakes
1 tbsp fresh ginger, grated

3 green onions, sliced

Directions and Total Time: approx. 45 minutes

Melt half of butter in a wok over medium heat, add bok choy, and stir-fry until softened. Season with salt, pepper, garlic and onion powders, and plain vinegar. Sauté for 2 minutes and set aside. Melt the remaining butter in the wok, and sauté garlic, chili flakes, and ginger until fragrant. Put in tofu and cook until browned. Add in green onions and bok choy, for 2 minutes and serve.

Per serving: Cal 686; Net Carbs 8g; Fat 64g; Protein 35g

Tofu Loaf with Walnuts

Ingredients for 4 servings

3 tbsp olive oil
2 white onions, chopped
4 garlic cloves, minced
1 lb tofu, pressed and cubed
2 tbsp soy sauce
¾ cup chopped walnuts
Salt and black pepper
1 tbsp Italian mixed herbs
½ tsp swerve sugar
¼ cup golden flaxseed meal
1 tbsp sesame seeds
1 green bell pepper, chopped
1 red bell pepper, chopped
½ cup tomato sauce

Directions and Total Time: approx. 70 minutes

Preheat oven to 350 F. In a bowl, combine olive oil, onion, garlic, tofu, soy sauce, walnuts, salt, pepper, Italian herbs, swerve sugar, golden flaxseed meal and mix with your hands. Pour the mixture into a bowl and stir in sesame seeds and bell peppers. Transfer the loaf into a greased and spoon tomato sauce on top. Bake for 45 minutes. Turn onto a chopping board, slice, and serve.

Per serving: Cal 432; Net Carbs 2.5g; Fat 31g; Protein 24g

Tofu & Spinach Lasagna with Red Sauce

Ingredients for 4 servings

2 tbsp butter
1 white onion, chopped
1 garlic clove, minced
2 ½ cups crumbled tofu

3 tbsp tomato paste
½ tbsp dried oregano
1 cup baby spinach
8 tbsp flax seed powder
1 ½ cups cream cheese
5 tbsp psyllium husk powder
2 cups coconut cream
5 oz grated mozzarella
2 oz grated Parmesan cheese
½ cup fresh parsley, chopped

Directions and Total Time: approx. 65 minutes

Melt butter in a pot and sauté onion and garlic for 3 minutes. Stir in tofu and cook until brown. Mix in tomato paste, oregano, salt, and pepper. Pour ½ cup water into the pot, stir, and simmer until most of the liquid has evaporated. Preheat oven to 300 F and mix the flax seed powder with 1 ½ cups water in a bowl to make flax egg. Let thicken for 5 minutes. Combine the flax egg with cream cheese and salt. Whisk in psyllium husk a bit at a time and let the mixture sit for 5 more minutes. Line a baking sheet with parchment paper and spread the mixture. Cover with another parchment paper and use a rolling pin to flatten the dough into the sheet. Bake for 12 minutes, remove, take off the parchment papers, and slice the pasta into sheets. In a bowl, combine coconut cream and two-thirds of mozzarella cheese. Fetch out 2 tbsp of the mixture and reserve. Mix in Parmesan, salt, pepper, and parsley; set aside. Grease a baking dish, lay a single line of pasta, spread with some tomato sauce, 1/3 of the spinach, and ¼ of the coconut cream mixture. Repeat the layering twice in the same manner making sure to top the final layer with the coconut cream mixture and the reserved cream cheese. Bake for 30 minutes at 400 F.

Per serving: Cal 775; Net Carbs 8g; Fat 64g; Protein 40g

Mushroom Pizza Bowls with Avocado

Ingredients for 4 servings
1 ½ cups cauli rice
2 tbsp water
Olive oil for brushing
2 cups pizza sauce
1 cup grated Monterey Jack
1 cup grated mozzarella
½ cup sliced mushrooms
2 large tomatoes, chopped
1 small red onion, chopped
1 tsp dried oregano
2 jalapeño peppers, chopped
Salt and black pepper to taste
1 avocado, chopped
¼ cup chopped cilantro

Directions and Total Time: approx. 40 minutes

Preheat oven to 400 F. Microwave cauli rice for 2 minutes. Fluff with a fork and set aside. Brush 4 ramekins with olive oil and spread half of pizza sauce at the bottom. Top with half of cauli rice and half of the cheeses. In a bowl, mix mushrooms, tomatoes, onions, oregano, jalapeños, salt, and pepper. Spoon half of the mixture into the ramekin and repeat the layering process, finishing off with cheese. Bake for 20 minutes. Top with avocados and cilantro.

Per serving: Cal 378; Net Carbs 3.4g; Fat 22g; Protein 21g

Pesto Tofu Zoodles

Ingredients for 4 servings
2/3 cup grated Pecorino Romano cheese
2 tbsp olive oil
1 white onion, chopped
1 garlic clove, minced
28 oz tofu, pressed and cubed
1 red bell pepper, sliced
6 zucchinis, spiralized
Salt and black pepper to taste
¼ cup basil pesto
½ cup shredded mozzarella
Toasted pine nuts to garnish

Directions and Total Time: approx. 20 minutes

Heat olive oil in a pot and sauté onion and garlic for 3 minutes. Add in tofu and cook until golden on all sides, then pour in the bell pepper and cook for 4 minutes. Mix in zucchinis, pour pesto on top, and season with salt and pepper. Cook for 3-4 minutes. Stir in the Pecorino cheese. Top with mozzarella, garnish with pine nuts, and serve.

Per serving: Cal 477; Net Carbs 5.4g; Fat 32g; Protein 20g

Veal Chops with Raspberry Sauce

Ingredients for 4 servings

3 tbsp olive oil
2 lb veal chops
Salt and black pepper to taste
2 cups raspberries
¼ cup water
1 ½ tbsp Italian Herb mix
3 tbsp balsamic vinegar
2 tsp Worcestershire sauce

Directions and Total Time: approx. 20 minutes

Heat oil in a skillet, season veal with salt and pepper and cook for 5 minutes on each side. Put on serving plates and reserve the pork drippings. Mash the raspberries in a bowl until jam-like. Pour into a saucepan, add water, and herb mix. Bring to boil on low heat for 4 minutes. Stir in veal drippings, vinegar, and Worcestershire sauce. Simmer for 1 minute. Spoon sauce over the veal chops and serve.

Per serving: Cal 413; Net Carbs 1.1g; Fat 32.5g; Protein 26g

Kale & Mushroom Pierogis

Ingredients for 4 servings
7 tbsp butter
2 garlic cloves, chopped
1 small red onion, chopped
3 oz bella mushrooms, sliced
2 oz fresh kale
Salt and black pepper to taste
½ cup cream cheese
2 cups Parmesan, grated
1 tbsp flax seed powder
½ cup almond flour
4 tbsp coconut flour
1 tsp baking powder

Directions and Total Time: approx. 45 minutes

Melt 2 tbsp of butter in a skillet and sauté garlic, red onion, mushrooms, and kale for 5 minutes. Season with salt and pepper and reduce the heat to low. Stir in cream cheese and ½ cup Parmesan; simmer for 1 minute. Set aside to cool. In a bowl, mix flax seed powder with 3 tbsp water and allow sitting for 5 minutes. In a another bowl, combine almond and coconut flours, salt, and baking powder. Put a pan over low heat and melt the remaining Parmesan and butter. Turn the heat off.

Pour the flax egg into the cream mixture, continue stirring, while adding the flour mixture until a firm dough forms. Mold the dough into four balls, place on a chopping board, and use a rolling pin to flatten each into ½ inch thin round pieces. Spread a generous amount of stuffing on one-half of each dough, then fold over the filling, and seal the dough with fingers. Brush with olive oil and bake for 20 minutes at 380 F. Serve.

Per serving: Cal 540; Net Carbs 6g; Fat 47g; Protein 18g

Cashew Quesadillas with Leafy Greens

Ingredients for 4 servings
3 tbsp flax seed powder
½ cup dairy-free cream cheese
1½ tsp psyllium husk powder
1 tbsp coconut flour
½ tsp salt
2 tbsp cashew butter
5 oz grated vegan cheddar
1 oz leafy greens

Directions and Total Time: approx. 30 minutes

Preheat oven to 400 F. In a bowl, mix flax seed powder with ½ cup water and allow sitting to thicken for 5 minutes. Whisk the cream cheese into the flax egg until the batter is smooth. In another bowl, combine psyllium husk, coconut flour, and salt. Add flour mixture to the flax egg batter and fold in until fully incorporated. Let sit for a few minutes. Line a baking sheet with parchment paper and pour in the mixture. Bake for 7 minutes until brown around the edges. Remove and slice into 8 pieces; set aside. Warm some cashew butter in a skillet and place a tortilla in the pan. Sprinkle with cheddar, leafy greens, and cover with another tortilla. Brown each side for 1 minute until the cheese melts. Repeat with the remaining cashew butter.

Per serving: Cal 470; Net Carbs 4g; Fat 40g; Protein 19g

BBQ Tofu Skewers with Squash Mash

Ingredients for 4 servings
7 tbsp fresh cilantro, chopped
4 tbsp fresh basil, chopped
2 garlic cloves

Juice of ½ a lemon
4 tbsp capers
2/3 cup olive oil
Salt and black pepper to taste
1 lb tofu, cubed
½ tbsp sugar-free BBQ sauce
½ cup vegan butter
3 cups butternut squash, cubed
2 oz grated vegan Parmesan

Directions and Total Time: approx. 30 minutes

In a blender, add cilantro, basil, garlic, lemon juice, capers, olive oil, salt, and pepper and process until smooth, 2 minutes. Set aside the salsa verde. Thread tofu cubes on wooden skewers. Season with salt and brush with BBQ sauce. Melt 1 tbsp vegan butter in a grill pan and fry tofu until browned on both sides; remove to a plate. Pour squash into a pot, add some salted water, and bring the vegetables to a boil for 15 minutes. Drain and pour the squash into a bowl. Add remaining vegan butter, vegan Parmesan cheese, salt, and pepper; mash vegetable. Serve tofu skewers with mashed squash and salsa verde.

Per serving: Cal 850; Net Carbs 5g; Fat 78g; Protein 26g

Roasted Chorizo & Mixed Greens

Ingredients for 4 servings
1 lb chorizo, cubed
1 lb asparagus, halved
2 mixed bell peppers, diced
1 cup green beans, trimmed
2 red onions, cut into wedges
1 head broccoli, cut into florets
Salt and black pepper to taste
4 tbsp olive oil
1 tbsp sugar-free maple syrup
1 lemon, juiced

Directions and Total Time: approx. 30 minutes

Preheat oven to 400 F. On a baking tray, add chorizo, asparagus, bell peppers, green beans, onions, and broccoli; season with salt, pepper, and drizzle with olive oil and maple syrup. Rub the seasoning onto the vegetables. Bake for 15 minutes. Drizzle with lemon juice and serve warm.

Per serving: Cal 300; Net Carbs 3.3g; Fat 18g; Protein 15g

Spicy Veggie Steaks with Green Salad

Ingredients for 2 servings
1/3 eggplant, sliced
½ zucchini, sliced
¼ cup coconut oil
Juice of ½ lemon
5 oz cheddar cheese, cubed
10 Kalamata olives
2 tbsp pecans
1 oz mixed salad greens
½ cup mayonnaise
½ tsp Cayenne pepper to taste

Directions and Total Time: approx. 35 minutes

Set the oven to broil and line a baking sheet with parchment paper. Arrange zucchini and eggplant slices on the sheet. Brush with coconut oil and sprinkle with salt and cayenne pepper. Broil until golden brown, about 18 minutes. Remove to a serving platter and drizzle with lemon juice. Arrange cheddar, olives, pecans, and mixed greens next to grilled veggies. Top with mayonnaise and serve.

Per serving: Cal 512g; Net Carbs 8g; Fat 31g; Protein 22g

Grilled Zucchini with Spinach Avocado Pesto

Ingredients for 4 servings
3 oz spinach, chopped
1 ripe avocado, chopped
Juice of 1 lemon
1 garlic clove, minced
2 oz pecans
Salt and black pepper to taste
¾ cup olive oil
2 zucchini, sliced
2 tbsp melted vegan butter
1 ½ lb tempeh slices

Directions and Total Time: approx. 20 minutes

Place spinach in a food processor along with avocado, half of lemon juice, garlic, and pecans and blend until smooth; season with salt and pepper. Add in olive oil and process a little more. Pour the pesto into a bowl and set aside. Season zucchini with the remaining lemon juice, salt, pepper, and vegan butter. Brush tempeh with some olive oil. Preheat a grill pan and cook both the tempeh and

zucchini slices until browned. Plate the tempeh and zucchini, spoon some pesto to the side, and serve.
Per serving: Cal 550; Net Carbs 6g; Fat 46g; Protein 25g

Seitan Cakes with Broccoli Mash

Ingredients for 4 servings
1 tbsp flax seed powder
1½ lbs crumbled seitan
½ white onion, chopped
2 oz olive oil
1 lb broccoli
5 tbsp vegan butter
2 oz grated vegan Parmesan
2 tbsp lemon juice

Directions and Total Time: approx. 30 minutes
Preheat oven to 220 F. In a bowl, mix flax seed powder with 3 tbsp water and let sit for 5 minutes. When the flax egg is ready, add crumbled seitan, onion, salt, and pepper. Mix and mold out 6-8 cakes out of the mixture. Warm olive oil in a skillet and fry the patties on both sides. Remove onto a wire rack to cool slightly. Pour lightly salted water into a pot, bring to a boil over medium heat, and add broccoli. Cook until tender but not too soft. Drain and transfer to a bowl. Add in 2 tbsp of vegan butter, and Parmesan. Use an immersion blender to puree the ingredients until smooth and creamy; set aside. To make the lemon butter, mix soft vegan butter with lemon juice, salt, and pepper in a bowl. Serve seitan cakes with broccoli mash and lemon butter.
Per serving: Cal 860; Net Carbs 6g; Fat 76g; Protein 35g

Greek-Style Pizza

Ingredients for 4 servings
½ cup almond flour
¼ tsp salt
2 tbsp ground psyllium husk
1 tbsp olive oil
¼ tsp red chili flakes
¼ tsp dried Greek seasoning
1 cup crumbled feta cheese
3 sliced plum tomatoes
6 Kalamata olives, chopped
5 basil leaves, chopped

Directions and Total Time: approx. 30 minutes
Preheat oven to 390 F and line a baking sheet with parchment paper. In a bowl, mix almond flour, salt, psyllium powder, olive oil, and 1 cup of lukewarm water until dough forms. Spread the mixture on the pizza pan and bake for 10 minutes. Sprinkle the red chili flakes and Greek seasoning on the crust and top with the feta cheese. Arrange the tomatoes and olives on top. Bake for 10 minutes. Garnish pizza with basil, slice and serve warm.
Per serving: Cal 276; Net Carbs 4.5g; Fats 12g; Protein 8g

Baked Stuffed Avocados

Ingredients for 4 servings
3 avocados, halved and pitted, skin on
½ cup mozzarella, shredded
½ cup Swiss cheese, grated
2 eggs, beaten
1 tbsp fresh basil, chopped

Directions and Total Time: approx. 20 minutes
Set oven to 360 F. Lay avocado halves in an ovenproof dish. In a bowl, mix both types of cheeses, pepper, eggs, and salt. Split the mixture into the avocado halves. Bake for 15 to 17 minutes. Decorate with basil before serving.
Per serving: Cal 342; Net Carbs: 7.5g; Fat: 30g; Protein: 11g

Curried Tofu with Buttery Cabbage

Ingredients for 4 servings
2 cups extra firm tofu, cubed
3 tbsp coconut oil
½ cup grated coconut
1 tsp yellow curry powder
½ tsp onion powder
2 cups Napa cabbage
4 oz vegan butter
Lemon wedges for serving

Directions and Total Time: approx. 55 minutes
In a bowl, mix shredded coconut, curry powder, salt, and onion powder. Toss in tofu. Heat coconut oil in a skillet and fry tofu until golden brown; transfer to a plate. In the same skillet, melt half of vegan butter, add, and sauté the cabbage until slightly caramelized.

Season with salt and pepper. Place the cabbage into plates with tofu and lemon wedges. Melt the remaining vegan butter in the skillet and drizzle over the cabbage and tofu. Serve immediately.

Per serving: Cal 733; Net Carbs 4g; Fat 61g; Protein 36g

Avocado Coconut Pie

Ingredients for 4 servings
1 egg
4 tbsp coconut flour
4 tbsp chia seeds
¾ cup almond flour
1 tbsp psyllium husk powder
1 tsp baking powder
3 tbsp coconut oil
2 ripe avocados, chopped
1 cup mayonnaise
2 tbsp fresh parsley, chopped
1 jalapeño pepper, chopped
½ tsp onion powder
½ cup cream cheese
1¼ cups grated Parmesan

Directions and Total Time: approx. 80 minutes
Preheat oven to 350 F. In a food processor, add coconut flour, chia seeds, almond flour, psyllium husk, baking powder, pinch of salt, coconut oil, and 4 tbsp water. Blend until the resulting dough forms into a ball. Line a springform pan with parchment paper and spread the dough. Bake for 15 minutes. In a bowl, put avocado, mayonnaise, egg, parsley, jalapeño, onion, salt, cream cheese, and vegan Parmesan; mix well. Remove the piecrust when ready and fill with creamy mixture. Continue baking for 35 minutes until lightly golden brown.

Per serving: Cal 876; Net Carbs 10g; Fat 67g; Protein 24g

Asparagus with Creamy Puree

Ingredients for 4 servings
4 tbsp flax seed powder
5 oz vegan butter, melted
3 oz grated cashew cheese
½ cup coconut cream
1 tbsp olive oil
½ lb asparagus, stalks removed
Juice of ½ lemon
½ tsp chili pepper

Directions and Total Time: approx. 15 minutes
In a microwave bowl, mix flax seed powder with ½ cup water and set aside for 5 minutes. Warm the flax egg in the microwave for 2 minutes, then, pour into a blender. Add in 2 oz butter, coconut cream, salt, and chili pepper; puree until smooth. Heat olive oil in a saucepan.

Roast the asparagus until lightly charred. Season with salt and pepper; set aside. Warm the remaining butter in a frying pan until nutty and golden brown. Stir in lemon juice and pour the mixture into a sauce cup. Spoon the creamy blend into four plates and spread out lightly. Top with asparagus and drizzle the lemon butter on top. Serve.

Per serving: Cal 520g; Net Carbs 6g; Fat 53g; Protein 6.3g

Caprese Casserole

Ingredients for 4 servings
1 cup mozzarella cheese, cut into pieces
1 cup cherry tomatoes, halved
2 tbsp basil pesto
1 cup mayonnaise
2 oz Parmesan cheese
1 cup arugula
4 tbsp olive oil

Directions and Total Time: approx. 25 minutes
Preheat oven to 350 F. In a baking dish, mix cherry tomatoes, mozzarella cheese, basil pesto, mayonnaise, and half of the Parmesan cheese. Level the ingredients with a spatula and sprinkle the remaining Parmesan on top. Bake for 20 minutes until the top is golden brown; let cool. Slice, top with arugula and olive oil, and serve.

Per serving: Cal 450; Net Carbs 5g; Fat 41g; Protein 12g

Mushroom Lettuce Wraps

Ingredients for 4 servings
4 oz baby bella mushrooms, sliced
1 iceberg lettuce, leaves extracted
1 cup grated cheddar cheese
2 tbsp vegan butter
1½ lbs tofu, crumbled
Salt and black pepper to taste
1 large tomato, sliced

Directions and Total Time: approx. 20 minutes

Melt butter in a skillet over medium heat. Add mushrooms and sauté until browned and tender, 6 minutes; set aside. Add in tofu, season with salt and pepper, and cook until brown, about 10 minutes. Spoon the tofu and mushrooms into the lettuce leaves, sprinkle with cheddar, and share tomato slices on top. Serve the burger immediately.

Per serving: Cal 620; Net Carbs 3g; Fat 52g; Protein 32g

Buttered Carrot Noodles with Kale

Ingredients for 4 servings
2 carrots, spiralized
¼ cup vegetable broth
4 tbsp butter
1 garlic clove, minced
1 cup chopped kale
Salt and black pepper to serve

Directions and Total Time: approx. 15 minutes

Pour broth into a saucepan over low heat and add in carrot noodles to simmer for 3 minutes; strain and set aside. Melt butter a skillet and sauté garlic and kale until the kale is wilted. Pour in carrots, season with to taste, and stir-fry for 4 minutes. Serve with grilled tofu.

Per serving: Cal 335; Net Carbs 8g; Fat 28g; Protein 6g

Eggplant Fries with Chili Aioli & Beet Salad

Ingredients for 4 servings
1 egg, beaten in a bowl
2 eggplants, sliced
2 cups almond flour
Salt and black pepper to taste
2 tbsp melted butter
2 egg yolks
2 garlic cloves, minced
1 cup olive oil
½ tsp red chili flakes
2 tbsp lemon juice
3 tbsp yogurt
3½ oz cooked beets, shredded
3½ oz red cabbage, grated
2 tbsp fresh cilantro

Directions and Total Time: approx. 25 minutes

Preheat oven to 400 F. In a deep plate, mix flour, salt, and pepper. Dip eggplants into the egg, then in the flour mixture. Place on a greased baking sheet and brush with butter. Bake for 15 minutes. To make aioli whisk egg yolks with garlic, gradually pouring ¾ cup olive oil. Stir in chili flakes, salt, pepper, 1 tbsp of lemon juice, and yogurt. In a salad bowl, mix beets, cabbage, cilantro, remaining oil, remaining lemon juice, salt, and pepper; toss to coat. Serve the fries with the chili aioli and beet salad.

Per serving: Cal 850; Net Carbs 8g; Fat 77g; Protein 26g

Baked Cheesy Spaghetti Squash

Ingredients for 4 servings
2 lb spaghetti squash
1 tbsp coconut oil
Salt and black pepper to taste
2 tbsp melted vegan butter
½ tbsp garlic powder
1/5 tsp chili powder
1 cup coconut cream
2 oz dairy-free cream cheese
1 cup vegan mozzarella
2 oz grated Parmesan
2 tbsp fresh cilantro, chopped
Olive oil for drizzling

Directions and Total Time: approx. 40 minutes

Preheat oven to 350 F. Cut squash in halves lengthwise and spoon out the seeds and fiber. Place the halves on a baking dish, brush each with coconut oil, and season with salt and pepper. Bake for 30 minutes. Remove and use two forks to shred the flesh into strands. Empty the spaghetti strands into a bowl and mix with vegan butter, garlic powder, chili powder, coconut cream, cream cheese, half of mozzarella cheese, and Parmesan. Spoon the mixture into the squash cups and sprinkle with the remaining mozzarella. Bake further for 5 minutes or until the cheese is golden brown. Season with black pepper, cilantro; drizzle with olive oil.

Per serving: Cal 515; Net Carbs 7g; Fat 45g; Protein 18g

Tempeh Garam Masala Bake

Ingredients for 4 servings
3 tbsp butter

3 cups tempeh slices
2 tbsp garam masala
1 green bell pepper, diced
1 ¼ cups coconut cream
1 tbsp fresh cilantro, chopped
Directions and Total Time: approx. 30 minutes
Preheat oven to 400 F. Melt butter in a skillet and fry tempeh until browned, about 4 minutes. Stir in half of garam masala; turn the heat off.
Transfer the tempeh to a baking dish. In a bowl, mix bell pepper, coconut cream, cilantro, and the remaining garam masala. Pour over tempeh and bake for 20 minutes. Garnish with cilantro to serve.
Per serving: Cal 610; Net Carbs 5g; Fat 47g; Protein 35g

Cheesy Cauliflower Casserole

Ingredients for 4 servings
2 oz vegan butter
1 white onion, finely chopped
½ cup celery stalks, chopped
1 green bell pepper, chopped
1 head cauliflower, chopped
1 cup mayonnaise
4 oz grated Parmesan
1 tsp red chili flakes
Directions and Total Time: approx. 35 minutes
Preheat oven to 400 F. Season onion, celery, and bell pepper with salt and pepper. In a bowl, mix cauliflower, mayo, Parmesan, and chili flakes. Pour the mixture into a greased baking dish, add and distribute the veggies evenly. Bake until golden, 20 minutes. Serve with baby spinach.
Per serving: Cal 464; Net Carbs 4g; Fat 37g; Protein 36g

Tempeh Coconut Curry Bake

Ingredients for 4 servings
15 oz cauliflower, cut into florets
Salt and black pepper to taste
2 ½ cups chopped tempeh
4 tbsp butter
2 tbsp red curry paste
1 ½ cups coconut cream
½ cup fresh parsley, chopped
Directions and Total Time: approx. 30 minutes

Preheat oven to 400 F. Arrange tempeh on a greased baking dish, sprinkle with salt and pepper, and top each tempeh with a slice of butter. In a bowl, mix curry paste with coconut cream and parsley. Pour the mixture over the tempeh. Bake for 20 minutes. Season cauliflower with salt and microwave for 3 minutes until soft and tender within. Remove the curry bake and serve with the cauliflower.
Per serving: Cal 860; Net Carbs 10g; Fat 56g; Protein 73g

Creamy Brussels Sprouts Bake

Ingredients for 4 servings
3 tbsp butter
1 cup tempeh, cubed
1½ lb halved Brussels sprouts
5 garlic cloves, minced
1¼ cups coconut cream
2 cups grated vegan cheddar
¼ cup grated vegan Parmesan
Salt and black pepper to taste
Directions and Total Time: approx. 40 minutes
Preheat oven to 400 F. Melt butter in a skillet and fry tempeh cubes for 6 minutes; remove to a plate. Pour the Brussels sprouts and garlic into the skillet and sauté until nice color forms. Mix in coconut cream and simmer for 4 minutes. Mix in tempeh cubes. Pour the sauté into a baking dish, sprinkle with cheddar and Parmesan cheeses. Bake for 10 minutes. Serve with tomato salad.
Per serving: Cal 420; Net Carbs 7g; Fat 34g; Protein 13g

Zoodle Bolognese

Ingredients for 4 servings
3 oz olive oil
1 white onion, chopped
1 garlic clove, minced
3 oz carrots, chopped
3 cups crumbled tofu
2 tbsp tomato paste
1 ½ cups crushed tomatoes
Salt and black pepper to taste
1 tbsp dried basil
1 tbsp Worcestershire sauce
2 lbs zucchini, spiralized
2 tbsp vegan butter
Directions and Total Time: approx. 45 minutes

Heat olive oil in a saucepan and sauté onion, garlic, and carrots for 3 minutes. Pour in tofu, tomato paste, tomatoes, salt, pepper, basil, some water, and Worcestershire sauce. Stir and cook for 15 minutes. Melt vegan butter in a skillet and toss in zoodles quickly, about 1 minute. Season with salt and pepper. Serve zoodles topped with the sauce.

Per serving: Cal 425; Net Carbs 6g; Fat 33g; Protein 20g

Baked Tofu with Roasted Peppers

Ingredients for 4 servings
3 oz dairy-free cream cheese
¾ cup vegan mayonnaise
2 oz cucumber, diced
1 large tomato, chopped
Salt and black pepper to taste
2 tsp dried parsley
4 orange bell peppers
2 ½ cups cubed tofu
1 tbsp melted vegan butter
1 tsp dried basil

Directions and Total Time: approx. 20 minutes
Preheat a broiler to 450 F and line a baking sheet with parchment paper. In a salad bowl, combine cream cheese, vegan mayonnaise, cucumber, tomato, salt, pepper, and parsley; refrigerate. Arrange bell peppers and tofu on the paper-lined baking sheet, drizzle with melted butter, and season with basil, salt, and pepper. Use hands to rub the ingredients until evenly coated. Bake for 15 minutes until the peppers have charred lightly and the tofu browned.

Per serving: Cal 840; Net Carbs 8g; Fat 76g; Protein 28g

Spicy Cheese with Tofu Balls

Ingredients for 4 servings
1/3 cup vegan mayonnaise
¼ cup pickled jalapenos
1 tsp paprika powder
1 tbsp mustard powder
1 pinch cayenne pepper
4 oz grated vegan cheddar
1 tbsp flax seed powder
2 ½ cup crumbled tofu
Salt and black pepper to taste
2 tbsp vegan butter, for frying

Directions and Total Time: approx. 40 minutes
In a bowl, mix mayonnaise, jalapenos, paprika, mustard, cayenne, and cheddar; set aside. In another bowl, combine flax seed powder with 3 tbsp water and allow absorbing for 5 minutes. Add the flax egg to the cheese mixture, crumbled tofu, salt, and pepper; mix well. Form meatballs out of the mix. Melt vegan butter in a skillet over medium heat and fry balls until cooked and browned on the outside.

Per serving: Cal 650; Net Carbs 2g; Fat 52g; Protein 43g

Zucchini Boats with Vegan Cheese

Ingredients for 2 servings
1 zucchini, halved
4 tbsp vegan butter
2 garlic cloves, minced
1½ oz baby kale
Salt and black pepper to taste
2 tbsp tomato sauce
1 cup vegan cheese
1 tbsp olive oil

Directions and Total Time: approx. 40 minutes
Preheat oven to 375 F. Scoop out zucchini pulp with a spoon. Keep the flesh. Grease a baking sheet with cooking spray and place the zucchini boats on top. Melt butter in a skillet and sauté garlic until fragrant and slightly browned, 4 minutes. Add in kale and zucchini pulp. Cook until the kale wilts; season with salt and pepper. Spoon tomato sauce into the boats and spread to coat evenly. Spoon kale mixture into the zucchinis and sprinkle with vegan cheese. Bake for 25 minutes. Drizzle with olive oil.

Per serving: Cal 620; Net Carbs 4g; Fat 57g; Protein 20g

Sweet & Spicy Brussel Sprout Stir-Fry

Ingredients for 4 servings
4 tbsp butter
4 shallots, chopped
1 tbsp apple cider vinegar
Salt and black pepper to taste
2 cups Brussels sprouts, halved
Hot chili sauce

Directions and Total Time: approx. 15 minutes

Melt half of butter in a saucepan over medium heat and sauté shallots for 2 minutes until slightly soften. Add in apple cider vinegar, salt, and pepper. Stir and reduce the heat to cook the shallots further with continuous stirring, about 5 minutes. Transfer to a plate. Pour Brussel sprouts into the saucepan and stir-fry with remaining vegan butter until softened. Season with salt and pepper, stir in the shallots and hot chili sauce, and heat for a few seconds.

Per serving: Cal 260; Net Carbs 7g; Fat 23g; Protein 3g

Roasted Butternut Squash with Chimichurri

Ingredients for 4 servings
Zest and juice of 1 lemon
½ red bell pepper, chopped
1 jalapeño pepper, chopped
1 cup olive oil
½ cup chopped fresh parsley
2 garlic cloves, minced
Salt and black pepper to taste
1 lb butternut squash
1 tbsp butter, melted
3 tbsp toasted pine nuts

Directions and Total Time: approx. 15 minutes
In a bowl, add lemon zest and juice, bell pepper, jalapeño, olive oil, parsley, garlic, salt, and pepper. Use an immersion blender to grind the ingredients until desired consistency is achieved; set chimichurri aside. Slice the squash into rounds and remove the seeds. Drizzle with butter and season with salt and pepper. Preheat grill pan over medium heat and cook the squash for 2 minutes on each side. Scatter pine nuts on top and serve with chimichurri.

Per serving: Cal 650; Net Carbs 6g; Fat 44g; Protein 55g

Tofu Eggplant Pizza

Ingredients for 4 servings
2 eggplants, sliced
1/3 cup melted butter
2 garlic cloves, minced
1 red onion
12 oz crumbled tofu
7 oz tomato sauce
Salt and black pepper to taste

½ tsp cinnamon powder
1 cup grated Parmesan
¼ cup chopped fresh oregano

Directions and Total Time: approx. 45 minutes
Preheat oven to 400 F and line a baking sheet with parchment paper. Brush eggplants with butter. Bake until lightly browned, 20 minutes. Heat the remaining butter in a skillet and sauté garlic and onion until fragrant and soft, about 3 minutes. Stir in tofu and cook for 3 minutes. Add tomato sauce and season with salt and pepper. Simmer for 10 minutes. Remove eggplants from the oven and spread the tofu sauce on top. Sprinkle with Parmesan cheese and oregano. Bake further for 10 minutes.

Per serving: Cal 600; Net Carbs 12g; Fat 46g; Protein 26g

Tomato Artichoke Pizza

Ingredients for 4 servings
2 oz canned artichokes, cut into wedges
2 tbsp flax seed powder
4¼ oz grated broccoli
6¼ oz grated Parmesan
½ tsp salt
2 tbsp tomato sauce
2 oz mozzarella cheese, grated
1 garlic clove, thinly sliced
1 tbsp dried oregano
Green olives for garnish

Directions and Total Time: approx. 40 minutes
Preheat oven to 350 F and line a baking sheet with parchment paper. In a bowl, mix flax seed powder and 6 tbsp water and allow thickening for 5 minutes. When the flax egg is ready, add broccoli, 4 ½ ounces of Parmesan cheese, salt, and stir to combine. Pour the mixture into the baking sheet and bake until the crust is lightly browned, 20 minutes. Remove from oven and spread tomato sauce on top, sprinkle with the remaining Parmesan and mozzarella cheeses, add artichokes and garlic. Spread oregano on top. Bake pizza for 10 minutes at 420 F. Garnish with olives.

Per serving: Cal 860; Net Carbs 10g; Fat 63g; Protein 55g

White Pizza with Mixed Mushrooms

Ingredients for 4 servings

2 tbsp flax seed powder
½ cup mayonnaise
¾ cup almond flour
1 tbsp psyllium husk powder
1 tsp baking powder
2 oz mixed mushrooms, sliced
1 tbsp basil pesto
2 tbsp olive oil
½ cup coconut cream
¾ cup grated Parmesan

Directions and Total Time: approx. 35 minutes

Preheat oven to 350 F. Combine flax seed powder with 6 tbsp water and allow sitting for 5 minutes. Whisk in mayonnaise, flour, psyllium husk, baking powder, and ½ tsp salt; let rest. Pour batter into a baking sheet. Bake for 10 minutes. In a bowl, mix mushrooms with pesto, olive oil, salt, and pepper. Remove crust from the oven and spread coconut cream on top. Add the mushroom mixture and Parmesan. Bake the pizza further until the cheese melts, about 5-10 minutes. Slice and serve.

Per serving: Cal 750; Net Carbs 6g; Fat 69g; Protein 22g

Pepperoni Fat Head Pizza

Ingredients for 4 servings
3 ½ cups grated mozzarella
2 tbsp cream cheese, softened
2 eggs, beaten
1/3 cup almond flour
1 tsp dried oregano
½ cup sliced pepperoni

Directions and Total Time: approx. 35 minutes

Preheat oven to 420 F and line a round pizza pan with parchment paper. Microwave 2 cups of the mozzarella cheese and cream cheese for 1 minute. Mix in eggs and almond flour. Transfer the pizza "dough" onto a flat surface and knead until smooth. Spread it on the pizza pan. Bake for 6 minutes. Top with remaining mozzarella, oregano, and pepperoni. Bake for 15 minutes.

Per serving: Cal 229; Net Carbs 0.4g; Fats 7g; Protein 36.4g

Vegan Cordon Bleu Casserole

Ingredients for 4 servings
2 cups grilled tofu, cubed

1 cup smoked seitan, cubed
1 cup cream cheese
1 tbsp mustard powder
1 tbsp plain vinegar
1 ¼ cup grated cheddar
½ cup baby spinach
4 tbsp olive oil

Directions and Total Time: approx. 30 minutes

Preheat oven to 400 F. Mix cream cheese, mustard powder, plain vinegar, and cheddar in a baking dish. Top with tofu and seitan. Bake until the casserole is golden brown, about 20 minutes. Drizzle with olive oil.

Per serving: Cal 980; Net Carbs 6g; Fat 92g; Protein 30g

Parmesan Meatballs

Ingredients for 4 servings
½ lb ground beef
½ lb ground Italian sausage
¾ cup pork rinds
½ cup grated Parmesan cheese
2 eggs
1 tsp onion powder
1 tsp garlic powder
1 tbsp chopped fresh basil
Salt and black pepper to taste
2 tsp dried Italian seasoning
3 tbsp olive oil
2 ½ cups marinara sauce

Directions and Total Time: approx. 1 hour

In a bowl, add beef, Italian sausage, pork rinds, Parmesan cheese, eggs, onion powder, garlic powder, basil, salt, pepper, and Italian seasoning. Form meatballs out of the mixture. Heat the remaining olive oil in a skillet and brown the meatballs for 10 minutes. Pour in marinara sauce and submerge the meatballs in the sauce; cook for 45 minutes.

Per serving: Cal 513; Net Carbs 8.2g; Fat 24g; Protein 35g

Seitan Cauliflower Gratin

Ingredients for 4 servings
2 oz butter
1 leek, coarsely chopped
1 onion, coarsely chopped
2 cups broccoli florets
1 cup cauliflower florets
2 cups crumbled seitan
1 cup coconut cream

2 tbsp mustard powder
5 oz grated Parmesan
4 tbsp fresh rosemary

Directions and Total Time: approx. 40 minutes

Preheat oven to 450 F. Put half of butter in a pot, set over medium heat to melt. Add leek, onion, broccoli, and cauliflower and cook until the vegetables have softened, about 6 minutes. Transfer them to a baking dish. Melt the remaining butter in a skillet over medium heat, and cook seitan until browned.
Mix coconut cream and mustard powder in a bowl. Pour the mixture over the veggies. Scatter seitan and Parmesan on top and sprinkle with rosemary. Bake for 15 minutes. Serve warm.

Per serving: Cal 480; Net Carbs 9.8g; Fat 40g; Protein 16g

Walnut Stuffed Mushrooms

Ingredients for 4 servings
½ cup grated Pecorino Romano cheese
12 button mushrooms, stemmed
¼ cup pork rinds
2 garlic cloves, minced
2 tbsp chopped fresh parsley
Salt and black pepper to taste
¼ cup ground walnuts
¼ cup olive oil

Directions and Total Time: approx. 30 minutes

Preheat oven to 400 F. In a bowl, mix pork rinds, Pecorino Romano cheese, garlic, parsley, salt, and pepper. Brush a baking sheet with 2 tablespoons of the olive oil. Spoon the cheese mixture into the mushrooms and arrange on the baking sheet. Top with the ground walnuts and drizzle the remaining olive oil on the mushrooms. Bake for 20 minutes or until golden. Transfer to a platter and serve.

Per serving: Cal 292; Net Carbs 7.1g; Fat 25g; Protein 8g

Kentucky Cauliflower with Mashed Parsnips

Ingredients for 6 servings
½ cup almond milk
¼ cup coconut flour
¼ tsp cayenne pepper
½ cup almond breadcrumbs
½ cup grated cheddar cheese
30 oz cauliflower florets
1 lb parsnips, quartered
3 tbsp melted butter
A pinch nutmeg
1 tsp cumin powder
1 cup coconut cream
2 tbsp sesame oil

Directions and Total Time: approx. 35 minutes

Preheat oven to 425 F and line a baking sheet with parchment paper. In a bowl, combine almond milk, coconut flour, and cayenne. In another bowl, mix breadcrumbs and cheddar cheese. Dip each cauliflower floret into the milk mixture, and then into the cheese mixture.
Place breaded cauliflower on the baking sheet and bake for 30 minutes, turning once. Pour 4 cups of slightly salted water in a pot and add in parsnips. Bring to boil for 15 minutes. Drain and transfer to a bowl. Add in melted butter, cumin, nutmeg, and coconut cream. Mash the ingredients using a potato mash. Spoon the mash into plates and drizzle with some sesame oil. Serve with baked cauliflower.

Per serving: Cal 385; Net Carbs 8g; Fat 35g; Protein 6g

Arugula & Pecan Pizza

Ingredients for 4 servings
½ cup almond flour
2 tbsp ground psyllium husk
1 tbsp olive oil
1 cup basil pesto
1 cup grated mozzarella
1 tomato, thinly sliced
1 zucchini, cut into half-moons
1 cup baby arugula
2 tbsp chopped pecans
¼ tsp red chili flakes

Directions and Total Time: approx. 30 minutes

Preheat oven to 390 F and line a baking sheet with parchment paper. In a bowl, mix almond flour, a pinch of salt, psyllium powder, olive oil, and 1 cup of lukewarm water until dough forms. Spread the mixture on the pizza pan and bake for 10 minutes.
Spread pesto on the crust and top with mozzarella cheese, tomato, and zucchini.

Bake until the cheese melts, 15 minutes. Top with arugula, pecans, and red chili flakes. Slice and serve.

Per serving: Cal 186; Net Carbs 3.4g; Fats 14g; Protein 11g

Curry Cauli Rice with Mushrooms

Ingredients for 4 servings

8 oz baby bella mushrooms, stemmed and sliced
2 heads cauliflower, chopped
2 tbsp toasted sesame oil
1 onion, chopped
3 garlic cloves, minced
Salt and black pepper to taste
½ tsp curry powder
1 tsp freshly chopped parsley
2 scallions, thinly sliced

Directions and Total Time: approx. 15 minutes

Place cauliflower in a food processor and pulse until rice-like consistency. Heat sesame oil in a skillet over medium heat, and sauté onion, garlic, and mushrooms for 5 minutes until the mushrooms are soft.

Pour in cauli rice and cook for 6 minutes. Season with salt, pepper, and curry powder. Remove from heat. Stir in parsley and scallions, and serve.

Per serving: Cal 305; Net Carbs 7g; Fat 25g; Protein 6g

POULTRY

Broccoli & Cheese Chicken Sausage

Ingredients for 4 servings
2 tbsp salted butter
4 links chicken sausages, sliced
3 cups broccoli florets
4 garlic cloves, minced
½ cup tomato sauce
¼ cup red wine
½ tsp red pepper flakes
3 cups chopped kale
½ cup Pecorino Romano
Salt and black pepper to taste
Directions and Total Time: approx. 30 minutes
Melt 1 tbsp of butter in a wok and fry the sausages until brown, 5 minutes; set aside. Melt the remaining butter and sauté broccoli for 5 minutes. Mix in garlic and cook for 3 minutes, then pour in tomato sauce, wine, red flakes, and season with salt and pepper. Cover the lid and cook for 10 minutes or until the tomato sauce reduces by one-third. Return the sausages to the pan and heat for 1 minute. Stir in kale to wilt. Spoon onto a platter and sprinkle with Pecorino cheese. Serve warm with cauliflower rice.
Per serving: Cal 263; Net Carbs 7.1g; Fat 17g; Protein 15g

Parmesan Chicken & Broccoli Casserole

Ingredients for 4 servings
5 tbsp butter
1 small white onion, chopped
2 garlic cloves, minced
1 lb ground chicken
1 lb broccoli rabe, chopped
1 cup grated Parmesan cheese
Directions and Total Time: approx. 40 minutes
Preheat oven to 350 F. Melt butter in a skillet and sauté onion and garlic for 3 minutes. Put in chicken and cook until no longer pink, 8 minutes. Add chicken and broccoli rabe to a greased baking dish and mix evenly. Top with butter from the skillet and sprinkle Parmesan on top. Bake for 20 minutes until the cheese melts. Serve.

Per serving: Cal 429; Net Carbs 4.3g; Fat 31g; Protein 31g

Smoked Chicken Tart with Baby Kale

Ingredients for 4 servings
1 cup shredded provolone cheese
1 lb ground chicken
2 cups powdered Parmesan
¼ tsp onion powder
¼ tsp garlic powder
½ cup tomato sauce
1 tsp white vinegar
½ tsp liquid smoke
¼ cup baby kale, chopped
Directions and Total Time: approx. 30 minutes
Preheat oven to 400 F and line a pizza pan with parchment paper and grease with cooking spray. In a bowl, combine chicken, salt, pepper, and Parmesan. Spread the mixture on the pan to fit. Bake for 15 minutes until the meat cooks. In a bowl, mix onion and garlic powder, tomato sauce, vinegar, and liquid smoke. Remove the meat crust from the oven and spread tomato mixture on top. Add kale and sprinkle with provolone cheese. Bake for 7 minutes or until the cheese melts. Slice and serve warm.
Per serving: Cal 517; Net Carbs 16.2g; Fat 28g; Protein 46g

Baked Cheese Chicken with Acorn Squash

Ingredients for 6 servings
6 chicken breasts
1 lb acorn squash, sliced
Salt and black pepper to taste
1 cup blue cheese, crumbled
Directions and Total Time: approx. 1 hour 15 minutes
Grease a baking dish, add in chicken breasts, salt, pepper, squash, and drizzle with olive oil. Transfer to the oven set at 420 F, and bake for 1 hour. Scatter blue cheese, and bake for 15 minutes. Remove to a plate and serve.
Per serving: Cal 235, Net Carbs 5g, Fat 16g, Protein 12g

Cheesy Chicken Tenders

Ingredients for 4 servings

2 eggs
3 tbsp butter, melted
3 cups Monterey Jack, crushed
½ cup pork rinds, crushed
1 lb chicken tenders
Salt to taste

Directions and Total Time: approx. 45 minutes

Preheat oven to 350 F and line a baking sheet with parchment paper. Whisk the eggs with the butter in one bowl and mix the cheese and pork rinds in another bowl. Season chicken with salt, dip in egg mixture, and coat in cheddar mixture. Place on baking sheet, cover with aluminium foil and bake for 25 minutes. Remove foil and bake further for 12 minutes to golden brown. Serve.

Per serving: Cal 507, Net Carbs 1.3g, Fat 54g, Protein 42g

Thyme Zucchini & Chicken Chunks Skillet

Ingredients for 4 servings
2 tbsp olive oil
1 tbsp unsalted butter
1 (4.6 oz) chicken chunks
¼ cup finely chopped onion
¼ cup chopped fresh parsley
3 zucchinis, cut into 1-inch dices
1 tsp dried thyme
Salt and black pepper to taste

Directions and Total Time: approx. 30 minutes

Heat olive oil and butter in a skillet and sauté chicken for 5 minutes. Add in onion and parsley and cook further for 3 minutes. Stir in zucchini and thyme, season with salt, pepper, cover, and cook for 8-10 minutes or until the vegetables soften. Serve immediately.

Per serving: Cal 157; Net Carbs 0.2g; Fat 12g; Protein 8g

Roasted Chicken with Yogurt Scallions Sauce

Ingredients for 4 servings
2 tbsp butter
4 scallions, chopped
4 chicken breasts
Salt and black pepper, to taste
6 ounces plain yogurt
2 tbsp fresh dill, chopped

Directions and Total Time: approx. 35 minutes

Heat a pan with butter, add in chicken, season with pepper and salt, and fry for 2-3 per side. Transfer to a baking dish and bake for 15 minutes at 390 F.

To the pan, add scallions and cook for 2 minutes. Pour in plain yogurt, warm through without boil. Slice the chicken and serve.

Per serving: Cal 236, Net Carbs 2.3g, Fat 9g, Protein 18g

Cheesy Chicken with Cauliflower Steaks

Ingredients for 4 servings
4 slices chicken luncheon meat
1 large head cauliflower
½ tsp smoked paprika
2 tbsp olive oil
½ cup grated cheddar cheese
4 tbsp ranch dressing
2 tbsp chopped parsley

Directions and Total Time: approx. 30 minutes

Stand cauliflower on a flat surface and into 4 steaks from top to bottom. Season with paprika, salt, and pepper. Heat olive oil in a grill pan over medium heat and cook cauliflower on both sides until softened, 4 minutes. Top one side with chicken and sprinkle with cheddar cheese. Heat to melt the cheese. Transfer to serving plates, drizzle with ranch dressing, and garnish with parsley. Serve.

Per serving: Cal 253; Net Carbs 1g; Fat 22g; Protein 9g

Savory Cheesy Chicken

Ingredients for 4 servings
1 ½ lb chicken breasts, halved lengthwise
½ cup sliced Pecorino Romano cheese
Salt and black pepper to taste
2 eggs
2 tbsp Italian seasoning
1 pinch red chili flakes
¼ cup fresh parsley, chopped
4 tbsp butter
2 garlic cloves, minced
2 cups crushed tomatoes
1 tbsp dried basil
½ lb sliced mozzarella cheese

Directions and Total Time: approx. 45 minutes

Preheat oven to 400 F. Season chicken with salt and pepper; set aside. In a bowl, whisk eggs with Italian seasoning and chili flakes. On a plate, combine Pecorino cheese with parsley. Melt butter in a skillet. Dip the chicken in the egg mixture and then dredge in the cheese mixture. Place in the butter and fry on both sides until the cheese melts and is golden brown, 10 minutes; set aside. Sauté garlic in the same pan and mix in tomatoes. Top with basil, salt, and pepper, and cook for 10 minutes. Pour the sauce into a greased baking dish. Lay the chicken pieces in the sauce and top with mozzarella. Bake for 15 minutes or until the cheese melts. Remove and serve with leafy green salad.

Per serving: Cal 674; Net Carbs 5.3g; Fat 43g; Protein 59g

Delicious Veggies & Chicken Casserole

Ingredients for 4 servings

¾ lb Brussels sprouts, halved
2 large zucchinis, chopped
2 red bell peppers, quartered
2 chicken breasts, cubed
¼ cup olive oil
1 tbsp balsamic vinegar
1 tsp chopped thyme leaves
1 tsp chopped rosemary
½ cup toasted walnuts

Directions and Total Time: approx. 30 minutes

Preheat oven to 400 F. Scatter Brussels sprouts, zucchinis, bell peppers, and chicken on a baking sheet. Season with salt and pepper, and drizzle with olive oil. Add balsamic vinegar and toss. Scatter thyme and rosemary on top. Bake for 25 minutes, shaking once. Top with walnuts and serve.

Per serving: Cal 485; Net Carbs 3.7g; Fat 34g; Protein 35g

Parsley Chicken & Cauliflower Stir-Fry

Ingredients for 4 servings

1 large head cauliflower, cut into florets
2 tbsp olive oil
2 chicken breasts, sliced

1 red bell pepper, diced
1 yellow bell pepper, diced
3 tbsp chicken broth
2 tbsp chopped parsley

Directions and Total Time: approx. 30 minutes

Heat olive oil in a skillet and season chicken with salt and pepper; cook until brown on all sides, 8 minutes. Transfer to a plate. Pour bell peppers into the pan and sauté until softened, 5 minutes. Add in cauliflower, broth, season to taste, and mix. Cover the pan and cook for 5 minutes or until cauliflower is tender. Mix in chicken, parsley. Serve.

Per serving: Cal 345; Net Carbs 3.5g; Fat 21g; Protein 32g

Baked Cheese Chicken

Ingredients for 6 servings

2 tbsp olive oil
8 oz cottage cheese, grated
1 lb ground chicken
1 cup buffalo sauce
1 cup ranch dressing
3 cups Monterey Jack, grated

Directions and Total Time: approx. 30 minutes

Preheat oven to 350 F. Warm oil in a skillet and brown chicken for a couple of minutes; set aside. Spread cottage cheese on a greased sheet, top with chicken, pour buffalo sauce, add ranch dressing, and sprinkle with Monterey cheese. Bake for 23 minutes. Serve with veggie sticks.

Per serving: Cal 216; Net Carbs 3g; Fat 16g; Protein 14g

Parsnip & Bacon Chicken Bake

Ingredients for 4 servings

6 bacon slices, chopped
2 tbsp butter
½ lb parsnips, diced
2 tbsp olive oil
1 lb ground chicken
2 tbsp butter
1 cup heavy cream
2 oz cream cheese, softened
1 ¼ cups grated Pepper Jack
¼ cup chopped scallions

Directions and Total Time: approx. 50 minutes

Preheat oven to 300 F. Put the bacon in a pot and fry on until brown and crispy, 7 minutes; set aside. Melt butter in a skillet and sauté parsnips until softened and lightly browned. Transfer to a greased baking sheet. Heat olive oil in the same pan and cook the chicken until no longer pink, 8 minutes. Spoon onto a plate and set aside too.

Add heavy cream, cream cheese, two-thirds of the Pepper Jack cheese, salt, and pepper to the pot. Melt the ingredients over medium heat, frequently stirring, 7 minutes. Spread the parsnips on the baking dish, top with chicken, pour the heavy cream mixture over, and scatter bacon and scallions. Sprinkle the remaining cheese on top and bake until the cheese melts and is golden, 30 minutes.

Per serving: Cal 757; Net Carbs 5.5g; Fat 66g; Protein 29g

Baked Chicken with Kale & Feta

Ingredients for 4 servings
4 chicken breasts, cut into strips
¼ cup shredded Monterey Jack cheese
2 tbsp olive oil
Salt and black pepper to taste
1 small onion, chopped
2 garlic cloves, minced
½ tbsp red wine vinegar
1 ½ crushed tomatoes
2 tbsp tomato paste
1 tsp Italian mixed herbs
2 medium zucchinis, chopped
1 cup baby kale
¼ cup crumbled feta cheese
½ cup grated Parmesan

Directions and Total Time: approx. 45 minutes
Preheat oven to 400 F. Heat olive oil in a skillet, season the chicken with salt and pepper, and cook for 8 minutes; set aside. Add in and sauté onion and garlic for 3 minutes. Mix in vinegar, tomatoes, tomato paste. Cook for 8 minutes. Season with salt, pepper, and mixed herbs. Stir in chicken, zucchinis, kale, and feta cheese. Pour the mixture into a baking dish and top with Monterey Jack cheese. Bake for 15 minutes or until the cheese melts and is golden. Garnish with Parmesan cheese and serve.

Per serving: Cal 681; Net Carbs 6.6g; Fat 39g; Protein 69g

Yummy Chicken Squash Lasagna

Ingredients for 4 servings
2 tbsp butter
1 ½ lb ground chicken
1 tsp garlic powder
1 tsp onion powder
2 tbsp coconut flour
1 ½ cups grated mozzarella
1/3 cup Parmesan cheese
2 cups crumbled ricotta
1 large egg, beaten
2 cups marinara sauce
1 tbsp Italian mixed herbs
¼ tsp red chili flakes
4 large yellow squash, sliced
¼ cup fresh basil leaves

Directions and Total Time: approx. 55 minutes
Preheat oven to 375 F. Melt butter in a skillet and cook chicken for 10 minutes; set aside. In a bowl, mix garlic and onion powders, coconut flour, salt, pepper, mozzarella, half of Parmesan, ricotta cheese, and egg. In another bowl, combine marinara sauce, mixed herbs, and chili flakes; set aside. Make a single layer of the squash slices in a greased baking dish; spread a quarter of the egg mixture on top, a layer of the chicken, then a quarter of the marinara sauce. Repeat the layering process in the same proportions and sprinkle with the remaining Parmesan. Bake for 30 minutes. Garnish with basil leaves, slice, and serve.

Per serving: Cal 664; Net Carbs 7g; Fat 39g; Protein 62g

Mustard Chicken Cordon Blue Casserole

Ingredients for 4 servings
1 rotisserie chicken, shredded
7 oz smoked deli ham, chopped
8 oz cream cheese
1 tbsp Dijon mustard
1 tbsp plain vinegar
10 oz shredded Gruyere

Directions and Total Time: approx. 30 minutes
Preheat oven to 350 F. Spread the chicken and ham on a greased baking dish. In a bowl, mix cream cheese, mustard, vinegar, and two-thirds of Gruyere cheese. Spread the mixture on top of chicken and ham, season with salt

and pepper, and cover with the remaining cheese. Bake for 20 minutes or until the cheese melts and is golden brown.
Per serving: Cal 692; Net Carbs 3.6g; Fat 48g; Protein 60g

Tasty Chicken Pot Pie with Vegetables

Ingredients for 4 servings
1/3 cup cremini mushrooms, sliced
3 tbsp butter
1 lb ground chicken
Salt and black pepper to taste
1 large yellow onion, chopped
2 baby zucchinis, chopped
1 cup green beans, chopped
½ cup chopped broccoli rabe
2 celery stalks, chopped
4 oz cream cheese
½ cup coconut cream
½ tsp dried rosemary
¼ tsp poultry seasoning
10 egg whites
4 tbsp coconut flour
2½ cups fine almond flour
2 tsp baking powder
½ cup shredded cheddar
6 tbsp butter

Directions and Total Time: approx. 60 minutes
Preheat oven to 350 F. Melt 1 tbsp of butter in a skillet, add chicken, season with salt and pepper, and cook for 8 minutes or until the chicken is no longer pink; set aside. Melt the remaining butter in the same skillet and sauté onion, zucchini, green beans, broccoli rabe, celery, and mushrooms. Cook until the vegetables soften, 5 minutes. Stir in chicken, cream cheese, and coconut cream. Simmer until the sauce thickens, 5 minutes. Season with rosemary and poultry seasoning and cook for 2 minutes. Turn the heat off and pour the mixture into a baking dish. Pour the egg whites into a bowl and using a hand mixer, beat the whites until frothy, but not stiff. Mix in coconut flour, almond flour, baking powder, cheddar, and salt until evenly combined. Beat the batter until smooth. Spoon the content in the baking dish and bake for 30 minutes or until the top browns. Remove from the oven and serve.

Per serving: Cal 808; Net Carbs 4.7g; Fat 68g; Protein 39g

Chili Pulled Chicken with Avocado

Ingredients for 4 servings
1 white onion, finely chopped
¼ cup chicken stock
3 tbsp coconut oil
3 tbsp tamari sauce
3 tbsp chili pepper
1 tbsp red wine vinegar
Salt and black pepper to taste
2 lb boneless chicken thighs
1 avocado, halved and pitted
½ lemon, juiced

Directions and Total Time: approx. 2 hours 30 minutes
In a pot, combine onion, stock, coconut oil, tamari sauce, chili, vinegar, salt, pepper. Add thighs, close the lid, and cook over low heat for 2 hours. Scoop avocado pulp into a bowl, add lemon juice, and mash the avocado into a puree; set aside. When the chicken is ready, open the lid and use two forks to shred it. Cook further for 15 minutes. Turn the heat off and mix in avocado. Serve with low carb tortillas.
Per serving: Cal 710; Net Carbs 4g; Fat 56g; Protein 40g

Savory Chicken Wings with Chimichurri

Ingredients for 4 servings
16 chicken wings, halved
Salt and black pepper to taste
½ cup butter, melted
3 garlic cloves, peeled
1 cup fresh parsley leaves
¼ cup fresh cilantro leaves
2 tbsp red wine vinegar
½ cup olive oil

Directions and Total Time: approx. 50 minutes
Preheat oven to 350 F. Put chicken in a bowl, season with salt and pepper, and pour butter all over. Toss to coat and transfer to a greased baking sheet. Bake for 40-45 minutes or until light brown and cooked within. Transfer to the same bowl. In a food processor, blend garlic, parsley, cilantro, salt, and pepper until smooth. Add in vinegar and gradually pour in olive oil while blending further. Pour the

mixture (chimichurri) over the chicken; toss well to serve.
Per serving: Cal 603; Net Carbs 1.4g; Fat 54g; Protein 27g

Scallion & Saffron Chicken with Pasta

Ingredients for 4 servings
1 cup shredded mozzarella cheese
4 chicken breasts, cut into strips
1 egg yolk
3 tbsp butter
½ tsp ground saffron threads
1 yellow onion, chopped
2 garlic cloves, minced
1 tbsp almond flour
1 pinch cardamom powder
1 pinch cinnamon powder
1 cup heavy cream
1 cup chicken stock
¼ cup chopped scallions
3 tbsp chopped parsley
Directions and Total Time: approx. 35 min + chilling time
Microwave mozzarella cheese for 2 minutes. Take out the bowl and allow cooling for 1 minute. Mix in egg yolk until well-combined. Lay a parchment paper on a flat surface, pour the cheese mixture on top and cover with another parchment paper. Flatten the dough into 1/8-inch thickness. Take off the parchment paper and cut the dough into thick fettuccine strands. Place in a bowl and refrigerate overnight. Bring 2 cups of water to a boil and add the keto fettuccine. Cook for 1 minute and drain; set aside. Melt butter in a skillet, season the chicken with salt and pepper, and cook for 5 minutes. Stir in saffron, onion, and garlic and cook until the onion softens, 3 minutes. Stir in almond flour, cardamom powder, and cinnamon powder and cook for 1 minute.
Add in heavy cream and chicken stock and cook for 2-3 minutes. Mix in fettuccine and scallions. Garnish with parsley and serve warm.
Per serving: Cal 775; Net Carbs 3.1g; Fats 48g; Protein 73g

Spiralized Zucchini with Chicken & Pine Nuts

Ingredients for 4 servings
2 ½ lb chicken breast, cut into strips
5 garlic cloves, minced
¼ tsp pureed onion
Salt and black pepper to taste
2 tbsp avocado oil
3 large eggs, lightly beaten
¼ cup chicken broth
2 tbsp coconut aminos
1 tbsp white vinegar
½ cup chopped scallions
1 tsp red chili flakes
4 zucchinis, spiralized
½ cup toasted pine nuts
Directions and Total Time: approx. 30 minutes
In a bowl, combine half of garlic, onion, salt, and pepper. Add chicken and mix well. Heat avocado oil in a deep skillet over medium heat and add the chicken. Cook for 8 minutes until no longer pink with a slight brown crust. Transfer to a plate. Pour the eggs into the pan and scramble for 1 minute. Spoon the eggs to the side of the chicken and set aside. Reduce the heat to low and in a bowl, mix broth, coconut aminos, vinegar, scallions, remaining garlic, and chili flakes; simmer for 3 minutes. Stir in chicken, zucchini, and eggs. Cook for 1 minute and turn the heat off. Spoon into plates, top with pine nuts and serve warm.
Per serving: Cal 766; Net Carbs 3.3g; Fat 50g; Protein 71g

Lovely Pulled Chicken Egg Bites

Ingredients for 4 servings
2 tbsp butter
1 chicken breast
2 tbsp chopped green onions
½ tsp red chili flakes
12 eggs
¼ cup grated Monterey Jack
Directions and Total Time: approx. 30 minutes
Preheat oven to 400 F and line a 12-hole muffin tin with cupcake liners. Melt butter in a skillet, season chicken with salt and pepper, and cook it until brown on each side, 10 minutes. Transfer to a plate and shred with 2 forks. Divide between muffin holes along with green onions and chili flakes. Crack an egg into each muffin hole and scatter the cheese on top. Bake for 15 minutes until eggs set.
Per serving: Cal 393; Net Carbs 0.5g; Fat 27g; Protein 34g

Buffalo Spinach Chicken Sliders

Ingredients for 4 servings
4 zero carb hamburger buns, halved
3 lb chicken thighs, boneless and skinless
1 tsp onion powder
2 tsp garlic powder
Salt and black pepper to taste
2 tbsp ranch dressing mix
¼ cup white vinegar
2 tbsp hot sauce
½ cup chicken broth
¼ cup melted butter
¼ cup baby spinach
4 slices cheddar cheese

Directions and Total Time: approx. 3 hours 30 minutes
In a bowl, combine onion and garlic powders, salt, pepper, and ranch dressing mix. Rub the mixture onto chicken and place into a pot. In another bowl, mix vinegar, hot sauce, broth, and butter. Pour the mixture all over the chicken and cook on low heat for 3 hours. Using two forks, shred the chicken into small strands. Mix and adjust the taste. Divide the spinach in the bottom half of each low carb bun, spoon the chicken on top, and add a slice of cheddar cheese. Cover with the remaining bun halves and serve.
Per serving: Cal 774; Net Carbs 15.7g; Fat 37g; Protein 87g

Creamy Mustard Chicken with Shirataki

Ingredients for 4 servings
2 (8 oz) packs angel hair shirataki
4 chicken breasts, cut into strips
1 cup chopped mustard greens
1 yellow bell pepper, sliced
1 tbsp olive oil
1 yellow onion, finely sliced
1 garlic clove, minced
1 tbsp wholegrain mustard
5 tbsp heavy cream
1 tbsp chopped parsley

Directions and Total Time: approx. 30 minutes
Boil 2 cups of water in a medium pot. Strain the shirataki pasta and rinse well under hot running water. Allow proper draining and pour the shirataki pasta into the boiling water. Cook for 3 minutes and strain again.

Place a dry skillet and stir-fry the shirataki pasta until visibly dry, 1-2 minutes; set aside. Heat olive oil in a skillet, season the chicken with salt and pepper and cook for 8-10 minutes; set aside. Stir in onion, bell pepper, and garlic and cook until softened, 5 minutes. Mix in mustard and heavy cream; simmer for 2 minutes and mix in the chicken and mustard greens for 2 minutes. Stir in shirataki pasta, garnish with parsley and serve.
Per serving: Cal 692; Net Carbs 15g; Fats 38g; Protein 65g

Creamy Chicken with Broccoli & Prosciutto

Ingredients for 4 servings
6 slices prosciutto, chopped
2 tbsp butter
4 chicken breasts, cubed
4 garlic cloves, minced
1 cup baby kale, chopped
1 ½ cups heavy cream
1 head broccoli, cut into florets
¼ cup shredded Parmesan

Directions and Total Time: approx. 30 minutes
Put prosciutto in a skillet and fry it until crispy and brown, 5 minutes; set aside. Melt butter in the same skillet and cook chicken until no longer pink. Add garlic to sauté for 1 minute. Mix in heavy cream, prosciutto, and kale and let simmer for 5 minutes until the sauce thickens. Pour broccoli into a safe-microwave bowl, sprinkle with some water, season with salt and pepper, and microwave for 2 minutes until broccoli softens. Spoon into the sauce, top with Parmesan, stir, and cook until the cheese melts.
Per serving: Cal 805; Net Carbs 4.5g; Fat 53g; Protein 71g

Chicken Bake with Onion & Parsnip

Ingredients for 6 servings
3 parsnips, sliced
1 onion, sliced
4 garlic cloves, crushed
2 tbsp olive oil
2 lb chicken breasts
½ cup chicken broth
¼ cup white wine
Salt and black pepper to taste

Directions and Total Time: approx. 30 minutes

Preheat oven to 360 F. Warm oil in a skillet over medium heat and brown chicken for a couple of minutes, and transfer to a baking dish. Arrange the vegetables around the chicken, add in wine and broth; season with salt and pepper. Bake for 25 minutes, stirring once. Serve.

Per serving: Cal 278; Net Carbs 5.1g; Fat 8.7g; Protein 35g

Cheddar Taco Chicken Bake

Ingredients for 4 servings
1 rotisserie chicken, shredded
1/3 cup mayonnaise
8 oz cream cheese
1 yellow onion, sliced
1 yellow bell pepper, chopped
2 tbsp taco seasoning
½ cup shredded cheddar
Salt and black pepper to taste

Directions and Total Time: approx. 30 minutes

Preheat oven to 400 F. Into a greased baking dish, add chicken, mayo, cream cheese, onion, bell pepper, taco seasoning, and two-thirds of cheese. Mix the ingredients and top with the remaining cheese. Bake for 20 minutes.

Per serving: Cal 477; Net Carbs 6.7g; Fat 33g; Protein 34g

Buttered Roast Chicken

Ingredients for 6 servings
3 lb chicken, whole bird
8 tbsp butter, melted
1 large lemon, juiced
2 large lemons, thinly sliced

Directions and Total Time: approx. 1 hour 30 minutes

Preheat oven to 400 F. Season the chicken with salt and pepper. Put the chicken, breast side up in a baking dish. In a bowl, combine butter and lemon juice. Allow to cool a little and spread the mixture all over the chicken. Arrange lemon slices at the bottom of the dish and bake for 1 to 1½ hours. Baste the chicken with the juice every 20 minutes. Remove the chicken and serve with mashed turnips.

Per serving: Cal 393; Net Carbs 1g; Fat 22g; Protein 46g

Baked Chicken Skewers with Rutabaga Fries

Ingredients for 4 servings
2 chicken breasts
½ tsp salt
¼ tsp ground black pepper
2 tbsp olive oil
¼ cup chicken broth
For the fries
1 lb rutabaga
2 tbsp olive oil
½ tsp salt
¼ tsp ground black pepper

Directions and Total Time: approx. 60 minutes

Set oven to 400 F. Grease and line a baking sheet. In a bowl, mix oil, spices and chicken; set in the fridge for 10 minutes. Peel and chop rutabaga to form fry shapes and place into a separate bowl. Apply oil to coat and season with pepper and salt. Arrange on the baking tray and bake for 10 minutes. Take the chicken from the refrigerator and thread onto the skewers. Place over the rutabaga, pour in the chicken broth, and bake for 30 minutes. Serve.

Per serving: Cal: 579, Net Carbs: 6g, Fat: 53g, Protein: 39g

Chicken Wraps in Bacon with Spinach

Ingredients for 4 servings
4 chicken breasts
8 slices bacon
Salt and black pepper to taste
2 tbsp olive oil
For the buttered spinach:
2 tbsp butter
1 lb spinach
4 garlic cloves

Directions and Total Time: approx. 30 minutes

Preheat oven to 450 F. Wrap each chicken breast with 2 bacon slices, season with salt and pepper; place on a baking sheet. Drizzle with olive oil and bake for 15 minutes until the bacon browns and chicken cooks within. Melt butter in a skillet, and sauté spinach and garlic until the leaves wilt, 5 minutes. Season with salt and pepper. Remove from the oven and serve with buttered spinach.

Per serving: Cal 856; Net Carbs 2.4g; Fat 60g; Protein 71g

Louisiana Chicken Fettuccine

Ingredients for 4 servings
1 medium red bell pepper, deseeded and thinly sliced
1 medium green bell pepper, deseeded and thinly sliced
2 cups grated mozzarella
½ cup grated Parmesan
1 cup shredded mozzarella
1 egg yolk
2 tbsp olive oil
4 chicken breasts, cubed
1 yellow onion, thinly sliced
4 garlic cloves, minced
4 tsp Cajun seasoning
1 cup Alfredo sauce
½ cup marinara sauce
2 tbsp chopped fresh parsley

Directions and Total Time: approx. 45 min + chilling time
Microwave mozzarella cheese for 2 minutes. Take out the bowl and allow cooling for 1 minute. Mix in egg yolk until well-combined. Lay a parchment paper on a flat surface, pour the cheese mixture on top and cover with another parchment paper. Flatten the dough into 1/8-inch thickness. Take off the parchment paper and cut the dough into thick fettuccine strands. Place in a bowl and refrigerate overnight. Bring 2 cups water to a boil and add fettuccine. Cook for 1 minute and drain; set aside. Preheat oven to 350 F. Heat olive oil in a skillet, season the chicken with salt and pepper, and cook for 6 minutes. Transfer to a plate. Add in onion, garlic and bell peppers and cook for 5 minutes. Return the chicken to the pot and stir in Cajun seasoning, Alfredo sauce, and marinara sauce. Cook for 3 minutes. Stir in fettuccine and transfer to a greased baking dish. Cover with the mozzarella and Parmesan cheeses and bake for 15 minutes. Garnish with parsley and serve warm.

Per serving: Cal 777; Net Carbs 4.6g; Fats 38g; Protein 93g

Mushroom Chicken Cheeseburgers

Ingredients for 4 servings
4 large Portobello caps, destemmed
1 ½ lb ground chicken
Salt and black pepper to taste
1 tbsp tomato sauce
1 tbsp olive oil
6 slices Gruyere cheese
4 lettuce leaves
4 large tomato slices
¼ cup mayonnaise

Directions and Total Time: approx. 30 minutes
In a bowl, combine chicken, salt, pepper, and tomato sauce. Mold into 4 patties and set aside. Heat olive oil in a skillet; place in Portobello caps and cook until softened, 3 minutes; set aside. Put the patties in the skillet and fry until brown and compacted, 8 minutes. Place Gruyere slices on the patties, allow melting for 1 minute and lift each patty onto each mushroom cap. Divide the lettuce on top, then tomato slices, and top with some mayonnaise.

Per serving: Cal 510; Net Carbs 2.2g; Fat 34g; Protein 45g

Stuffed Peppers with Chicken & Broccoli

Ingredients for 6 servings
6 yellow bell peppers, halved
1 ½ tbsp olive oil
3 tbsp butter
3 garlic cloves, minced
½ white onion, chopped
2 lb ground chicken
3 tsp taco seasoning
1 cup riced broccoli
¼ cup grated cheddar cheese
Crème fraiche for serving

Directions and Total Time: approx. 2 hours
Preheat oven to 400 F. Drizzle bell peppers with olive oil and season with salt; set aside. Melt butter in a skillet and sauté garlic and onion for 3 minutes. Stir in chicken and taco seasoning. Cook for 8 minutes. Mix in broccoli. Spoon the mixture into the peppers, top with cheddar cheese, and place in a greased baking dish. Bake until the cheese melts and is bubbly, 30 minutes. Plate the peppers. Top with the crème fraiche and serve.

Per serving: Cal 386; Net Carbs 11.5g; Fat 24g; Protein 30g

Grilled Chicken Kebabs with Curry & Yogurt

Ingredients for 4 servings4
1 ½ lb boneless chicken thighs, cut into 1-inch pieces
½ cup Greek yogurt
Salt and black pepper to taste
2 tbsp curry powder
1 tbsp olive oil

Directions and Total Time: approx. 30 minutes
Preheat oven to 400 F. In a bowl, combine Greek yogurt, salt, pepper, curry, and olive oil. Mix in chicken, cover the bowl with a plastic wrap and marinate for 20 minutes. Remove the wrap and thread the chicken onto skewers. Grill in the middle rack of the oven for 4 minutes on each side or until fully cooked. Remove the chicken skewers and serve with cauliflower rice or steamed green beans.

Per serving: Cal 440; Net Carbs 0.5g; Fat 29g; Protein 41g

Herby Chicken Meatloaf

Ingredients for 6 servings
2 ½ lb ground chicken
3 tbsp flaxseed meal
2 large eggs
2 tbsp olive oil
1 lemon,1 tbsp juiced
¼ cup chopped parsley
¼ cup chopped oregano
4 garlic cloves, minced
Lemon slices to garnish

Directions and Total Time: approx. 50 minutes
Preheat oven to 400 F. In a bowl, combine chicken, salt, pepper, and flaxseed meal; set aside. In a small bowl, whisk the eggs with olive oil, lemon juice, parsley, oregano, and garlic. Pour the mixture onto the chicken mixture and mix well. Spoon into a greased loaf pan and press to fit. Bake for 40 minutes. Remove the pan, drain the liquid, and let cool a bit. Slice, garnish with lemon slices and serve.

Per serving: Cal 362; Net Carbs 1.3g; Fat 24g; Protein 35g

Eggplant Chicken Gratin With Swiss Cheese

Ingredients for 4 servings
3 tbsp butter
1 eggplant, chopped
2 tbsp Swiss cheese, grated
Salt and black pepper, to taste
2 garlic cloves, minced
6 chicken thighs

Directions and Total Time: approx. 55 minutes
Warm butter in a pan and cook chicken for 3 minutes per side. Transfer to a baking dish and season with salt and pepper. In the same pan, cook garlic, eggplant, pepper, and salt for 10 minutes. Ladle this mixture over the chicken, spread with the cheese, set in oven at 350 F, and bake for 30 minutes. Turn on the broiler, and broil for 2 minutes.

Per serving: Cal 412, Net Carbs 5g, Fat 37g, Protein 34g

Chicken with Tomato and Zucchini

Ingredients for 4 servings
2 tbsp ghee
1 lb chicken thighs
2 cloves garlic, minced
1 (14 oz) can whole tomatoes
1 zucchini, diced
10 fresh basil leaves, chopped

Directions and Total Time: approx. 45 minutes
Melt ghee in a saucepan, season the chicken with salt and pepper, and fry for 4 minutes on each side. Remove to a plate. Sauté garlic in the ghee for 2 minutes, pour in tomatoes, and cook for 8 minutes. Add in zucchini and cook for 4 minutes. Season the sauce with salt and pepper, stir, and add the chicken. Coat with sauce and simmer for 3 minutes. Serve chicken with sauce garnished with basil.

Per serving: Cal 468, Net Carbs 2g, Fat 39g, Protein 26g

Cauli Rice & Chicken Collard Wraps

Ingredients for 4 servings
2 tbsp avocado oil
1 large yellow onion, chopped
2 garlic cloves, minced
Salt and black pepper to taste
1 jalapeño pepper, chopped

1 ½ lb chicken breasts, cubed
1 cup cauliflower rice
2 tsp hot sauce
8 collard leaves
¼ cup crème fraiche

Directions and Total Time: approx. 30 minutes

Heat avocado oil in a deep skillet and sauté onion and garlic until softened, 3 minutes. Stir in jalapeño pepper salt, and pepper. Mix in chicken and cook until no longer pink on all sides, 10 minutes. Add in cauliflower rice and hot sauce. Sauté until the cauliflower slightly softens, 3 minutes. Lay out the collards on a clean flat surface and spoon the curried mixture onto the middle part of the leaves, about 3 tbsp per leaf. Spoon crème fraiche on top, wrap the leaves, and serve immediately.

Per serving: Cal 437; Net Carbs 1.8g; Fat 28g; Protein 38g

Almond Crusted Chicken Zucchini Stacks

Ingredients for 4 servings
1 ½ lb chicken thighs, skinless and boneless, cut into strips
3 tbsp almond flour
Salt and black pepper to taste
2 large zucchinis, sliced
4 tbsp olive oil
2 tsp Italian mixed herb blend
½ cup chicken broth

Directions and Total Time: approx. 30 minutes

Preheat oven to 400 F. In a zipper bag, add almond flour, salt, and pepper. Mix and add the chicken slices. Seal the bag and shake to coat. Arrange the zucchinis on a greased baking sheet. Season with salt and pepper, and drizzle with 2 tbsp of olive oil. Remove the chicken from the almond flour mixture, shake off, and put 2-3 chicken strips on each zucchini. Season with herb blend and drizzle again with olive oil. Bake for 8 minutes; remove the sheet and pour in broth. Bake further for 10 minutes. Serve warm.

Per serving: Cal 512; Net Carbs 1.2g; Fat 42g; Protein 29g

Paleo Coconut Flour Chicken Nuggets

Ingredients for 2 servings

½ cup coconut flour
1 egg
2 tbsp garlic powder
2 chicken breasts, cubed
Salt and black pepper, to taste
½ cup butter

Directions and Total Time: approx. 30 minutes

In a bowl, combine salt, garlic powder, flour, and pepper, and stir. In a separate bowl, beat the egg. Add the chicken in egg mixture, then in the flour mixture. Set a pan over medium heat and warm butter. Add in chicken nuggets, and cook for 6 minutes on each side. Remove to paper towels, drain the excess grease and serve.

Per serving: Cal 417, Net Carbs 4.3g, Fat 37g, Protein 35g

Bacon Chicken Skillet with Bok Choy

Ingredients for 4 servings
2 lb ground chicken, cubed
Salt and black pepper to taste
4 bacon slices, chopped
1 tbsp coconut oil
1 orange bell pepper, chopped
2 cups baby bok choy
2 tbsp chopped oregano
2 garlic cloves, pressed

Directions and Total Time: approx. 30 minutes

Season the chicken with salt and pepper; set aside. Heat a skillet over medium heat and fry bacon until brown and crispy. Transfer to a plate. Melt coconut oil in the skillet and cook chicken until no longer pink, 10 minutes. Remove to the bacon plate. Add bell pepper and bok choy and sauté until softened, 5 minutes. Stir in bacon, chicken, oregano, and garlic, for 3 minutes. Serve with cauli rice.

Per serving: Cal 639; Net Carbs 1.2g; Fat 48g; Protein 46g

Celery Chicken Sausage Frittata

Ingredients for 4 servings
12 whole eggs
1 cup crème fraiche
2 tbsp butter
1 celery stalk, chopped
12 oz ground chicken sausages
¼ cup shredded Swiss cheese

Directions and Total Time: approx. 45 minutes

Preheat oven to 350 F. In a bowl, whisk eggs, crème fraiche, salt, and pepper. Melt butter in a safe oven skillet over medium heat. Sauté celery until soft, 5 minutes; set aside. Add the sausages to the skillet and cook until brown with frequent stirring to break the lumps that form, 8 minutes. Scatter celery on top, pour the egg mixture all over, and sprinkle with Swiss cheese. Put the skillet in the oven and bake until the eggs set and cheese melts, 20 minutes. Slice the frittata, and serve warm.

Per serving: Cal 529; Net Carbs 3g; Fat 44g; Protein 28g

Rosemary Turkey Brussels Sprouts Cakes

Ingredients for 4 servings

For the burgers

1 pound ground turkey
1 egg
1 onion, chopped
1 garlic clove, minced
1 tsp fresh rosemary, chopped
4 tbsp olive oil

For the fried Brussels sprouts

1 ½ lb Brussels sprouts
4 tbsp olive oil
2 tbsp balsamic vinegar
Salt to taste

Directions and Total Time: approx. 35 minutes

Preheat oven to 320 F and arrange Brussels sprouts in a baking dish. Toss to coat with olive oil and season with salt. Bake for 20 minutes, stirring once. Pour vinegar over and cook for 5 minutes. Combine burger ingredients in a bowl. Form patties out of the mixture. Set a pan, warm olive oil, and fry patties until cooked through. Serve.

Per serving: Cal 535; Net Carbs 6.7g; Fat 38g; Protein 31g

Jerk Chicken Drumsticks

Ingredients for 4 servings

½ cup Greek yogurt
2 tbsp melted butter
2 tbsp Jamaican seasoning
2 lb chicken drumsticks
3 tbsp pork rinds
¼ cup almond meal

Directions and Total Time: approx. 45 minutes

Preheat oven to 350 F. In a bowl, combine Greek yogurt, butter, Jamaican seasoning, salt, and pepper. Add the chicken and toss to coat evenly. Marinate for 15 minutes. In a food processor, blend the pork rinds with almond meal until well combined. Pour the mixture onto a wide plate. Remove chicken from the marinade, shake off any excess liquid, and coat generously in the pork rind mixture. Place on a greased baking sheet and bake for 30 minutes until golden brown and crispy, turning once. Serve warm.

Per serving: Cal 453; Net Carbs 1.8g; Fat 27g; Protein 45g

Creamy Chicken Thighs

Ingredients for 4 servings

1 pound chicken thighs
Salt and black pepper, to taste
1 tsp onion powder
¼ cup half-and-half
2 tbsp butter
2 tbsp sweet paprika

Directions and Total Time: approx. 50 minutes

In a bowl, combine paprika with onion, pepper, and salt. Season chicken pieces with this mixture and lay on a lined baking sheet; bake for 40 minutes in the oven at 400 F. Split the chicken in serving plates. Add the cooking juices to a skillet over medium heat, and mix with the half-and-half and butter. Cook for 6 minutes until the sauce thickens. Drizzle the sauce over the chicken and serve.

Per serving: Cal 381, Net Carbs 2.6g, Fat 33g, Protein 31g

Chicken Breasts with Jarred Pickle Juice

Ingredients for 4 servings

2 chicken breasts, cut into strips
4 oz chicken crisps, crushed
2 cups coconut oil
16 ounces jarred pickle juice
2 eggs, whisked

Directions and Total Time: approx. 30 min + chilling time

In a bowl, combine chicken with pickle juice; refrigerate for 12 hours. Place eggs in a bowl, and chicken crisps in a separate one. Dip the

chicken pieces in the eggs, and then in chicken crisps until well coated. Set a pan and warm oil. Fry chicken for 3 minutes per side, remove to paper towels, drain the excess grease, and serve.
Per serving: Cal 387, Net Carbs 2.5g, Fat 16g, Protein 23g

Cream Cheese & Turkey Tortilla Rolls

Ingredients for 4 servings
10 canned pepperoncini peppers, sliced and drained
8 oz softened cream cheese
10 oz turkey pastrami, sliced
Directions and Total Time: approx. 2 hours 40 minutes
Lay a plastic wrap on a flat surface and arrange the pastrami all over, slightly overlapping each other. Spread the cheese on top of the salami layers and arrange the pepperoncini on top. Hold 2 opposite ends of the plastic wrap and roll the pastrami. Twist both ends to tighten and refrigerate for 2 hours. Slice into 2-inch pinwheels. Serve.
Per serving: Cal 266; Net Carbs 1g; Fat 24g; Protein 13g

Cucumber-Turkey Canapes

Ingredients for 6 servings
2 cucumbers, sliced
2 cups dices leftover turkey
¼ jalapeño pepper, minced
1 tbsp Dijon mustard
¼ cup mayonnaise
Salt and black pepper to taste
Directions and Total Time: approx. 5 minutes
Cut mid-level holes in cucumber slices with a knife and set aside. Combine turkey, jalapeno, mustard, mayonnaise, salt, and black pepper to be evenly mixed. Fill cucumber holes with turkey mixture and serve.
Per serving: Cal 170; Net Carbs 1.3g; Fat 14g; Protein 10g

Provolone Chicken Spinach Bake

Ingredients for 6 servings
1 ¼ cups provolone cheese, shredded
6 chicken breasts
1 tsp mixed spice seasoning
Salt and black pepper to taste

2 loose cups baby spinach
3 tsp olive oil
4 oz cream cheese, cubed
Directions and Total Time: approx. 45 minutes
Preheat oven to 370 F. Season chicken with spice mix, salt, and pepper. Put in a greased casserole dish and layer spinach over the chicken. Mix oil with cream cheese, provolone cheese, salt, and pepper and stir in 4 tbsp of water, one tbsp at a time. Pour the mixture over the chicken and cover the pot with aluminium foil. Bake for 20 minutes, remove foil and cook for 15 minutes. Serve.
Per serving: Cal 340, Net Carbs 3.1g, Fat 30g, Protein 15g

Italian Chicken-Basil Pizza

Ingredients for 4 servings
1 ½ cups grated mozzarella cheese
1 lb ground chicken
1 tsp Italian seasoning
1 cup tomato sauce
½ cup fresh basil leaves
Directions and Total Time: approx. 40 minutes
Preheat oven to 390 F and line a round pizza pan with parchment paper. In a bowl, mix ground chicken, Italian seasoning, and 1 cup of mozzarella cheese. Spread the pizza "dough" on the pizza pan and bake for 18 minutes. Spread tomato sauce on top. Scatter the mozzarella cheese and basil all over and bake for 15 minutes. Slice and serve.
Per serving: Cal 316; Net Carbs 0.4g; Fats 17g; Protein 35g

Tomato Basil Stuffed Chicken Breasts

Ingredients for 6 servings
4 ounces cream cheese
3 oz provolone cheese slices
10 ounces spinach
½ cup mozzarella, shredded
1 tbsp olive oil
1 cup tomato basil sauce
3 whole chicken breasts
Directions and Total Time: approx. 45 minutes
Preheat oven to 400 F. Microwave cream cheese, provolone cheese slices, and spinach for 2 minutes. Cut the chicken with the knife a

couple of times horizontally. Stuff with the cheese filling. Brush the top with olive oil. Place on a lined baking dish and bake for 25 minutes. Pour the sauce over and top with mozzarella cheese. Return to oven and cook for 5 minutes. Serve.
Per serving: Cal 338, Net Carbs: 2.5g, Fat: 28g, Protein: 37g

Cranberry Glazed Chicken with Onions

Ingredients for 6 servings
4 green onions, chopped diagonally
4 tbsp unsweetened cranberry puree
2 lb chicken wings
2 tbsp olive oil
Chili sauce to taste
Juice from 1 lime

Directions and Total Time: approx. 50 minutes
Preheat the oven (broiler side) to 400 F. Then, in a bowl, mix the cranberry puree, olive oil, salt, sweet chili sauce, and lime juice. After, add in the wings and toss to coat. Place the chicken under the broiler, and cook for 45 minutes, turning once halfway. Remove the chicken after and serve warm with a cranberry puree and cheese dipping sauce. Top with green onions to serve.
Per serving: Cal 152, Net Carbs 1.6g, Fat 8.5g, Protein 17g

Acorn Squash Chicken Traybake

Ingredients for 4 servings
2 lb chicken thighs
1 lb acorn squash, cubed
½ cup black olives, pitted
¼ cup olive oil
5 garlic cloves, sliced
1 tbsp dried oregano

Directions and Total Time: approx. 60 minutes
Set oven to 400 F. Place the chicken with the skin down in a greased baking dish. Set garlic, olives and acorn squash around the chicken then drizzle with oil. Spread pepper, salt, and thyme over the mixture. Bake for 45 minutes.
Per serving: Cal: 411, Net Carbs: 5g, Fat: 15g, Protein: 31g

Turkey Bolognese Veggie Pasta

Ingredients for 6 servings

2 cups sliced mushrooms
2 tsp olive oil
1 pound ground turkey
3 tbsp pesto sauce
1 cup diced onion
2 cups sliced zucchini
6 cups veggie pasta, spiralized
Salt and black pepper to taste

Directions and Total Time: approx. 30 minutes
Heat oil in a skillet. Add turkey and cook until browned. Transfer to a plate. Add onions to the skillet, and cook until translucent, about 3 minutes. Add zucchini and mushrooms and cook for 7 more minutes. Return the turkey to skillet and stir in pesto sauce. Cover the pan, lower the heat, and simmer for 5 minutes. Serve immediately.
Per serving: Cal 273; Net Carbs 3.8g Fat 16g; Protein 19g

Grilled Garlic Chicken with Cauliflower

Ingredients for 6 servings
1 head cauliflower, cut into florets
3 tbsp smoked paprika
2 tsp garlic powder
1 tbsp olive oil
6 chicken breasts

Directions and Total Time: approx. 30 minutes
Place the cauliflower florets onto the steamer basket over boiling water and steam for approximately 8 minutes or until crisp-tender; set aside. Grease grill grate with cooking spray and preheat to 400 F. Combine paprika, salt, black pepper, and garlic powder in a bowl. Brush chicken with olive oil and sprinkle spice mixture over and massage with hands. Grill chicken for 7 minutes per side until well-cooked, and plate. Serve warm.
Per serving: Cal 422, Net Carbs 2g, Fat 35g, Protein 26g

Cucumber Salsa Topped Turkey Patties

Ingredients for 4 servings
2 spring onions, thinly sliced
1 pound ground turkey
1 egg
4 garlic cloves, minced

1 tbsp chopped herbs
2 tbsp ghee
1 tbsp apple cider vinegar
1 tbsp chopped dill
2 cucumbers, grated
1 cup sour cream
1 jalapeño pepper, minced
2 tbsp olive oil

Directions and Total Time: approx. 30 minutes

In a bowl, place spring onions, turkey, egg, two garlic cloves, and herbs; mix to combine. Make patties out of the mixture. Melt ghee in a skillet over medium heat. Cook the patties for 3 minutes per side. In a bowl, combine vinegar, dill, remaining garlic, cucumber, sour cream, jalapeño, and olive oil; toss well. Serve patties topped with salsa.

Per serving: Cal 475; Net Carbs 5g; Fat 38g; Protein 26g

Turkey with Avocado Sauce

Ingredients for 4 servings

1 avocado, pitted
½ cup mayonnaise
3 tbsp ghee
1 pound turkey breasts
1 cup chopped cilantro leaves
½ cup chicken broth

Directions and Total Time: approx. 25 minutes

Spoon avocado, mayo, and salt into a food processor and puree until smooth. Season with salt. Pour sauce into a jar and refrigerate. Melt ghee in a skillet, fry turkey for 4 minutes on each side. Remove to a plate. Pour broth in the same skillet and add cilantro. Bring to a simmer for 15 minutes and add the turkey. Cook on low heat for 5 minutes until liquid reduces by half. Dish and spoon mayo-avocado sauce over.

Per serving: Cal 398, Net Carbs 4g, Fat 32g, Protein 24g

Bell Pepper Turkey Keto Carnitas

Ingredients for 4 servings

1 lb turkey breasts, sliced
1 garlic clove, minced
1 red onion, sliced
1 green chili, minced
2 tsp ground cumin
2 tbsp lime juice

1 tsp sweet paprika
2 tbsp olive oil
1 tsp ground coriander
1 green bell pepper, sliced
1 red bell pepper, sliced
1 tbsp fresh cilantro, chopped

Directions and Total Time: approx. 25 minutes

In a bowl, combine lime juice, cumin, garlic, coriander, paprika, salt, green chili, and pepper. Toss in the turkey pieces to coat well. Place a pan over medium heat and warm oil. Cook in turkey on each side, for 3 minutes; set aside. In the same pan, sauté bell peppers, cilantro, and onion for 6 minutes. Serve keto carnitas in lettuce leaves.

Per serving: Cal 262; Net Carbs 4.2g; Fat 15.2g; Protein 26g

Caprese Turkey Meatballs

Ingredients for 4 servings

2 tbsp chopped sun-dried tomatoes
1 pound ground turkey
2 tbsp chopped basil
½ tsp garlic powder
1 egg
¼ cup almond flour
2 tbsp olive oil
½ cup shredded mozzarella
Salt and black pepper to taste

Directions and Total Time: approx. 15 minutes

Place everything except for the oil in a bowl; mix well. Form 16 meatballs out of the mixture. Heat the olive oil in a skillet. Cook the meatballs for about 6 minutes. Serve.

Per serving: Cal 310; Net Carbs 2g; Fat 26g; Protein 22g

Tasty Curried Chicken Meatballs

Ingredients for 4 servings

3 lb ground chicken
1 yellow onion, chopped
2 green bell peppers, chopped
3 garlic cloves, minced
2 tbsp melted butter
1 tsp dried parsley
2 tbsp hot sauce
Salt and black pepper to taste
1 tbsp red curry powder
3 tbsp olive oil

Directions and Total Time: approx. 30 minutes

Preheat oven to 400 F. In a bowl, combine chicken, onion, bell peppers, garlic, butter, parsley, hot sauce, salt, pepper, and curry. Form meatballs and place on a greased baking sheet. Drizzle with olive oil and bake until the meatballs brown on the outside and cook within, 25 minutes. Serve.

Per serving: Cal 908; Net Carbs 2.7g; Fat 67g; Protein 65g

Hot Chicken Meatball Tray

Ingredients for 4 servings

1 egg
1 pound ground chicken
Salt and black pepper, to taste
1 red pepper, chopped
2 spring onions, chopped
¼ cup Pecorino, grated
1 tbsp dry Italian seasoning
2 tbsp olive oil
¼ cup hot sauce
2 tbsp parsley, chopped

Directions and Total Time: approx. 25 minutes

Preheat oven to 480 F. In a bowl, combine ground chicken, red pepper, onions, Italian seasoning, Pecorino cheese, salt, black pepper, parsley, and egg, and mix well with hands. Form into meatballs, arrange them on a greased with olive oil baking tray and bake for 16 minutes. Remove from the oven to a bowl and cover with hot sauce. Serve.

Per serving: Cal 383; Net Carbs 4.4g; Fat 28.1g; Protein 26g

Creamy Turkey & Broccoli Bake

Ingredients for 4 servings

1 lb turkey breasts, cooked
2 tbsp butter, melted
1 head broccoli, cut into florets
½ cup buttermilk
1 carrot, sliced
½ cup heavy cream
1 cup cheddar cheese, grated
4 tbsp pork rinds, crushed
Salt and black pepper, to taste
1 tsp oregano

Directions and Total Time: approx. 40 minutes

Cook broccoli in salted water for 4 minutes. Shred the turkey and place into a bowl together with buttermilk, butter, oregano, carrot, and broccoli; mix to combine. Season with salt and pepper, and transfer the mixture to a greased pan. Pour in heavy cream and top with cheese. Cover with pork rinds. Bake for 25 minutes at 450 F.

Per serving: Cal 469; Net Carbs 6.2g; Fat 3g; Protein 38.4g

Cheesy Turkey Sausage Egg Cups

Ingredients for 4 servings

1 cup Pecorino Romano cheese, grated
1 tsp butter
6 eggs
Salt and black pepper, to taste
½ tsp dried thyme
3 turkey sausages, chopped

Directions and Total Time: approx. 15 minutes

Preheat oven to 400 F and grease muffin cups with cooking spray.

In a skillet over medium heat add the butter and cook the turkey sausages for 4-5 minutes. Beat 3 eggs with a fork. Add in sausages, cheese, and seasonings. Divide between the ups and bake for 4 minutes. Crack in an egg to each of the cups. Bake for an additional 4 minutes. Allow cooling before serving.

Per serving: Cal 423; Net Carbs 2.2g; Fat 34g; Protein 26.4g

BEEF

Easy Beef Burger Bake

Ingredients for 4 servings
¼ cup shredded Monterey Jack cheese
1 tbsp butter
1 lb ground beef
1 garlic clove, minced
1 medium red onion, chopped
2 tomatoes
1 tbsp dried basil
Salt and black pepper to taste
2 eggs
2 tbsp tomato paste
1 cup coconut cream

Directions and Total Time: approx. 35 minutes
Preheat oven to 400 F. Melt the butter in a large skillet and add the beef. Cook for 10 minutes. Stir in garlic and onion and cook for another 3 minutes. Mix in tomatoes, basil, salt, and pepper until the tomatoes soften. Add 2/3 of Monterey Jack cheese and stir to melt. In a bowl, crack the eggs and whisk with tomato paste, salt, and coconut cream. Spoon the beef mixture into a greased baking sheet and spread the egg mixture on top. Sprinkle with the remaining cheese and bake for 20 minutes. Serve.
Per serving: Cal 469; Net Carbs 4.5g; Fat 34g; Protein 33g

Awesome Zucchini Boats Stuffed with Beef

Ingredients for 4 servings4
2 zucchinis
2 tbsp butter
1 lb ground beef
1 red bell pepper, chopped
2 garlic cloves, minced
1 shallot, finely chopped
2 tbsp taco seasoning
½ cup finely chopped parsley
1 tbsp olive oil
1¼ cups shredded cheddar

Directions and Total Time: approx. 50 minutes
Preheat oven to 400 F and grease a baking sheet with cooking spray. Using a knife, cut zucchinis into halves and scoop out the pulp using to form 4 vegetable boats. Set aside and chop the flesh. Melt the butter in a skillet over medium heat and cook the beef until brown, frequently stirring and breaking the lumps, 10 minutes. Stir in bell pepper, pulp, garlic, shallot, taco seasoning, and cook until softened, 5 minutes. Turn the heat off. Place the boats on the baking sheet with the open side up. Spoon in the beef mixture, divide the parsley on top, drizzle with olive oil, and top with cheddar cheese. Bake for 20 minutes until the cheese melts and is golden brown on top. Plate the boats, and serve warm with tangy lettuce salad.
Per serving: Cal 423; Net Carbs 2.9g; Fat 29g; Protein 35g

Sage Beef Meatloaf with Pecans

Ingredients for 4 servings
2 tbsp olive oil
1 white onion, finely chopped
1 ½ lb ground beef
½ cup coconut cream
½ cup shredded Parmesan
1 egg, lightly beaten
1 tbsp dried sage
4 tbsp toasted pecans, chopped
Salt and black pepper to taste
6 bacon slices

Directions and Total Time: approx. 45 minutes
Preheat oven to 400 F. Heat olive oil in a skillet and sauté the onion for 3 minutes. In a bowl, mix ground beef, onion, coconut cream, Parmesan cheese, eggs, sage, pecans, salt, and pepper. Form into a loaf, wrap it with bacon slices, secure with toothpicks, and place on a greased baking sheet. Bake for 30 minutes. Serve sliced.
Per serving: Cal 617; Net Carbs 6.6g; Fat 43g; Protein 48g

Tangy Cabbage & Beef Bowl with Creamy Blue Cheese

Ingredients for 4 servings
3 tbsp butter
1 canon cabbage, shredded
1 tsp onion powder
1 tsp garlic powder
2 tsp dried oregano
1 tbsp red wine vinegar

1 ½ lb ground beef
1 cup coconut cream
¼ cup blue cheese
½ cup fresh parsley, chopped

Directions and Total Time: approx. 25 minutes

Melt 1 tbsp of butter in a deep skillet, and sauté cabbage, onion and garlic powders, oregano, salt, pepper, and vinegar, for 5 minutes; set aside. Melt the 2 tbsp butter in the skillet and cook the beef until browned, frequently stirring and breaking the lumps, 10 minutes. Stir in coconut cream and blue cheese until the cheese melts, 3 minutes. Return the cabbage mixture, and add parsley. Stir-fry for 2 minutes. Dish into serving bowls with low carb bread.

Per serving: Cal 542; Net Carbs 4.2g; Fat 41g; Protein 41g

Cheesy Tomato Beef Tart

Ingredients for 4 servings
2 tbsp olive oil
1 small brown onion, chopped
1 garlic clove, finely chopped
2 lb ground beef
1 tbsp Italian mixed herbs
4 tbsp tomato paste
4 tbsp coconut flour
¾ cup almond flour
4 tbsp flaxseeds
1 tsp baking powder
3 tbsp coconut oil, melted
1 egg
¼ cup ricotta, crumbled
¼ cup shredded cheddar

Directions and Total Time: approx. 1 hour 30 minutes

Preheat oven to 350 F. Line a pie dish with parchment paper and grease with cooking spray; set aside. Heat olive oil in a large skillet over medium heat; and sauté onion and garlic until softened. Add in beef and cook until brown. Season with herbs, salt, and pepper. Stir in tomato paste and ½ cup water, reduce the heat to low.
Simmer for 20 minutes; set aside. In a food processor, add the flours, flaxseeds, baking powder, a pinch of salt, coconut oil, egg, and 4 tbsp water. Mix starting on low speed to medium until evenly combined and dough is formed. Spread the dough in the pie pan and

bake for 12 minutes. Remove and spread the meat filling on top. In a small bowl, mix ricotta and cheddar cheeses, and scatter on top. Bake until the cheeses melt and are golden brown on top, 35 minutes. Remove the pie, let cool for 3 minutes, slice, and serve with green salad and garlic vinaigrette.

Per serving: Cal 603; Net Carbs 2.3g; Fat 39g; Protein 57g

Olive & Pesto Beef Casserole with Goat Cheese

Ingredients for 4 servings
2 tbsp ghee
1 ½ lb ground beef
Salt and black pepper to taste
3 oz pitted green olives
5 oz goat cheese, crumbled
1 garlic clove, minced
3 oz basil pesto
1¼ cups coconut cream

Directions and Total Time: approx. 45 minutes

Preheat oven to 400 F and grease a casserole dish with cooking spray. Melt ghee in a deep, medium skillet, and cook the beef until brown; season to taste. Stir frequently. Spoon and spread the beef at the bottom of the casserole dish. Top with olives, goat cheese, and garlic. In a bowl, mix pesto and coconut cream and pour the mixture all over the beef. Bake until lightly brown around the edges and bubbly, 25 minutes. Serve with a leafy green salad.

Per serving: Cal 656; Net Carbs 4g; Fat 51g; Protein 47g

Maple Jalapeño Beef Plate

Ingredients for 4 servings
1 lb ribeye steak, sliced into ¼-inch strips
2 tsp sugar-free maple syrup
Salt and black pepper to taste
1 tbsp coconut flour
1/2 tsp xanthan gum
½ cup olive oil, for frying
1 tbsp coconut oil
1 tsp freshly pureed ginger
1 clove garlic, minced
1 red chili, minced
4 tbsp tamari sauce
1 tsp sesame oil
1 tsp fish sauce
2 tbsp white wine vinegar

1 tsp hot sauce
1 small bok choy, quartered
½ jalapeño, sliced into rings
1 tbsp toasted sesame seeds
1 scallion, chopped

Directions and Total Time: approx. 40 minutes

Season the beef with salt and pepper, and rub with coconut flour and xanthan gum; set aside. Heat olive oil in a skillet and fry the beef until brown on all sides. Heat coconut oil in a wok and sauté ginger, garlic, red chili, and bok choy for 5 minutes. Mix in tamari sauce, sesame oil, fish sauce, vinegar, hot sauce, and maple syrup; cook for 2 minutes. Add the beef and cook for 2 minutes. Spoon into bowls, top with jalapeños, scallion and sesame seeds. Serve.

Per serving: Cal 507; Net Carbs 2.9g; Fat 43g; Protein 25g

Cheese & Beef Avocado Boats

Ingredients for 4 servings
4 tbsp avocado oil
1 lb ground beef
Salt and black pepper to taste
1 tsp onion powder
1 tsp cumin powder
1 tsp garlic powder
2 tsp taco seasoning
2 tsp smoked paprika
1 cup raw pecans, chopped
1 tbsp hemp seeds, hulled
7 tbsp shredded Monterey Jack
2 avocados, halved and pitted
1 medium tomato, sliced
¼ cup shredded iceberg lettuce
4 tbsp sour cream
4 tbsp shredded Monterey Jack

Directions and Total Time: approx. 30 minutes

Heat half of avocado oil in a skillet and cook beef for 10 minutes. Season with salt, pepper, onion powder, cumin, garlic, taco seasoning, and paprika. Add the pecans and hemp seeds; stir-fry for 10 minutes. Fold in 3 tbsp Monterey Jack cheese to melt. Spoon the filling into avocado holes, top with 1-2 slices of tomatoes, some lettuce, a tbsp each of sour cream, and the remaining Monterey Jack cheese, and serve immediately.

Per serving: Cal 840; Net Carbs 4g; Fat 70g; Protein 42g

Morning Beef Bowl

Ingredients for 4 servings
1 lb beef sirloin, cut into strips
¼ cup tamari sauce
2 tbsp lemon juice
3 tsp garlic powder
1 tbsp swerve sugar
1 cup coconut oil
6 garlic cloves, minced
1 lb cauliflower rice
2 tbsp olive oil
4 large eggs
2 tbsp chopped scallions

Directions and Total Time: approx. 35 min + chilling time

In a bowl, mix tamari sauce, lemon juice, garlic powder, and swerve. Pour beef into a zipper bag and add in seasoning. Massage the meat to coat well. Refrigerate overnight. The next day, heat coconut oil in a wok, and fry the beef until the liquid evaporates and the meat cooks through, 12 minutes; set aside. Sauté garlic for 2 minutes. Mix in cauli rice until softened, 5 minutes. Season with salt and pepper; spoon into 4 serving bowls and set aside. Wipe the pan clean and heat 1 tbsp of olive oil. Crack in two eggs and fry sunshine-style, 1 minute. Place an egg on each cauliflower rice bowl and fry the other 2 eggs with the remaining olive oil. Serve garnished with scallions.

Per serving: Cal 908; Net Carbs 5.1g; Fat 83g; Protein 34g

Rosemary Beef Meatza

Ingredients for 4 servings
1 ½ lb ground beef
Salt and black pepper to taste
1 large egg
1 tsp rosemary
1 tsp thyme
3 garlic cloves, minced
1 tsp basil
½ tbsp oregano
¾ cup low-carb tomato sauce
¼ cup shredded Parmesan
1 cup shredded Pepper Jack
1 cup shredded mozzarella

Directions and Total Time: approx. 30 minutes

Preheat oven to 350 F and grease a pizza pan with cooking spray. In a bowl, combine beef, salt, pepper, egg, rosemary, thyme, garlic, basil, and oregano. Transfer the mixture into pan and using hands, flatten to a two-inch thickness. Bake for 15 minutes until the beef has a lightly brown crust. Remove and spread tomato sauce on top. Sprinkle with Parmesan, Pepper Jack, and mozzarella cheeses. Return to oven to bake until the cheeses melt, 5 minutes.

Per serving: Cal 319; Net Carbs 3.6g; Fat 10g; Protein 49g

Homemade Philly Cheesesteak in Omelet

Ingredients for 2 servings
4 large eggs
2 tbsp almond milk
2 tbsp olive oil
1 yellow onion, sliced
½ green bell pepper, sliced
¼ lb beef ribeye shaved steak
Salt and black pepper to taste
2 oz provolone cheese, sliced

Directions and Total Time: approx. 35 minutes

In a bowl, beat the eggs with milk. Heat half of the oil in a skillet and pour in half of the eggs. Fry until cooked on one side, flip, and cook until well done. Slide into a plate and fry the remaining eggs. Place them into another plate. Heat the remaining olive oil in the same skillet and sauté the onion and bell pepper for 5 minutes; set aside. Season beef with salt and pepper, and cook in the skillet until brown with no crust. Add onion and pepper back to the pan and cook for 1 minute. Lay provolone cheese in the omelet and top with the hot meat mixture. Roll the eggs and place back to the skillet to melt the cheese. Serve.

Per serving: Cal 497; Net Carbs 3.6g; Fat 36g; Protein 34g

Celery & Beef Stuffed Mushrooms

Ingredients for 4 servings
½ cup shredded Pecorino Romano cheese
2 tbsp olive oil
½ celery stalk, chopped
1 shallot, finely chopped

1 lb ground beef
2 tbsp mayonnaise
1 tsp Old Bay seasoning
½ tsp garlic powder
2 large eggs
4 caps Portobello mushrooms
1 tbsp flaxseed meal
2 tbsp shredded Parmesan
1 tbsp chopped parsley

Directions and Total Time: approx. 55 minutes

Preheat oven to 350 F. Heat olive oil in a skillet and sauté celery and shallot for 3 minutes. Transfer to a bowl. Add beef to the skillet and cook for 10 minutes; transfer to the bowl. Pour in mayo, Old Bay seasoning, garlic powder, Pecorino cheese, and crack in the eggs. Combine the mixture evenly. Arrange the mushrooms on a greased baking sheet and fill with the meat mixture. Combine flaxseed meal and Parmesan in a bowl, and sprinkle over the mushroom filling. Bake until the cheese melts, 30 minutes. Garnish with parsley to serve.

Per serving: Cal 375; Net Carbs 3.5g; Fat 22g; Protein 37g

Korean Braised Beef with Kelp Noodles

Ingredients for 4 servings
1 ½ lb sirloin steak, cut into strips
2 (16- oz) packs kelp noodles, thoroughly rinsed
1 tbsp coconut oil
2 pieces star anise
1 cinnamon stick
1 garlic clove, minced
1-inch ginger, grated
3 tbsp coconut aminos
2 tbsp swerve brown sugar
¼ cup red wine
4 cups beef broth
1 head napa cabbage, steamed
Scallions, thinly sliced

Directions and Total Time: approx. 2 hours 15 minutes

Heat oil in a pot over and sauté anise, cinnamon, garlic, and ginger until fragrant, 5 minutes. Add in beef, season with salt and pepper, and sear on both sides, 10 minutes. In a bowl, combine aminos, sugar, wine, and ¼ cup water. Pour the mixture into the pot, close the lid, and bring to a boil. Reduce the heat and simmer for 1 to 1 ½ hours or until the meat is tender. Strain the pot's content through a colander into a bowl and pour the braising liquid back into the pot. Discard cinnamon and anise and set aside. Add broth and simmer until hot, 10 minutes. Put kelp noodles in the broth and cook until softened and separated, 6 minutes. Spoon the noodles and some broth into bowls, add beef strips, and top with cabbage and scallions.

Per serving: Cal 548; Net Carbs 26.6g; Fat 27g; Protein 44g

Homemade Pasta with Meatballs

Ingredients for 4 servings
1 cup shredded mozzarella
1 egg yolk
½ cup olive oil
2 yellow onions, chopped
6 garlic cloves, minced
2 tbsp tomato paste
2 large tomatoes, chopped
¼ tsp saffron powder
2 cinnamon sticks
4 ½ cups chicken broth
Salt and black pepper to taste
2 cups pork rinds
1 lb ground beef
1 egg
¼ cup almond milk
¼ tsp nutmeg powder
1 tbsp smoked paprika
1 ½ tsp fresh ginger paste
1 tsp cumin powder
½ tsp cayenne pepper
½ tsp cloves powder
4 tbsp chopped cilantro
4 tbsp chopped scallions
4 tbsp chopped parsley
¼ cup almond flour
1 cup crumbled feta cheese

Directions and Total Time: approx. 1 hour + chilling time
Microwave mozzarella cheese for 2 minutes. Mix in egg yolk until combined. Lay parchment paper on a flat surface, pour the cheese mixture on top and cover with another piece of parchment paper. Flatten the dough into 1/8-inch thickness. Take off the parchment paper and cut the dough into

spaghetti strands; refrigerate overnight. When ready, bring 2 cups of water to a boil in a saucepan and add the pasta. Cook for 1 minute, drain, and let cool. In a pot, heat 3 tbsp of olive oil and sauté onions and half of the garlic for 3 minutes. Stir in tomato paste, tomatoes, saffron, and cinnamon sticks; cook for 2 minutes. Mix in chicken broth, salt, and pepper. Simmer for 25 minutes.
In a bowl, mix pork rinds, beef, egg, almond milk, remaining garlic, salt, pepper, nutmeg, paprika, ginger, cumin, cayenne, cloves powder, cilantro, parsley, 3 tbsp of scallions, and almond flour. Form balls out of the mixture. Heat the remaining olive oil in a skillet and fry the meatballs for 10 minutes. Place them into the sauce and continue cooking for 5-10 minutes. Divide the pasta onto serving plates and spoon the meatballs with sauce on top. Garnish with feta cheese and scallions and serve.

Per serving: Cal 783; Net Carbs 6.3g; Fats 56g; Protein 55g

Mustard Beef Collard Rolls

Ingredients for 4 servings
2 lb corned beef
1 tbsp butter
Salt and black pepper to taste
2 tsp Worcestershire sauce
1 tsp Dijon mustard
1 tsp whole peppercorns
¼ tsp cloves
¼ tsp allspice
½ tsp red pepper flakes
1 large bay leaf
1 lemon, zested and juiced
¼ cup white wine
¼ cup freshly brewed coffee
2/3 tbsp swerve sugar
8 large Swiss collard leaves
1 medium red onion, sliced

Directions and Total Time: approx. 70 minutes
In a pot, add beef, butter, salt, pepper, Worcestershire sauce, mustard, peppercorns, cloves, allspice, flakes, bay leaf, lemon zest, lemon juice, wine, coffee, and swerve. Close the lid and cook over low heat for 1 hour. Ten minutes before the end, bring a pot of water to a boil, add collards with one slice of onion for 30 seconds and transfer to ice bath to

blanch for 2-3 minutes. Remove, pat dry, and lay on a flat surface. Remove the meat from the pot, place on a cutting board, and slice. Divide meat onto the collards, top with onion slices, and roll the leaves. Serve with tomato gravy and pickled cabbages.

Per serving: Cal 349; Net Carbs 1.5g; Fat 16g; Protein 47g

Parsley Steak Bites with Shirataki Fettucine

Ingredients for 4 servings
2 (8 oz) packs shirataki fettuccine
1 lb thick-cut New York strip steaks, cut into 1-inch cubes
1 cup freshly grated Pecorino Romano cheese
4 tbsp butter
Salt and black pepper to taste
4 garlic cloves, minced
2 tbsp chopped fresh parsley

Directions and Total Time: approx. 30 minutes
Boil 2 cups of water in a pot. Strain the shirataki pasta and rinse well under hot running water. Allow proper draining and pour into the boiling water. Cook for 3 minutes and strain again. Place a dry skillet and stir-fry the shirataki pasta until visibly dry, 1-2 minutes; set aside. Melt butter in a skillet, season the steaks with salt and pepper, and cook for 10 minutes. Stir in garlic and cook for 1 minute. Mix in parsley and shirataki; toss and season with salt and pepper. Top with the Pecorino Romano cheese and serve.

Per serving: Cal 422; Net Carbs 7.3g; Fats 22g; Protein 36g

Cheddar Zucchini & Beef Mugs

Ingredients for 2 servings
4 oz roast beef deli slices, torn apart
3 tbsp sour cream
1 small zucchini, chopped
2 tbsp chopped green chilies
3 oz shredded cheddar cheese

Directions and Total Time: approx. 10 minutes
Divide the beef slices at the bottom of 2 wide mugs and spread 1 tbsp of sour cream. Top with 2 zucchini slices, season with salt and pepper, add green chilies, top with the remaining sour cream and then cheddar

cheese. Place the mugs in the microwave for 1-2 minutes until the cheese melts. Remove the mugs, let cool for 1 minute, and serve.

Per serving: Cal 188; Net Carbs 3.7g; Fat 9g; Protein 18g

Balsamic Meatloaf

Ingredients for 8 servings
3 pounds ground beef
½ cup chopped onion
½ cup almond flour
2 garlic cloves, minced
1 cup sliced mushrooms
3 eggs
2 tbsp chopped parsley
¼ cup chopped bell peppers
⅓ cup grated Parmesan
1 tsp balsamic vinegar
Glaze:
2 cups balsamic vinegar
1 tbsp sweetener
2 tbsp sugar-free ketchup

Directions and Total Time: approx. 1 hour 15 minutes
Combine all meatloaf ingredients in a large bowl. Press this mixture into 2 greased loaf pans. Bake at 370 F for about 30 minutes. Combining all glaze ingredients in a saucepan over medium heat. Simmer for 20 minutes, until the glaze is thickened. Pour ¼ cup of the glaze over the meatloaf. Save the extra for future use. Put the meatloaf back in the oven and cook for 20 more minutes.

Per serving: Cal 264; Net Carbs 6g; Fat 19g; Protein 23g

Sautéed Thai Beef Shirataki

Ingredients for 4 servings
2 (8 oz) packs angel hair shirataki
1 cup sliced shiitake mushrooms
2 tbsp olive oil, divided
1 ¼ lb flank steak, sliced
1 white onion, thinly sliced
1 red bell pepper, sliced
4 garlic cloves, minced
1 ½ cups Thai basil leaves
2 tbsp toasted sesame seeds
1 tbsp chopped peanuts
1 tbsp chopped scallions
3 tbsp coconut aminos
2 tbsp fish sauce
1 tbsp hot sauce

Directions and Total Time: approx. 35 minutes

Boil 2 cups of water. Strain the shirataki pasta and rinse very well under hot running water. Allow proper draining and pour the shirataki pasta into the boiling water. Cook for 3 minutes and strain again. Place a dry skillet and stir-fry the shirataki pasta until visibly dry, 1-2 minutes; set aside.

Heat olive oil in a skillet, season the meat with salt and pepper and sear on both sides until brown, 5 minutes; set aside. Add onion, bell pepper, garlic, and mushrooms to the skillet; cook for 5 minutes. Return the beef to the skillet and add the pasta. Combine aminos, fish sauce, and hot sauce in a bowl. Pour the mixture over the beef. Top with Thai basil and toss to coat. Cook for 1-2 minutes. Serve garnished with sesame seeds, peanuts, and scallions.

Per serving: Cal 358; Net Carbs 7.5g; Fats 16g; Protein 30g

Bacon-Wrapped Beef Hot Dogs

Ingredients for 4 servings
8 large beef hot dogs
½ cup grated Gruyere cheese
16 slices bacon
1 tsp onion powder
1 tsp garlic powder
Salt and black pepper to taste

Directions and Total Time: approx. 45 minutes

Preheat oven to 400 F. Cut a slit in the middle of each hot dog and stuff evenly with the cheese. Wrap each hot dog with 2 bacon slices each and secure with toothpicks. Season with onion and garlic powders, salt, and pepper. Place the hot dogs in the middle rack of the oven and slide in the cookie sheet beneath the rack to catch dripping grease. Grill for 40 minutes until the bacon browns and crisps. Serve with creamy spinach puree.

Per serving: Cal 958; Net Carbs 4.1g; Fat 86g; Protein 37g

Parsley Beef Carbonara

Ingredients for 4 servings
1 cup shredded mozzarella
1 ¼ cups grated Parmesan
4 bacon slices, chopped
1 ¼ cups heavy cream

¼ cup mayonnaise
4 egg yolks
2 tbsp parsley, chopped
Salt and black pepper to taste

Directions and Total Time: approx. 30 minutes

Microwave mozzarella cheese for 2 minutes. Remove and let cool for 1 minute. Mix in 1 egg yolk until combined. Lay a parchment paper on a flat surface, pour the cheese mixture on top and cover with another parchment paper. Flatten the dough into 1/8-inch thickness. Take off the parchment paper and cut the dough into thin spaghetti strands. Place in a bowl and refrigerate overnight. When ready, bring 2 cups water to a boil in saucepan and add pasta. Cook for 1 minute and drain; divide between serving bowls. Add bacon to a skillet and cook until crispy, 5 minutes; set aside. Pour heavy cream into a pot and let simmer for 5 minutes. Whisk in mayo and season with salt and pepper. Cook for 1 minute. Spoon 2 tbsp of the mixture into a bowl and mix in remaining egg yolks. Pour the mixture in the pot and mix. Stir in 1 cup of Parmesan cheese and fold in the pasta. Spoon into pasta bowls and top with Parmesan cheese and parsley to serve.

Per serving: Cal 470; Net Carbs 8.9g; Fats 35g; Protein 25g

Salisbury Steak

Ingredients for 6 servings
2 pounds ground beef
1 tbsp onion flakes
¾ almond flour
¼ cup beef broth
1 tbsp chopped parsley
1 tbsp Worcestershire sauce

Directions and Total Time: approx. 25 minutes

Combine all ingredients in a bowl. Mix well and make 6 patties out of the mixture. Arrange on a lined baking sheet. Bake at 375 F for about 18 minutes. Serve.

Per serving: Cal 354; Net Carbs 2.5g; Fat 28g; Protein 27g

Beef Alfredo Squash Spaghetti

Ingredients for 4 servings
2 medium spaghetti squashes, halved
2 tbsp olive oil

2 tbsp butter
1 lb ground beef
½ tsp garlic powder
Salt and black pepper to taste
1 tsp arrowroot starch
1 ½ cups heavy cream
A pinch of nutmeg
1/3 cup grated Parmesan
1/3 cup grated mozzarella

Directions and Total Time: approx. 1 hour 20 minutes

Preheat oven to 375 F. Season the squash with olive oil, salt, and pepper. Place on a lined with foil baking dish and roast for 45 minutes. Let cool and shred the inner part of the noodles; set aside. Melt butter in a pot, add in beef, garlic powder, salt, and pepper, and cook for 10 minutes. Stir in arrowroot starch, heavy cream, and nutmeg.
Cook until the sauce thickens, 2-3 minutes. Spoon the sauce into the squashes and cover with Parmesan and mozzarella cheeses. Cook under the broiler for 3 minutes.

Per serving: Cal 563; Net Carbs 4g; Fats 42g; Protein 36g

Cheesy Beef-Asparagus Shirataki Mix

Ingredients for 4 servings
2 (8 oz) packs angel hair shirataki
1 lb fresh asparagus, cut into 1-inch pieces
1 lb ground beef
3 tbsp olive oil
2 shallots, finely chopped
3 garlic cloves, minced
Salt and black pepper to taste
1 cup grated Parmesan cheese

Directions and Total Time: approx. 40 minutes

Bring 2 cups of water to a boil. Strain the shirataki pasta and rinse well under hot running water. Drain and transfer to the boiling water. Cook for 3 minutes and strain again. Place a dry skillet and stir-fry the shirataki pasta until visibly dry, 1 to 2 minutes; set aside. Heat olive oil in a skillet and add the beef. Cook for 10 minutes. Transfer to a plate. In the same skillet sauté for 7 minutes. Stir in shallots and garlic and cook until fragrant, 2 minutes. Season with salt and pepper. Stir in beef and shirataki and toss until combined. Top with Parmesan cheese and serve.

Per serving: Cal 513; Net Carbs 7.2g; Fat 25g; Protein 44g

Classic Beef Ragu with Veggie Pasta

Ingredients for 4 servings
8 mixed bell peppers, spiralized
2 tbsp butter
1 lb ground beef
Salt and black pepper to taste
¼ cup tomato sauce
1 small red onion, spiralized
1 cup grated Parmesan cheese

Directions and Total Time: approx. 20 minutes

Heat the butter in a skillet and cook the beef until brown, 5 minutes. Season with salt and pepper. Stir in tomato sauce and cook for 10 minutes, until the sauce reduces by a quarter. Stir in bell peppers and onion noodles; cook for 1 minute. Top with Parmesan cheese and serve.

Per serving: Cal 451; Net Carbs 7.2g; Fats 25g; Protein 40g

Barbecued Beef Pizza

Ingredients for 4 servings
1 cup grated mozzarella cheese
1 ½ cups grated Gruyere cheese
1 lb ground beef
2 eggs, beaten
¼ cup sugar-free BBQ sauce
¼ cup sliced red onion
2 bacon slices, chopped
2 tbsp chopped parsley

Directions and Total Time: approx. 40 minutes

Preheat oven to 390 F and line a round pizza pan with parchment paper. Mix beef, mozzarella cheese and eggs, and salt. Spread the pizza "dough" on the pan and bake for 20 minutes. Spread BBQ sauce on top, scatter Gruyere cheese all over, followed by the red onion, and bacon slices. Bake for 15 minutes or until the cheese has melted and the back is crispy. Serve warm sprinkled with parsley.

Per serving: Cal 538; Net Carbs 0.4g; Fats 32g; Protein 56g

Beef with Parsnip Noodles

Ingredients for 4 servings
1 lb beef stew meat, cut into strips
1 cup sun-dried tomatoes in oil, chopped

1 cup shaved Parmesan cheese
3 tbsp butter
Salt and black pepper to taste
4 large parsnips, spiralized
4 garlic cloves, minced
1 ¼ cups heavy cream
¼ tsp dried basil
¼ tsp red chili flakes
2 tbsp chopped parsley

Directions and Total Time: approx. 35 minutes

Melt butter in a skillet and sauté the parsnips until softened, 5-7 minutes. Set aside. Season the beef with salt and pepper and add to the same skillet; cook until brown, and cooked within, 8-10 minutes. Stir in sun-dried tomatoes and garlic and cook until fragrant, 1 minute. Reduce the heat to low and stir in heavy cream and Parmesan cheese. Simmer until the cheese melts. Season with basil and red chili flakes. Fold in the parsnips until well coated and cook for 2 more minutes. Garnish with parsley and serve.

Per serving: Cal 596; Net Carbs 6.5g; Fats 35g; Protein 37g

Assorted Grilled Veggies & Beef Steaks

Ingredients for 4 servings
1 red and 1 green bell peppers, cut into strips
4 tbsp olive oil
1 ¼ pounds sirloin steaks
Salt and black pepper to taste
3 tbsp balsamic vinegar
½ lb asparagus, trimmed
1 eggplant, sliced
2 zucchinis, sliced
1 red onion, sliced

Directions and Total Time: approx. 30 minutes

Divide the meat and vegetables between 2 bowls. Mix salt, pepper, olive oil, and balsamic vinegar in a 2 bowl. Rub the beef all over with half of this mixture. Pour the remaining mixture over the vegetables. Preheat a grill pan. Drain the steaks and reserve the marinade. Sear the steaks on both sides for 10 minutes, flipping once halfway through; set aside. Pour the vegetables and marinade in the pan; and cook for 5 minutes, turning once. Serve.

Per serving: Cal 459; Net Carbs 4.5g; Fat 31g; Protein 32.8g

Classic Swedish Coconut Meatballs

Ingredients for 4 servings
1 ½ lb ground beef
2 tsp garlic powder
1 tsp onion powder
Salt and black pepper to taste
2 tbsp olive oil
2 tbsp butter
2 tbsp almond flour
1 cup beef broth
½ cup coconut cream
¼ freshly chopped dill
¼ cup chopped parsley

Directions and Total Time: approx. 30 minutes

Preheat oven to 400 F. In a bowl, combine beef, garlic powder, onion powder, salt, and pepper. Form meatballs from the mixture and place on a greased baking sheet. Drizzle with olive oil and bake until the meat cooks, 10-15 minutes. Remove the baking sheet. Melt butter in a saucepan and stir in almond flour until smooth. Gradually mix in broth, while stirring until thickened, 2 minutes. Stir in coconut cream and dill, simmer for 1 minute and stir in meatballs. Spoon the meatballs with sauce onto a serving platter and garnish with parsley. Serve immediately.

Per serving: Cal 459; Net Carbs 3.2g; Fat 32g; Protein 40g

Herbed Bolognese Sauce

Ingredients for 5 servings
1 pound ground beef
2 garlic cloves
1 onion, chopped
1 tsp oregano
1 tsp marjoram
1 tsp rosemary
7 oz canned chopped tomatoes
1 tbsp olive oil

Directions and Total Time: approx. 35 minutes

Heat olive oil in a saucepan. Cook onions and garlic for 3 minutes. Add beef and cook until browned, about 5 minutes. Stir in herbs and tomatoes. Cook for 15 minutes.

Per serving: Cal 318; Net Carbs 9g; Fat 20g; Protein 26g

Cheese & Beef Bake

Ingredients for 6 servings
2 lb ground beef
Salt and black pepper to taste
1 cup cauli rice
2 cups chopped cabbage
14 oz can diced tomatoes
1 cup shredded Gouda cheese
Directions and Total Time: approx. 30 minutes
Preheat oven to 370 F. Put beef in a pot, season with salt and pepper, and cook for 6 minutes. Add cauli rice, cabbage, tomatoes, and ¼ cup water. Stir and bring to boil for 5 minutes to thicken the sauce. Spoon the beef mixture into a greased baking dish. Sprinkle with cheese and bake for 15 minutes. Cool for 4 minutes and serve.
Per serving: Cal 385, Net Carbs 5g, Fat 25g, Protein 20g

Beef Burgers with Roasted Brussels Sprouts

Ingredients for 4 servings
1 ½ lb Brussels sprouts, halved
1 pound ground beef
1 egg
½ onion, chopped
1 tsp dried thyme
4 oz butter
Salt and black pepper to taste
Directions and Total Time: approx. 30 minutes
Combine beef, egg, onion, thyme, salt, and pepper in a mixing bowl. Create patties out of the mixture. Set a pan over medium heat, warm half of the butter, and fry the patties until browned. Remove to a plate and cover with aluminium foil. Fry Brussels sprouts in the remaining butter, season to taste, then set into a bowl. Plate the burgers and Brussels sprouts and serve.
Per serving: Cal: 443, Net Carbs: 5g, Fat: 25g, Protein: 31g

Smoked Paprika Grilled Ribs

Ingredients for 4 servings
4 tbsp sugar-free BBQ sauce + extra for serving
2 tbsp erythritol
Salt and black pepper to taste
1 tbsp olive oil
3 tsp smoked paprika
1 tsp garlic powder
1 lb beef spare ribs
Directions and Total Time: approx. 35 minutes
Mix erythritol, salt, pepper, oil, smoked paprika, and garlic powder. Brush on the meaty sides of the ribs and wrap in foil. Sit for 30 minutes to marinate.
Preheat oven to 400 F, place wrapped ribs on a baking sheet, and cook for 40 minutes. Remove ribs and aluminium foil, brush with BBQ sauce, and brown under the broiler for 10 minutes on both sides. Slice and serve with extra BBQ sauce and lettuce tomato salad.
Per serving: Cal 395; Net Carbs 3g; Fat 33g; Protein 21g

Beef Broccoli Curry

Ingredients for 6 servings
1 head broccoli, cut into florets
1 tbsp olive oil
1 ½ lb ground beef
1 tbsp ginger-garlic paste
1 tsp garam masala
1 (7 oz) can whole tomatoes
Salt and chili pepper to taste
Directions and Total Time: approx. 30 minutes
Heat oil in a saucepan, add beef, ginger-garlic paste and season with garam masala. Cook for 5 minutes. Stir in tomatoes and broccoli, season with salt and chili pepper, and cook for 6 minutes. Add ¼ cup of water and bring to a boil for 10 minutes or until the water has reduced by half. Adjust taste with salt. Spoon into serving bowls and serve.
Per serving: Cal 374, Net Carbs 2g, Fat 33g, Protein 22g

Shitake Butter Steak

Ingredients for 4 servings
2 cups shitake mushrooms, sliced
4 ribeye steaks
2 tbsp butter
2 tsp olive oil
Salt and black pepper to taste
Directions and Total Time: approx. 25 minutes

Heat olive oil in a pan over medium heat. Rub the steaks with salt and pepper and cook for 4 minutes per side. Set aside. Melt butter in the pan and cook the shitakes for 4 minutes. Pour the butter and mushrooms over the steak.

Per serving: Cal 370; Net Carbs 3g; Fat 31g; Protein 33g

Gruyere Beef Burgers with Sweet Onion

Ingredients for 4 servings
4 zero carb hamburger buns, halved
1 medium white onion, sliced
3 tbsp olive oil
2 tbsp balsamic vinegar
2 tsp erythritol
1 lb ground beef
Salt and black pepper to taste
4 slices Gruyere cheese
Mayonnaise to serve

Directions and Total Time: approx. 35 minutes
Heat 2 tbsp of olive oil in a skillet and add onion. Sauté for 15 minutes until golden brown and add erythritol, balsamic vinegar, and salt. Cook for 3 more minutes; set aside.Make 4 patties out of the ground beef and season with salt and pepper. Then, heat the remaining olive oil in a skillet and cook the patties for 4 minutes on each side. Place a Gruyere slice on each patty and top with the caramelized onions. Put the patties with cheese and onions into two halves of the buns. Serve with mayonnaise.

Per serving: Cal 487; Net Carbs 7.8g; Fat 32g; Protein 38g

PORK

Pancetta & Egg Plate with Cherry Tomatoes

Ingredients for 4 servings
5 oz pancetta, chopped
2 tbsp olive oil
8 eggs
1 tbsp butter, softened
¼ cup cherry tomatoes, halved
2 tbsp chopped oregano

Directions and Total Time: approx. 30 minutes

Pour pancetta in a skillet and fry until crispy, 7 minutes; set aside. Heat half of olive oil in the skillet and crack 4 eggs in. Cook until the whites set, but the yolk are still runny, 1 minute. Spoon two eggs next to pancetta in two plates and fry the remaining eggs with the remaining oil; plate as well. Melt butter in the skillet, fry tomatoes until brown around the edges, 8 minutes. Remove to the same plates. Season to taste, garnish with oregano and serve.

Per serving: Cal 278; Net Carbs 0.5g; Fat 23g; Protein 20g

Chorizo in Cabbage Sauce with Pine Nuts

Ingredients for 4 servings
25 oz green canon cabbage, shredded
6 tbsp butter
25 oz chorizo sausages
1 ¼ cups coconut cream
½ cup fresh sage, chopped
½ lemon, zested
2 tbsp toasted pine nuts

Directions and Total Time: approx. 30 minutes

Melt 2 tbsp of butter in a skillet and fry chorizo until lightly brown on the outside, 10 minutes. Remove to a plate. Melt the remaining butter and sauté cabbage, occasionally stirring until golden brown, 4 minutes. Mix in coconut cream and simmer until the cream reduces. Season with sage, salt, pepper, and lemon zest. Divide the chorizo into four plates, spoon the cabbage to the side of the chorizo, and sprinkle the pine nuts on the cabbage. Serve warm.

Per serving: Cal 914; Net Carbs 16.9g; Fat 76g; Protein 38g

Hawaiian Pork Loco Moco

Ingredients for 4 servings
1 ½ lb ground pork
1/3 cup flaxseed meal
½ tsp nutmeg powder
1 tsp onion powder
5 large egg
2 tbsp heavy cream
3 tbsp coconut oil
1 tbsp salted butter
1 shallot, finely chopped
1 cup sliced oyster mushrooms
1 cup vegetable stock
1 tsp Worcestershire sauce
1 tsp tamari sauce
½ tsp xanthan gum
2 tbsp olive oil
4 large eggs

Directions and Total Time: approx. 40 minutes

In a bowl, combine pork, flaxseed meal, nutmeg and onion powders, salt, and pepper. In another bowl, whisk 1 egg with heavy cream and mix into the pork mixture. The batter will be sticky. Mold 8 patties from the mixture and set aside. Heat coconut oil in a skillet.

Fry the patties on both sides until no longer pink, 16 minutes; set aside. Melt the butter in the same skillet and cook shallot and mushrooms until softened, 7 minutes. In a bowl, mix stock, Worcestershire and tamari sauces, salt, and pepper. Pour the mixture over the mushrooms and cook for 3 minutes. Stir in xanthan gum, and allow thickening, 1 minute. Heat half of olive oil in a skillet, crack in an egg, and fry sunshine style, 1 minute. Plate and fry the remaining eggs using the remaining olive oil. Serve pork with mushroom gravy and top with fried eggs.

Per serving: Cal 655; Net Carbs 2.2g; Fat 46g; Protein 55g

Pork Sausage Omelet with Mushrooms

Ingredients for 2 servings
¼ cup sliced cremini mushrooms

2 tbsp olive oil
2 oz pork sausage, crumbled
1 small white onion, chopped
2 tbsp butter
6 eggs
2 oz shredded cheddar cheese

Directions and Total Time: approx. 30 minutes

Heat olive oil in a pan, add in pork sausage, and fry for 10 minutes; set aside. In the same pan sauté the onion and mushrooms, 8 minutes; set aside. Melt the butter over low heat. Meanwhile, crack the eggs into a bowl and beat with some salt and black pepper until smooth and frothy. Pour the eggs into the pan, swirl to spread around and omelet begins to firm, top with pork, mushroom-onion mixture, and cheese. Using a spatula, carefully remove the egg around the edges of the pan and flip over the stuffing, for 2 minutes. Serve warm for breakfast or brunch.

Per serving: Cal 534; Net Carbs 2.7g; Fat 43g; Protein 29g

British Pork Pie with Broccoli Topping

Ingredients for 4 servings
1 head broccoli, cut into florets
½ cup crème fraîche
1 whole egg
½ celery, finely chopped
3 oz butter, melted
5 oz shredded Swiss cheese
2 tbsp butter, cold
2 lb ground pork
2 tbsp tamari sauce
2 tbsp Worcestershire sauce
½ tbsp hot sauce
1 tsp onion powder

Directions and Total Time: approx. 55 minutes

Preheat oven to 400 F. Bring a pot of salted water to boil and cook broccoli for 3-5 minutes. Drain and transfer to a food processor; grind until rice-like. Pour the broccoli into a bowl. Add crème fraiche, egg, celery, butter, half of Swiss cheese, salt, and pepper. Mix until evenly combined. Melt cold butter in a pot, add and cook the pork until brown, 10 minutes. Mix in tamari, hot and Worcestershire sauces, onion powder, salt,

and pepper; cook for 3 minutes. Spread the mixture in a greased baking dish and cover with broccoli mixture. Sprinkle with the remaining cheese and bake for 20 minutes. Serve with leafy greens.

Per serving: Cal 701; Net Carbs 3.3g; Fat 49g; Protein 60g

Hot Tex-Mex Pork Casserole

Ingredients for 4 servings
2 tbsp butter
1 ½ lb ground pork
3 tbsp Tex-Mex seasoning
2 tbsp chopped jalapeños
½ cup crushed tomatoes
½ cup shredded Monterey Jack
1 scallion, chopped to garnish
1 cup sour cream, for serving

Directions and Total Time: approx. 40 minutes

Preheat oven to 330 F and grease a baking dish with cooking spray. Melt butter in a skillet and cook the pork until brown, 8 minutes. Stir in Tex-Mex seasoning, jalapeños, and tomatoes; simmer for 5 minutes and season to taste. Transfer the mixture to the dish and use a spoon to level at the bottom of the dish. Sprinkle the cheese on top and bake for 20 until the cheese melts is golden brown. Serve, garnished with scallions and sour cream.

Per serving: Cal 431; Net Carbs 7.8g; Fat 24g; Protein 43g

Thyme Pork Roast with Brussels Sprouts

Ingredients for 4 servings
2 lb pork roast
Salt and black pepper to taste
2 tsp dried thyme
1 bay leaf
5 black peppercorns
2 ½ cups beef broth
2 garlic cloves, minced
1 ½ oz fresh ginger, grated
1 tbsp coconut oil
1 tbsp smoked paprika
½ lb Brussel sprouts, halved
1 ½ cups coconut cream

Directions and Total Time: approx. 2 hours

Preheat oven to 360 F. Place the meat in a deep baking dish and season with salt, pepper, thyme, bay leaf, and peppercorns. Pour the broth over and cover with aluminum foil. Bake for 90 minutes. Remove the foil, and carefully lift the pork onto a cutting board. Pour the juices into a bowl and reserve. In a bowl, combine garlic, ginger, coconut oil, and paprika. Rub the mixture onto meat and return the meat to the dish. Roast for 10 minutes or until golden brown. Remove, slice thinly, and set aside. Meanwhile, strain the juices through a colander into a pot and bring to boil until reduced to 1 ½ cups. Pour in Brussel sprouts and cook for 8 minutes or until softened. Stir in coconut cream, and simmer for 15 minutes. Serve creamy Brussel sprouts with pork roast.
Per serving: Cal 691; Net Carbs 9.6g; Fat 45g; Protein 59g

Cheesy Pork Quiche

Ingredients for 4 servings
1 ¼ cups almond flour
1 tbsp psyllium husk powder
4 tbsp chia seeds
2 tbsp melted butter
6 egg
1 tbsp butter
½ lb smoked pork shoulder
1 yellow onion, chopped
1 tsp dried thyme
Salt and black pepper to taste
1 cup coconut cream
¼ cup shredded Swiss cheese
Directions and Total Time: approx. 70 minutes
Preheat oven to 350 F, grease a springform pan with cooking spray, and line with parchment paper; set aside. To a food processor, add almond flour, psyllium husk, chia seeds, ½ tsp of salt, butter, and 1 egg. Mix until a firm dough forms. Oil your hands and spread the dough at the bottom of the springform pan. Refrigerate while you make the filling. Melt butter in a skillet, and cook the pork and onion until the meat browns, 10-12 minutes. Stir in thyme, salt, and pepper; cook further for 2 minutes. Remove the piecrust from the fridge and spoon pork and onion onto the crust. In a bowl, whisk coconut cream, half of Swiss cheese, and the

remaining 5 eggs. Pour the mixture over the meat filling and top with the remaining Swiss cheese. Bake until the cheese melts and a toothpick inserted into the quiche comes out clean, 45 minutes. Remove the pan, release the lock, and take off the ring. Slice and serve.
Per serving: Cal 498; Net Carbs 4.6g; Fat 42g; Protein 24g

Parmesan & Pimiento Pork Meatballs

Ingredients for 4 servings
¼ cup chopped pimientos
1/3 cup mayonnaise
3 tbsp softened cream cheese
1 tsp paprika powder
1 pinch cayenne pepper
1 tbsp Dijon mustard
4 oz grated Parmesan cheese
1 ½ lb ground pork
1 large egg
2 tbsp olive oil, for frying
Directions and Total Time: approx. 30 minutes
In a bowl, mix pimientos, mayo, cream cheese, paprika, cayenne, mustard, Parmesan, pork, salt, pepper, and egg. Mix with hands, and form large meatballs. Heat olive oil in a non-stick skillet and fry the meatballs in batches on both sides until brown, 10 minutes in total. Transfer to a plate and serve on a bed of leafy green salad.
Per serving: Cal 485; Net Carbs 6.8g; Fat 30g; Protein 47g

Pork Bake with Cottage Cheese & Olives

Ingredients for 4 servings
½ cup cottage cheese, crumbled
2 tbsp avocado oil
1 ½ lb ground pork
¼ cup sliced Kalamata olives
2 garlic cloves, minced
½ cup marinara sauce
1 ¼ cups heavy cream
Directions and Total Time: approx. 40 minutes
Preheat oven to 400 F and grease a casserole dish with cooking spray. Heat avocado oil in a deep skillet, add the pork, and cook until brown, 10 minutes. Stir frequently and break

any lumps that form. Spread the pork at the bottom of the casserole dish. Scatter olives, cottage cheese, and garlic on top. In a bowl, mix marinara sauce and heavy cream, and pour all over the meat. Bake until the top is bubbly and lightly brown, 20-25 minutes. Serve warm.

Per serving: Cal 451; Net Carbs 1.5g; Fat 30g; Protein 40g

Buttered Pork Chops with Lemon Asparagus

Ingredients for 4 servings
7 tbsp butter
4 pork chops
Salt and black pepper to taste
4 tbsp butter, softened
2 garlic cloves, minced
1 lb asparagus, trimmed
1 tbsp dried cilantro
1 small lemon, juice

Directions and Total Time: approx. 30 minutes
Melt 3 tbsp of butter in a skillet over medium heat. Season pork with salt and pepper and fry on both sides until brown, 10 minutes in total; set aside. Melt the remaining butter in a skillet, and sauté garlic until fragrant, 1 minute. Add in asparagus, and cook until slightly softened with some crunch, 4 minutes. Add cilantro and lemon juice, toss to coat well. Serve the asparagus with the pork chops.

Per serving: Cal 538; Net Carbs 1.2g; Fat 38g; Protein 42g

Tasty Pork Chops with Cauliflower Steaks

Ingredients for 4 servings
2 heads cauliflower, cut into 4 steaks
4 pork chops
1 tbsp mesquite seasoning
2 tbsp butter
2 tbsp olive oil
½ cup Parmesan cheese

Directions and Total Time: approx. 30 minutes
Season pork with mesquite flavoring, salt, and pepper. Melt butter in a skillet and fry pork on both sides for 10 minutes; set aside. Heat olive oil in a grill pan and cook cauli

steaks on all sides for 4 minutes. Sprinkle with Parmesan to melt. Serve the steaks with pork chops.

Per serving: Cal 429; Net Carbs 3.9g; Fat 23g; Protein 45g

Zucchini & Tomato Pork Omelet

Ingredients for 4 servings
3 zucchinis, halved lengthwise
4 tbsp olive oil
1 garlic clove, crushed
1 small plum tomato, diced
2 tbsp chopped scallions
1 tsp dried basil
1 tsp cumin powder
1 tsp smoked paprika
1 lb ground pork
3 large eggs, beaten
3 tsp crushed pork rinds
1/3 cup chopped cilantro

Directions and Total Time: approx. 50 minutes
Preheat a grill to medium, place the zucchinis on top, drizzle with 1 tbsp of olive oil and broil until brown, 5 minutes; set aside. Heat 1 tbsp of olive oil in a skillet and sauté garlic, tomato, and scallions, 8 minutes. Mix in basil, cumin, paprika, and salt. Add the pork and cook until brown, 10 minutes; set aside. Spread the pork mixture onto the grilled zucchini slices; flatten the mixture. In the same skillet, heat the remaining oil over medium and carefully place in the loaded zucchinis. Divide the eggs onto the zucchinis, cover the pan and cook until set, 3 minutes. Sprinkle pork rinds and cilantro on top, and serve.

Per serving: Cal 332; Net Carbs 1.1g; Fat 22g; Protein 30g

Italian Pork with Capers

Ingredients for 4 servings
1 ½ lb thin cut pork chops, boneless
½ lemon, juiced + 1 lemon, sliced
Salt and black pepper to taste
1 tbsp avocado oil
3 tbsp butter
2 tbsp capers
1 cup beef broth
2 tbsp chopped parsley

Directions and Total Time: approx. 30 minutes

Heat avocado oil in a skillet and cook pork chops on both sides until brown, 14 minutes. Transfer to a plate, cover to keep warm. Melt butter in the pan and cook capers until hot and sizzling; keep stirring to avoid burning, 3 minutes.

Pour in broth and lemon juice, use a spatula to scrape any bits stuck at the bottom, and boil until the sauce reduces by half. Add back the pork, arrange lemon slices on top, and sprinkle with 1 tbsp parsley. Simmer for 3 minutes. Serve garnished with parsley and with creamy mashed cauliflower.

Per serving: Cal 341; Net Carbs 0.8g; Fat 18g; Protein 40g

Avocado & Green Bean Pork Sauté

Ingredients for 4 servings
4 tbsp avocado oil
4 pork shoulder chops
2 tbsp avocado oil
1 ½ cups green beans
2 large avocados, chopped
Salt and black pepper to taste
6 green onions, chopped
1 tbsp chopped parsley

Directions and Total Time: approx. 30 minutes
Heat oil in a skillet, season pork with salt and pepper, and fry in the oil until brown, 12 minutes; set aside. To the same skillet, sauté green beans until sweating and slightly softened, 10 minutes. Mix in avocados and half of green onions for 2 minutes. Dish into plates, garnish with the remaining onions and parsley, and serve with pork chops.

Per serving: Cal 557; Net Carbs 1.9g; Fat 36g; Protein 43g

Savory Pork Tacos

Ingredients for 4 servings
2 tbsp olive oil
½ cup sliced yellow onion
2 lb pork shoulder
4 tbsp ras el hanout seasoning
Salt to taste
3 ½ cups beef broth
5 tbsp psyllium husk powder
1 ¼ cups almond flour
2 eggs, cracked into a bowl
2 tbsp butter, for frying

Directions and Total Time: approx. 7 hours
In a pot, heat olive oil and sauté onion for 3 minutes or until softened. Season pork shoulder with ras el hanout, salt, and place in the onion. Sear on each side for 3 minutes and pour the broth on top. Cover the lid, reduce heat to low, and cook for 4 to 5 hours or until the pork softens. Shred the pork with two forks. Cook further over low heat for 1 hour; set aside. In a bowl, combine psyllium husk powder, almond flour, and 1 tsp of salt. Mix in eggs until a thick dough forms and add 1 cup of water.

Separate the dough into 8 pieces. Lay a parchment paper on a flat surface, grease with cooking spray, and put a dough piece on top. Cover with another parchment paper and, using a rolling pin, flatten the dough into a circle. Repeat the same process for the remaining dough balls. Melt a quarter of the butter in a skillet over and fry the flattened dough one after another on both sides until light brown, 40 minutes in total. Transfer the keto tortillas to plates, spoon shredded meat and serve.

Per serving: Cal 520; Net Carbs 3.8g; Fat 30g; Protein 50g

Yummy Spareribs in Béarnaise Sauce

Ingredients for 4 servings
3 tbsp butter, melted
4 egg yolks, beaten
2 tbsp chopped tarragon
2 tsp white wine vinegar
½ tsp onion powder
Salt and black pepper to taste
4 tbsp butter
2 lb spareribs, divided into 16

Directions and Total Time: approx. 30 minutes
In a bowl, whisk butter gradually into the egg yolks until evenly mixed. In another bowl, combine tarragon, white wine vinegar, and onion powder. Mix into the egg mixture and season with salt and black pepper; set aside. Melt the butter in a skillet over medium heat. Season the spareribs on both sides with salt and pepper. Cook in the butter on both sides until brown with a crust, 12 minutes. Divide the spareribs between plates and serve with

béarnaise sauce to the side, along with some braised asparagus.
Per serving: Cal 878; Net Carbs 1g; Fat 78g; Protein 41g

Pork & Pecan in Camembert Bake

Ingredients for 4 servings
9 oz whole Camembert cheese
½ lb boneless pork chops, cut into small cubes
3 tbsp olive oil
2 oz pecans
1 garlic clove, minced
1 tbsp chopped parsley
Directions and Total Time: approx. 30 minutes
Preheat the oven to 400 F. While the cheese is in its box, using a knife, score around the top and side of about a ¼-inch and take off the top layer of the skin. Place the cheese on a baking tray and melt in the oven for 10 minutes. Meanwhile, heat olive oil in a skillet, season the pork with salt and black pepper, and fry until brown on all sides, 12 minutes. Transfer to a bowl and add pecans, garlic, and parsley. Spoon the mixture onto the cheese and bake for 10 minutes until the cheese softens and nuts toast.
Per serving: Cal 452; Net Carbs 0.2g; Fat 38g; Protein 27g

Cheddar Pork Burrito Bowl

Ingredients for 4 servings
1 tbsp butter
1 lb ground pork
½ cup beef broth
4 tbsp taco seasoning
Salt and black pepper to taste
½ cup sharp cheddar, shredded
½ cup sour cream
¼ cup sliced black olives
1 avocado, cubed
¼ cup tomatoes, diced
1 green onion, sliced
1 tbsp fresh cilantro, chopped
Directions and Total Time: approx. 30 minutes
Melt butter in a skillet over medium heat. Cook the pork until brown while breaking any lumps, 10 minutes. Mix in broth, taco seasoning, salt, and pepper; cook until most of the liquid evaporates, 5 minutes. Mix in

half of cheddar cheese to melt. Spoon into a bowl and top with olives, avocado, tomatoes, green onion, and cilantro to serve.
Per serving: Cal 386; Net Carbs 8.8g; Fat 23g; Protein 30g

Parmesan Pork Stuffed Mushrooms

Ingredients for 4 servings
12 medium portabella mushrooms, stalks removed
2 tbsp butter
½ lb ground pork
1 tsp paprika
3 tbsp chives, finely chopped
7 oz cream cheese
¼ cup shredded Parmesan
Directions and Total Time: approx. 30 minutes
Preheat oven to 400 F and grease a baking sheet with cooking spray. Melt butter in a skillet, add the pork, season with salt, pepper, and paprika. Stir-fry until brown, 10 minutes. Mix in two-thirds of chives and cream cheese until evenly combined. Place mushrooms on the baking sheet and spoon the mixture into the mushrooms. Top with the Parmesan and bake until mushrooms turn golden and the cheese melts, 10 minutes. Remove to plates, garnish with the remaining chives, and serve immediately.
Per serving: Cal 299; Net Carbs 2.2g; Fat 23g; Protein 19g

Florentine-Style Pizza with Bacon

Ingredients for 2 servings
1 cup shredded provolone cheese
1 (7 oz) can sliced mushrooms, drained
10 eggs
1 tsp Italian seasoning
6 bacon slices
2/3 cup tomato sauce
2 cups chopped kale, wilted
½ cup grated mozzarella
4 eggs
Olive oil for drizzling
Directions and Total Time: approx. 45 minutes
Preheat oven to 400 F and line a pizza-baking pan with parchment paper. Crack 6 eggs into a bowl; whisk in provolone cheese, and Italian seasoning. Spread the mixture on a pizza-baking pan and bake until golden, 15

minutes. Remove from oven and let cool for 2 minutes. Increase temperature to 450 F. Fry bacon in a skillet until brown and crispy, 5 minutes. Transfer to a plate. Spread tomato sauce on the crust, top with kale, mozzarella, and mushrooms. Bake in the oven for 8 minutes. Crack the remaining 4 eggs on top, cover with bacon, and continue baking until the eggs set, 2-3 minutes. Serve warm.

Per serving: Cal 1093; Net Carbs 6.1g; Fat 77g; Protein 69g

Cheesy Mushrooms & Bacon Lettuce Rolls

Ingredients for 4 servings
½ cup sliced cremini mushrooms
1 iceberg lettuce, leaves separated
8 bacon slices, chopped
2 tbsp olive oil
1 ½ lb ground pork
1 cup shredded cheddar

Directions and Total Time: approx. 30 minutes

In a skillet, cook bacon until brown and crispy. Transfer onto a paper-towel-lined plate. Heat the 1 tbsp of olive oil in the skillet and sauté the mushrooms. Season with salt and pepper; cook for 5 minutes or until softened. Heat the remaining oil and cook the pork until brown, 10 minutes, while breaking the lumps that form. Divide the pork between lettuce leaves, sprinkle with cheddar cheese, top with bacon and mushrooms. Wrap and serve with mayo.

Per serving: Cal 630; Net Carbs 0.5g; Fat 45g; Protein 52g

Saucy Thai Pork Medallions

Ingredients for 4 servings
1 ½ pork tenderloin, sliced into ½ -inch medallions
6 tbsp butter
1 canon cabbage, shredded
Salt and black pepper to taste
1 celery, chopped
1 tbsp red curry powder
1 ¼ cups coconut cream

Directions and Total Time: approx. 45 minutes

Melt 2 tbsp of butter in a skillet, and sauté cabbage until soft and slightly golden; set aside. Melt 2 tbsp of butter in the skillet,

season the pork with salt and pepper, and fry until brown on the outside and cooked within 10 minutes; set aside. Add the remaining butter to the skillet and sauté celery until softened. Mix in curry, heat for 30 seconds, and stir in coconut cream. Simmer for 10 minutes. Put the meat into heat. Serve with buttered cabbage.

Per serving: Cal 626; Net Carbs 3.9g; Fat 48g; Protein 43g

Barbecue Baked Pork Chops

Ingredients for 4 servings
½ cup grated flaxseed meal
1 tsp dried thyme
1 tsp paprika
Salt and black pepper to taste
¼ tsp chili powder
1 ½ tsp garlic powder
1 tbsp dried parsley
1/2 tsp onion powder
1/8 tsp basil
4 pork chops
1 tbsp melted butter
½ cup BBQ sauce

Directions and Total Time: approx. 70 minutes

Preheat oven to 400 F. In a bowl, mix flaxseed meal, thyme, paprika, salt, pepper, chili, garlic powder, parsley, onion powder, and basil. Rub the pork chops with the mixture. Melt butter in a skillet and sear pork on both sides, 8 minutes. Transfer to a greased baking sheet, baste with BBQ sauce and bake for 50 minutes. Allow resting for 10 minutes, slice, and serve with buttered parsnips.

Per serving: Cal 385; Net Carbs 1.6g; Fat 19g; Protein 44g

Dijon Pork Loin Roast

Ingredients for 6 servings
3 lb boneless pork loin roast
5 cloves garlic, minced
Salt and black pepper to taste
1 tbsp Dijon mustard
1 tsp dried basil
2 tsp garlic powder

Directions and Total Time: approx. 30 minutes

Preheat oven to 400 F and place the pork in a baking dish. In a bowl, mix minced garlic, salt, pepper, mustard, basil, and garlic powder.

Rub the mixture onto pork. Drizzle with olive oil and bake for 15 minutes or until cooked within and brown outside. Transfer onto a flat surface, and let cool for 5 minutes. Serve sliced with steamed greens.

Per serving: Cal 311; Net Carbs 2g; Fat 9g; Protein 51g

Tender Pork Chops with Basil & Beet Greens

Ingredients for 4 servings
2 cups chopped beetroot greens
2 tbsp balsamic vinegar
2 tsp freshly pureed garlic
2 tbsp freshly chopped basil
4 thyme sprigs
1 tbsp olive oil
4 pork chops
2 tbsp butter

Directions and Total Time: approx. 30 minutes
Preheat oven to 400 F. In a saucepan, add vinegar, salt, pepper, garlic, and basil. Cook over low heat until the mixture is syrupy. Heat olive oil in a skillet and sear pork on both sides for 8 minutes. Brush the vinegar glaze on the pork, add thyme, and bake for 8 minutes. Melt butter in another skillet and sauté beetroot greens for 5 minutes. Serve pork with beetroot greens.

Per serving: Cal 391; Net Carbs 0.8g; Fat 16g; Protein 40g

Ground Pork & Scrambled Eggs with Cabbage

Ingredients for 4 servings
2 tbsp sesame oil
2 large eggs
2 tbsp minced garlic
½ tsp ginger puree
1 medium white onion, diced
1 lb ground pork
1 habanero pepper, chopped
1 green cabbage, shredded
5 scallions, chopped
3 tbsp coconut aminos
1 tbsp white vinegar
2 tbsp sesame seeds

Directions and Total Time: approx. 30 minutes

Heat 1 tbsp of sesame oil in a skillet over and scramble the eggs until set, 1 minute; set aside. Heat 1 tbsp sesame oil in the same skillet and sauté garlic, ginger, and onion until soft and fragrant, 4 minutes. Add ground pork and habanero pepper and season with salt, pepper. Cook for 10 minutes. Mix in cabbage, scallions, aminos, and vinegar and cook until the cabbage is tender. Stir in the eggs. Serve garnished with sesame seeds, and some low carb tortillas.

Per serving: Cal 295; Net Carbs 3.6g; Fat 16g; Protein 29g

Sweet Pork Chops with Brie Cheese

Ingredients for 4 servings
3 tbsp olive oil
2 large red onions, sliced
2 tbsp balsamic vinegar
1 tsp maple (sugar-free) syrup
Salt and black pepper to taste
4 pork chops
4 slices brie cheese
2 tbsp chopped mint leaves

Directions and Total Time: approx. 45 minutes
Heat 1 tbsp olive oil in a skillet until smoky. Reduce to low and sauté onions until brown. Pour in vinegar, maple syrup, and salt. Cook with frequent stirring to prevent burning until the onions caramelize, 15 minutes; set aside. Heat the remaining olive oil in the same skillet, season the pork with salt and black pepper, and cook for 12 minutes. Put a brie slice on each meat and top with the caramelized onions; let the cheese to melt for 2 minutes. Spoon the meat with the topping onto plates and garnish with mint.

Per serving: Cal 457; Net Carbs 3.1g; Fat 25g; Protein 46g

Sesame Pork Meatballs

Ingredients for 4 servings
1 lb ground pork
2 scallions, chopped
1 zucchini, grated
4 garlic cloves, minced
1 tsp freshly pureed ginger
1 tsp red chili flakes
2 tbsp tamari sauce
2 tbsp sesame oil
3 tbsp coconut oil, for frying

Directions and Total Time: approx. 30 minutes

In a bowl, combine pork, scallions, zucchini, garlic, ginger, chili flakes, tamari sauce, and sesame oil. With hands, form 1-inch oval shapes and place on a plate. Heat coconut oil in a skillet over medium heat and brown the balls for 12 minutes. Transfer to a paper towel-lined plate to drain and serve with creamy spinach puree.

Per serving: Cal 296; Net Carbs 1.5g; Fat 22g; Protein 24g

Hot Pork Stir-Fry with Walnuts

Ingredients for 4 servings
1 ½ lb pork tenderloin, cut into strips
2 tbsp coconut oil
Salt and black pepper to taste
1 green bell pepper, diced
1 small red onion, diced
1/3 cup walnuts
1 tbsp freshly grated ginger
3 garlic cloves, minced
1 tsp sesame oil
1 habanero pepper, minced
2 tbsp tamari sauce

Directions and Total Time: approx. 30 minutes

Heat coconut oil in a wok, season pork with salt and pepper, and cook until no longer pink, 10 minutes. Shift to one side of the wok and add bell pepper, onion, walnuts, ginger, garlic, sesame oil, and habanero pepper. Sauté until fragrant and onion softened, 5 minutes. Mix and season with tamari sauce. Stir-fry until well combined and cook for 1 minute. Serve with cauliflower rice.

Per serving: Cal 325; Net Carbs 2.8g; Fat 16g; Protein 38g

Lemony Greek Pork Tenderloin

Ingredients for 4 servings
¼ cup olive oil
2 lemon, juiced
2 tbsp Greek seasoning
2 tbsp red wine vinegar
1 ½ lb pork tenderloin
2 tbsp lard

Directions and Total Time: approx. 2 hours

Preheat oven to 425 F. In a bowl, combine olive oil, lemon juice, Greek seasoning,

vinegar, salt, and pepper. Place the pork on a clean flat surface, cut a few incisions, and brush the marinade all over. Cover in plastic wrap and refrigerate for 1 hour. Melt lard in a skillet, remove and unwrap the pork, and sear until brown on the outside. Place in a greased baking dish, brush with any reserved marinade, and bake for 45 minutes. Serve.

Per serving: Cal 383; Net Carbs 2.5g; Fat 24g; Protein 36g

Flavorful Chipotle-Coffee Pork Chops

Ingredients for 4 servings
1 tbsp finely ground coffee
½ tsp chipotle powder
½ tsp garlic powder
½ tsp cinnamon powder
½ tsp cumin powder
1 ½ tsp swerve brown sugar
4 bone-in pork chops
2 tbsp lard

Directions and Total Time: approx. 20 minutes

In a bowl, mix coffee, chipotle, garlic, cinnamon, cumin, salt, pepper, and swerve. Rub spices all over the pork. Cover with plastic wraps and refrigerate overnight. Preheat oven to 350 F. Melt lard in a skillet and sear pork on both sides for 3 minutes. Transfer the skillet to the oven and bake for 10 minutes. Remove to a cutting board, let cool, slice, and serve with buttered snap peas.

Per serving: Cal 291; Net Carbs 0.5g; Fat 13g; Protein 39g

Pork Belly with Creamy Coconut Kale

Ingredients for 4 servings
2 lb pork belly, chopped
Salt and black pepper to taste
1 tbsp coconut oil
1 white onion, chopped
6 cloves garlic, minced
¼ cup ginger thinly sliced
4 long red chilies, halved
1 cup coconut milk
1 cup coconut cream
2 cups chopped kale

Directions and Total Time: approx. 40 minutes

Season pork belly with salt and pepper and refrigerate for 30 minutes. Pour 2 cups water in a pot, add in pork and bring to a boil for 15

minutes. Drain and transfer to a skillet. Fry for 15 minutes until the skin browns and crackles. Turn a few times to prevent from burning. Spoon onto a plate and discard the fat. Heat coconut oil in the same skillet and sauté onion, garlic, ginger, and chilies for 5 minutes. Pour in coconut milk and coconut cream and cook for 1 minute. Add kale and cook until wilted, stirring occasionally. Stir in the pork. Cook for 2 minutes. Serve.
Per serving: Cal 608; Net Carbs 6.7g; Fat 36g; Protein 57g

Pork Medallions with & Morels

Ingredients for 4 servings4
1 ½ lb pork tenderloin, cut into 8 medallions
2 tbsp olive oil
16 fresh morels, rinsed
4 large green onions, chopped
½ cup red wine
¾ cup beef broth
2 tbsp unsalted butter
Directions and Total Time: approx. 25 minutes
Heat olive oil in a pot, season the pork medallions with salt and pepper, and sear until brown, 5 minutes; set aside. Add morels and green onions and cook until softened, 2 minutes. Mix in red wine and broth. Place the pork in the sauce to simmer for 5 minutes. Swirl in butter, adjust the taste, and serve hot with creamy mashed turnips.
Per serving: Cal 328; Net Carbs 1.2g; Fat 15g; Protein 39g

Mozzarella Baked Pork

Ingredients for 4 servings
4 boneless pork chops
Salt and black pepper to taste
1 cup golden flaxseed meal
1 large egg, beaten
1 cup tomato sauce
1 cup shredded mozzarella
Directions and Total Time: approx. 30 minutes
Preheat oven to 400 F and grease a baking sheet. Season the pork with salt and pepper, and add flaxseed meal to a plate. Coat the meat in the egg, then in flaxseed, and place on the baking sheet. Pour tomato sauce over and sprinkle with mozzarella. Bake for 15

minutes or until the cheese melts and pork cooks through. Serve hot with salad.
Per serving: Cal 592; Net Carbs 2.7g; Fat 25g; Protein 62g

Juicy Pork Chops with Parmesan

Ingredients for 4 servings
1 lb pork tenderloin, cut into ½-inch medallions
2 cups fresh raspberries
¼ cup water
1 tsp chicken bouillon granules
½ cup almond flour
2 large eggs, lightly beaten
2/3 cup grated Parmesan
Salt and black pepper to taste
6 tbsp butter, divided
1 tsp minced garlic
Sliced fresh raspberries
Directions and Total Time: approx. 30 minutes
To a blender, add raspberries, water, and chicken granules; process until smooth and set aside. In two separate bowls, pour almond flour and Parmesan cheese. Season the meat with salt and pepper. Coat in the flour, then in the eggs, and then in the cheese. Melt 2 tbsp of butter in a skillet and fry the pork for 3 minutes per side or until the cheese melts and the meat cooks within. Transfer to a plate, cover to keep warm. In the same skillet, melt the remaining butter and sauté garlic for 1 minute. Stir in raspberry mixture and cook for 3 minutes. Dish the pork and spoon sauce on top. Garnish with raspberries and serve with baby spinach.
Per serving: Cal 488; Net Carbs 6.1g; Fat 23g; Protein 34g

Mushroom Pork Meatballs with Parsnips

Ingredients for 4 servings
1 cup cremini mushrooms, chopped
1 ½ lb ground pork
2 garlic cloves, minced
2 small red onions, chopped
1 tsp dried basil
Salt and black pepper to taste
1 cup grated Parmesan
½ almond milk
2 tbsp olive oil
2 cups tomato sauce

6 fresh basil leaves to garnish
1 lb parsnips, chopped
1 cup water
2 tbsp butter
½ cup coconut cream

Directions and Total Time: approx. 60 minutes

Preheat oven to 350 F and line a baking tray with parchment paper. In a bowl, add pork, half of garlic, half of onion, mushrooms, basil, salt, and pepper; mix with hands until evenly combined. Mold bite-size balls out of the mixture. Pour ½ cup Parmesan and almond milk each in 2 separate bowls. Dip each ball in the milk and then in the cheese. Place on the tray and bake for 20 minutes.

Heat olive oil in a saucepan and sauté the remaining onion and garlic; sauté until fragrant and soft. Pour in tomato sauce and cook for 20 minutes. Add the meatballs, spoon some sauce to cover, and simmer for 7 minutes. In a pot, add parsnips, 1 cup water, and salt. Bring to a boil for 10 minutes until the parsnips soften. Drain and pour into a bowl. Add butter, salt, and pepper; mash into a puree using a mash. Stir in coconut cream and remaining Parmesan until combined. Spoon mashed parsnip into bowls, top with meatballs and sauce, and garnish with basil leaves.

Per serving: Cal 642; Net Carbs 21.1g; Fat 32g; Protein 50g

Smoked Paprika-Coconut Tenderloin

Ingredients for 4 servings
1 lb pork tenderloin, cubed
4 tsp smoked paprika
Salt and black pepper to taste
1 tsp almond flour
1 tbsp butter
3/4 cup coconut cream

Directions and Total Time: approx. 30 minutes

Pat dry the pork pieces with a paper towel and season with paprika, salt, pepper, and sprinkle with almond flour. Melt butter in a skillet and sauté the pork until lightly browned, 5 minutes. Stir in cream; let boil. Cook until the sauce slightly thickens, 7 minutes. Serve over a bed of cauli rice.

Per serving: Cal 310; Net Carbs 2.5g; Fat 21g; Protein 26g

Mushroom & Pork Casserole

Ingredients for 4 servings
1 cup portobello mushrooms, chopped
1 cup ricotta, crumbled
1 cup Italian cheese blend
4 carrots, thinly sliced
Salt and black pepper to taste
1 clove garlic, minced
1 ¼ pounds ground pork
4 green onions, chopped
15 oz canned tomatoes
4 tbsp pork rinds, crushed
¼ cup chopped parsley
3 tbsp olive oil
⅓ cup water

Directions and Total Time: approx. 38 minutes

Mix parsley, ricotta cheese, and Italian cheese blend in a bowl; set aside. Heat olive oil in a skillet and cook pork for 3 minutes. Add garlic, half of the green onions, mushrooms, and 2 tbsp of pork rinds. Continue cooking for 3 minutes. Stir in tomatoes and water and cook for 3 minutes. Sprinkle a baking dish with 2 tbsp of pork rinds, top with half of the carrots and a season of salt, 2/3 of the pork mixture, and the cheese mixture. Repeat the layering process a second time to exhaust the ingredients. Cover the baking dish with foil and bake for 20 minutes at 370 F. Remove the foil and brown the top of the casserole with the broiler side of the oven for 2 minutes.

Per serving: Cal 672; Net Carbs 7.9g; Fat 56g; Protein 34.8g

Tangy Lemon Pork Steaks with Mushrooms

Ingredients for 4 servings
8 oz white button mushrooms, chopped
4 large, bone-in pork steaks
2 tsp lemon pepper seasoning
3 tbsp olive oil
3 tbsp butter
1 cup beef stock
6 garlic cloves, minced
2 tbsp chopped parsley
1 lemon, thinly sliced

Directions and Total Time: approx. 30 minutes

Pat the pork dry with a paper towel and season with salt and lemon pepper. Heat 2 tbsp each of olive oil and butter in a skillet over medium heat and cook the meat until brown, 10 minutes; set aside. Add the remaining oil and butter to the skillet, pour in half of the stock to deglaze the bottom of the pan, add garlic and mushrooms, and cook until softened, 5 minutes. Return the pork, add lemon slices, and cook until the liquid reduces by two-thirds. Garnish with parsley, and serve with steamed green beans.

Per serving: Cal 505; Net Carbs 3.2g; Fat 32g; Protein 46g

Celery Braised Pork Shanks in Wine Sauce

Ingredients for 4 servings
3 tbsp olive oil
3 lb pork shanks
3 celery stalks, chopped
5 garlic cloves, minced
1 ½ cups crushed tomatoes
½ cup red wine
¼ tsp red chili flakes
¼ cup chopped parsley

Directions and Total Time: approx. 2 hours 30 minutes
Preheat oven to 300 F. Heat olive oil in a Dutch oven and brown pork on all sides for 4 minutes; set aside. Add celery and garlic and sauté for 3 minutes. Return the pork and top with tomatoes, red wine, and chili flakes. Cover the lid and put the pot in the oven. Cook for 2 hours, turning the meat every 30 minutes. In the last 15 minutes, open the lid and increase the temperature to 450 F. Take out the pot, stir in parsley, and serve the meat with sauce on a bed of creamy mashed cauliflower.

Per serving: Cal 520; Net Carbs 1.4g; Fat 20g; Protein 75g

Tuscan Pork Tenderloin with Cauli Rice

Ingredients for 4 servings
1 cup loosely packed fresh baby spinach
2 tbsp olive oil
1 ½ lb pork tenderloin, cubed
Salt and black pepper to taste
½ tsp cumin powder
2 cups cauliflower rice
½ cup water

1 cup grape tomatoes, halved
3/4 cup crumbled feta cheese
Directions and Total Time: approx. 30 minutes
Heat olive oil in a skillet, season the pork with salt, pepper, and cumin, and sear on both sides for 5 minutes until brown. Stir in cauli rice and pour in water. Cook for 5 minutes or until cauliflower softens. Mix in spinach to wilt, 1 minute, and add the tomatoes. Spoon the dish into bowls, sprinkle with feta cheese, and serve with hot sauce.

Per serving: Cal 377; Net Carbs 1.9g; Fat 17g; Protein 43g

Indian Pork Masala

Ingredients for 4 servings
1 ½ lb pork shoulder, cut into bite-size pieces
2 tbsp ghee
1 tbsp freshly grated ginger
2 tbsp freshly pureed garlic
6 medium red onions, sliced
1 cup crushed tomatoes
2 tbsp Greek yogurt
½ tsp chili powder
2 tbsp garam masala
1 bunch cilantro, chopped
2 green chilies, sliced

Directions and Total Time: approx. 30 minutes
Bring a pot of water to a boil to blanch meat for 3 minutes; drain and set aside. Melt ghee in a skillet and sauté ginger, garlic, and onions until caramelized, 5 minutes. Mix in tomatoes, yogurt, and pork. Season with chili, garam masala, salt, and pepper. Stir and cook for 10 minutes. Stir in cilantro and green chilies. Serve masala with cauli rice.

Per serving: Cal 302; Net Carbs 2.2g; Fat 16g; Protein 33g

Cheesy Sausages in Creamy Onion Sauce

Ingredients for 4 servings
2 tsp almond flour
1 (16 oz) pork sausages
6 tbsp golden flaxseed meal
1 egg, beaten
1 tbsp olive oil
8 oz cream cheese, softened
3 tbsp freshly chopped chives
3 tsp freshly pureed onion

3 tbsp chicken broth
2 tbsp almond milk

Directions and Total Time: approx. 30 minutes

In a plate, mix flour with salt and pepper, and pour flaxseed meal to a plate. Prick the sausages with a fork all around, roll in the flour, in the egg, and then in the flaxseed meal. Heat olive oil in a skillet and fry sausages until brown, 15 minutes. Transfer to a plate and keep warm. In a saucepan, combine cream cheese, chives, onion, broth, and milk. Cook and stir over medium heat until smooth and evenly mixed, 5 minutes. Plate the sausages and spoon the sauce on top. Serve immediately with steamed broccoli.

Per serving: Cal 461; Net Carbs 0.5g; Fat 32g; Protein 34g

Savory Jalapeño Pork Meatballs

Ingredients for 4 servings

3 green onions, chopped
1 tbsp garlic powder
1 pound ground pork
1 jalapeño pepper, chopped
1 tsp dried oregano
2 tsp parsley
½ tsp Italian seasoning
2 tsp cumin
Salt and black pepper to taste
3 tbsp butter melted + 2 tbsp
4 ounces cream cheese
1 tsp turmeric
¼ tsp xylitol
½ tsp baking powder
1 ½ cups flax meal
½ cup almond flour

Directions and Total Time: approx. 45 minutes

Preheat oven to 350 F. In a food processor, add green onions, garlic powder, jalapeño pepper, and ½ cup water; blend well. Set a pan, warm in 2 tbsp of butter and cook ground pork for 3 minutes. Stir in onion mixture, and cook for 2 minutes. Stir in parsley, cloves, salt, cumin, ½ teaspoon turmeric, oregano, Italian seasoning, and pepper, and cook for 3 minutes. In a bowl, combine the remaining turmeric with almond flour, xylitol, flax meal, and baking powder. In a separate bowl, combine 3 tbsp melted butter with cream cheese. Combine the 2

mixtures to obtain a dough. Form balls from this mixture, set on a parchment paper, and roll each into a circle. Split the pork mixture on one-half of the dough circles, cover with the other half, seal edges, and lay on a lined sheet. Bake for 25 minutes.

Per serving: Cal 598; Net Carbs 5.3g; Fat 45.8g; Protein 35g

Greek-Style Pork Packets with Halloumi

Ingredients for 4 servings

1 lb turnips, cubed
½ cup salsa verde
2 tsp chili powder
1 tsp cumin powder
4 boneless pork chops
Salt and black pepper to taste
3 tbsp olive oil
4 slices halloumi cheese, cubed

Directions and Total Time: approx. 30 minutes

Preheat the grill to 400 F. Cut out four 18x12-inch sheets of heavy-duty aluminum foil. Grease the sheets with cooking spray. In a bowl, combine turnips, salsa verde, chili, and cumin. Season with salt and pepper. Place a pork chop on each foil sheet, spoon the turnip mixture on the meat, divide olive oil on top, and then halloumi cheese. Wrap the foil and place on the grill grate and cook for 10 minutes. Turn the foil packs over and cook further for 8 minutes. Remove the packs onto plates, and serve.

Per serving: Cal 501; Net Carbs 2.1g; Fat 27g; Protein 52g

Pork & Bacon Parcels

Ingredients for 4 servings

4 bacon strips
2 tbsp fresh parsley, chopped
4 pork loin chops, boneless
⅓ cup cottage cheese
1 tbsp olive oil
1 onion, chopped
1 tbsp garlic powder
2 tomatoes, chopped
⅓ cup chicken stock
Salt and black pepper, to taste

Directions and Total Time: approx. 40 minutes

Lay a bacon strip on top of each pork chop, then divide the parsley and cottage cheese on top. Roll each pork piece and secure with toothpicks. Set a pan over medium heat and warm oil, cook the pork parcels until browned, and remove to a plate. Add in the onion, and cook for 5 minutes. Pour in the chicken stock and garlic powder, and cook for 3 minutes. Get rid of the toothpicks from the rolls and return them to the pan. Stir in black pepper, salt, parsley, and tomatoes, bring to a boil, set heat to medium-low, and cook for 25 minutes while covered. Serve.

Per serving: Cal 433; Net Carbs 6.8g; Fat 23g; Protein 44.6g

Hot Pork Chops with Satay Sauce

Ingredients for 4 servings
2 lb boneless pork loin chops, cut into 2-inch pieces
Salt and black pepper to taste
1 medium white onion, sliced
1/3 cup peanut butter
¼ cup tamari sauce
½ tsp garlic powder
½ tsp onion powder
½ tsp hot sauce
1 cup chicken broth, divided
3 tbsp xanthan gum
1 tbsp chopped peanuts

Directions and Total Time: approx. 80 minutes
Season pork with salt and pepper; put into a pot and add onion. In a bowl, combine peanut butter, tamari sauce, garlic and onion powders, hot sauce, and two-thirds of the chicken broth. Pour the mixture over the meat. Bring to a boil over high heat, reduce the heat, and simmer for 1 hour or until the meat becomes tender. In a bowl, combine the remaining broth and xanthan gum. Stir the mixture into the meat and simmer until the sauce thickens, 2 minutes. Spoon onto a plate, garnish with peanuts and serve.

Per serving: Cal 455; Net Carbs 6.7g; Fat 17g; Protein 61g

Turnip Pork Pie

Ingredients for 8 servings
1 cup turnip mash
2 pounds ground pork
½ cup water

1 onion, chopped
1 tbsp sage
2 tbsp butter
Crust:
2 oz butter
1 egg
2 oz cheddar, shredded
2 cups almond flour
¼ tsp xanthan gum
A pinch of salt

Directions and Total Time: approx. 50 minutes
Stir all crust ingredients in a bowl. Make 2 balls out of the mixture and refrigerate for 10 minutes. In a pan, warm 2 tbsp of butter and sauté onion and ground pork for 8 minutes. Let cool for a few minutes and add in turnip mash and sage. Mix with hands. Roll out the pie crusts and place one at the bottom of a greased pie pan. Spread filling over the crust and top with the other coat. Bake in the oven for 30 minutes at 350 F. Serve.

Per serving: Cal 477; Net Carbs 1.7g; Fat 36.1g; Protein 33g

Sweet Pork Chops with Hoisin Sauce

Ingredients for 4 servings
4 oz hoisin sauce, sugar-free
1 ¼ pounds pork chops
Salt and black pepper to taste
1 tbsp xylitol
½ tsp ginger powder
2 tsp smoked paprika

Directions and Total Time: approx. 2 hours 20 minutes
In a bowl, mix pepper, xylitol, ginger, and paprika; rub pork chops with the mixture. Cover with plastic wraps and refrigerate for 2 hours. Preheat grill. Grill the meat for 2 minutes per side. Reduce the heat and brush with the hoisin sauce, cover, and grill for 5 minutes. Turn the meat and brush again with hoisin sauce. Cook for 5 minutes.

Per serving: Cal 352; Net Carbs 2.5g; Fat 22.9g; Protein 37g

Basil Pork Meatballs in Tomato Sauce

Ingredients for 6 servings
1 pound ground pork
2 green onions, chopped
1 tbsp olive oil

1 cup pork rinds, crushed
3 cloves garlic, minced
½ cup buttermilk
2 eggs, beaten
1 cup asiago cheese, shredded
Salt and black pepper to taste
1 can (29-ounce) tomato sauce
1 cup pecorino cheese, grated
Chopped basil to garnish

Directions and Total Time: approx. 45 minutes

Preheat oven to 370 F. Mix buttermilk, ground pork, garlic, asiago cheese, eggs, salt, pepper, and pork rinds in a bowl, until combined. Shape pork mixture into balls and place into a greased baking pan. Bake for 20 minutes. Remove and pour in tomato sauce and sprinkle with Pecorino cheese. Cover the pan with foil and put it back in the oven for 10 minutes. Remove the foil and cooking for 5 more minutes. Garnish with basil and serve.

Per serving: Cal 623; Net Carbs 4.6g; Fat 51.8g; Protein 53g

Canadian Pork Pie

Ingredients for 8 servings

1 cup cooked and mashed cauliflower
1 egg
¼ cup butter
2 cups almond flour
¼ tsp xanthan gum
¼ cup shredded mozzarella
2 pounds ground pork
⅓ cup pureed onion
¾ tsp allspice
1 tbsp ground sage
2 tbsp butter

Directions and Total Time: approx. 1 hour 40 minutes

Preheat oven to 350 F. Whisk egg, butter, almond flour, mozzarella cheese, and salt in a bowl. Make 2 balls out of the mixture and refrigerate for 10 minutes. Melt butter in a pan and cook ground pork, salt, onion, and allspice for 5-6 minutes. Remove to a bowl and mix in cauliflower and sage. Roll out the pie balls and place one at the bottom of a greased pie pan. Spread the pork mixture over the crust. Top with the other coat. Bake for 50 minutes then serve.

Per serving: Cal 485; Net Carbs 4g; Fat 41g; Protein 29g

Quick Pork Lo Mein

Ingredients for 4 servings

4 boneless pork chops, cut into ¼-inch strips
1 cup green beans, halved
1 cup shredded mozzarella
1 egg yolk
1-inch ginger knob, grated
3 tbsp sesame oil
Salt and black pepper to taste
1 red bell pepper, sliced
1 yellow bell pepper, sliced
1 garlic clove, minced
4 green onions, chopped
1 tsp toasted sesame seeds
3 tbsp coconut aminos
2 tsp sugar-free maple syrup
1 tsp fresh ginger paste

Directions and Total Time: approx. 25 min + chilling time

Microwave mozzarella cheese for 2 minutes. Let cool for 1 minute and mix in the egg yolk until well-combined. Lay a parchment paper on a flat surface, pour the cheese mixture on top and cover with another parchment paper. Flatten the dough into 1/8-inch thickness. Take off the parchment paper and cut the dough into thin spaghetti strands. Place in a bowl and refrigerate overnight. Bring 2 cups water to a boil in saucepan and add in pasta. Cook for 1 minute and drain; set aside. Heat sesame oil in a skillet, season pork with salt and pepper, and sear on both sides for 5 minutes. Transfer to a plate. In the same skillet, mix in bell peppers, green beans and cook for 3 minutes. Stir in garlic, ginger, and green onions and cook for 1 minute. Add pork and pasta to the skillet and toss well. In a bowl, toss coconut aminos, remaining sesame oil, maple syrup, and ginger paste. Pour the mixture over the pork mixture; cook for 1 minute. Garnish with sesame seeds to serve.

Per serving: Cal 338; Fats 12g; Net Carbs 4.6g; Protein 43g

Tasty Sambal Pork Noodles

Ingredients for 4 servings

2 (8 oz) packs Miracle noodles, garlic, and herb
1 tbsp olive oil
1 lb ground pork
4 garlic cloves, minced

1-inch ginger, grated
1 tsp liquid stevia
1 tbsp tomato paste
2 fresh basil leaves, chopped
2 tbsp sambal oelek
2 tbsp plain vinegar
2 tbsp coconut aminos
Salt to taste
1 tbsp unsalted butter

Directions and Total Time: approx. 60 minutes

Bring 2 cups water to a boil Strain the Miracle noodles and rinse well under hot running water. Allow proper draining and pour them into the boiling water. Cook for 3 minutes and strain again. Place a dry skillet and stir-fry the shirataki noodles until visibly dry, 1-2 minutes. Season with salt and set aside. Heat olive oil in a pot and cook for 5 minutes. Stir in garlic, ginger, and stevia and cook for 1 minute. Add in tomato paste and mix in sambal oelek, vinegar, 1 cup water, aminos, and salt. Continue cooking over low heat for 30 minutes. Add in shirataki, butter; mix well into the sauce. Garnish with basil and serve.

Per serving: Cal 505; Fats 30g; Net Carbs 8.2g; Protein 34g

Pasta & Cheese Pulled Pork

Ingredients for 4 servings

1 cup shredded mozzarella cheese1
lb pork shoulders, divided into 3 pieces
1 egg yolk
2 tbsp olive oil
Salt and black pepper to taste
1 tsp dried thyme
1 cup chicken broth
2 tbsp butter
2 medium shallots, minced
2 garlic cloves, minced
1 cup grated Monterey Jack
4 oz cream cheese, softened
1 cup heavy cream
½ tsp white pepper
½ tsp nutmeg powder
2 tbsp chopped parsley

Directions and Total Time: approx. 100 min + chilling time

Microwave mozzarella cheese for 2 minutes. Take out the bowl and allow cooling for 1 minute. Mix in egg yolk until well-combined. Lay a parchment paper on a flat surface, pour the cheese mixture on top and cover with another parchment paper. Flatten the dough into 1/8-inch thickness. Take off the parchment paper and cut the dough into small cubes of the size of macaroni. Place in a bowl and refrigerate overnight. Bring 2 cups water to a boil and add in keto macaroni. Cook for 1 minute and drain; set aside. Heat olive oil in a pot, season pork with salt, pepper, and thyme and sear on both sides until brown. Pour in broth, cover, and cook over low heat for 1 hour or until softened. Remove to a plate and shred into small strands. Set aside. Preheat oven to 380 F. Melt butter in a skillet and sauté shallots and garlic for 3 minutes. Pour in 1 cup water to deglaze the pot and stir in half of Monterey Jack and cream cheeses for 4 minutes. Mix in heavy cream and season with salt, pepper, white pepper, and nutmeg powder. Mix in pasta and pork. Pour mixture into a baking dish and cover with remaining Monterey Jack cheese. Bake for 20 minutes. Garnish with parsley and serve.

Per serving: Cal 603; Fats 43g; Net Carbs 4.5g; Protein 46g

Baked Tenderloin with Lime Chimichurri

Ingredients for 4 servings

1 lime, juiced
¼ cup chopped mint leaves
¼ cup rosemary, chopped
2 cloves garlic, minced
¼ cup olive oil
4 lb pork tenderloin
Salt and black pepper to taste
Olive oil for rubbing

Directions and Total Time: approx. 1 hour 10 minutes

In a bowl, mix mint, rosemary, garlic, lime juice, olive oil, and salt, and combine well; set aside. Preheat charcoal grill to 450 F creating a direct heat area and indirect heat area. Rub the pork with olive oil, season with salt and pepper. Place the meat over direct heat and sear for 3 minutes on each side; then move to the indirect heat area. Close the lid and cook for 25 minutes on one side, then open, flip, and grill closed for 20 minutes. Remove from the grill and let sit for 5 minutes before

slicing. Spoon lemon chimichurri over the pork and serve.
Per serving: Cal 388, Net Carbs 2.1g, Fat 18g, Protein 28g

Green Bean Creamy Pork with Fettuccine

Ingredients for 4 servings
4 pork loin medallions, cut into thin strips
1 cup shredded mozzarella
1 cup shaved Parmesan cheese
1 egg yolk
1 tbsp olive oil
Salt and black pepper to taste
½ cup green beans, chopped
1 lemon, zested and juiced
¼ cup chicken broth
1 cup crème fraiche
6 basil leaves, chopped

Directions and Total Time: approx. 40 min + chilling time
Microwave mozzarella cheese for 2 minutes. Allow cooling for 1 minute. Mix in egg yolk until well-combined. Lay a parchment paper on a flat surface, pour the cheese mixture on top and cover with another parchment paper. Flatten the dough into 1/8-inch thickness. Take off the parchment paper and cut the dough into thick fettuccine strands. Place in a bowl and refrigerate overnight. Bring 2 cups water to a boil in saucepan and add the fettuccine. Cook for 1 minute and drain; set aside. Heat olive oil in a skillet, season the pork with salt and pepper, and cook for 10 minutes. Mix in green beans and cook for 5 minutes. Stir in lemon zest, lemon juice, and chicken broth. Cook for 5 more minutes. Add crème fraiche, fettuccine, and basil and cook for 1 minute. Top with Parmesan cheese.
Per serving: Cal 586; Fats 32.3g; Net Carbs 9g; Protein 59g

Cauliflower Pork Goulash

Ingredients for 4 servings
2 tbsp butter
1 cup mushrooms, sliced
1 ½ pounds ground pork
Salt and black pepper, to taste
2 cups cauliflower florets
1 onion, chopped
14 ounces canned tomatoes
1 garlic clove, minced

1 tbsp smoked paprika
2 tbsp parsley, chopped
1 tbsp tomato puree
1 ½ cups water

Directions and Total Time: approx. 30 minutes
Melt butter in a pan over medium heat, stir in pork, and brown for 5 minutes. Place in mushrooms, garlic, and onion, and cook for 4 minutes. Stir in paprika, water, tomatoes, tomato paste, and cauliflower, bring to a simmer and cook for 20 minutes. Add in pepper, salt and parsley.
Per serving: Cal 533; Net Carbs 7g; Fat 41.8g; Protein 35.5g

Basil Prosciutto Pizza

Ingredients for 4 servings
4 prosciutto slices, cut into thirds
2 cups grated mozzarella cheese
2 tbsp cream cheese, softened
½ cup almond flour
1 egg, beaten
⅓ cup tomato sauce
⅓ cup sliced mozzarella
6 fresh basil leaves, to serve

Directions and Total Time: approx. 45 minutes
Preheat oven to 390 F and line a pizza pan with parchment paper. Microwave mozzarella cheese and 2 tbsp of cream cheese for 1 minute. Mix in almond meal and egg. Spread the mixture on the pizza pan and bake for 15 minutes; set aside. Spread the tomato sauce on the crust. Arrange the mozzarella slices on the sauce and then the prosciutto. Bake again for 15 minutes or until the cheese melts. Remove and top with the basil. Slice and serve.
Per serving: Cal 160; Net Carbs 0.5g; Fats 6.2g; Protein 22g

Bell Pepper Noodles with Pork Avocado

Ingredients for 4 servings
2 lb red and yellow bell peppers, spiralized
2 tbsp butter
1 lb ground pork
Salt and black pepper to taste
1 tsp garlic powder
2 avocados, pitted, mashed
2 tbsp chopped pecans

Directions and Total Time: approx. 15 minutes

Melt butter in a skillet and cook the pork until brown, 5 minutes. Season with salt and pepper. Stir in bell peppers, garlic powder and cook until the peppers are slightly tender, 2 minutes. Mix in mashed avocados and cook for 1 minute. Garnish with the pecans and serve warm.

Per serving: Cal 704; Fats 49g; Net Carbs 9.3g; Protein 35g

Caribbean Jerk Pork

Ingredients for 4 servings

1 ½ pounds pork roast
1 tbsp olive oil
¼ cup jerk seasoning
2 tbsp soy sauce, sugar-free
½ cup vegetable stock

Directions and Total Time: approx. 4 hours 20 minutes

Preheat oven to 350 F and rub the pork with olive oil and jerk seasoning. Heat olive oil in a pan over medium heat and sear the meat well on all sides, about 4-5 minutes. Put the pork in a baking dish, add in the vegetable stock and soy sauce, cover with aluminium foil and bake for 45 minutes, turning once halfway. Then, remove the foil and continue cooking until completely cooked through. Serve.

Per serving: Cal 407; Net Carbs 5.6g; Fat 20g; Protein 46g

Parmesan Pork with Green Pasta

Ingredients for 4 servings

4 boneless pork chops
Salt and black pepper to taste
½ cup basil pesto
1 cup grated Parmesan cheese
1 tbsp butter
4 large turnips, spiralized

Directions and Total Time: approx. 1 hour 30 minutes

Preheat oven to 350 F. Season pork with salt and pepper and place on a greased baking sheet. Spread pesto on the pork and bake for 45 minutes. Pull out the baking sheet and divide half of Parmesan cheese on top of the pork. Cook further for 5 minutes; set aside. Melt butter in a skillet and sauté the turnips for 7 minutes. Stir in the remaining Parmesan and serve in plates, topped with the pork.

Per serving: Cal 532; Fats 28g; Net Carbs 4.9g; Protein 54g

Grilled BBQ Pork Chops

Ingredients for 4 servings

4 pork loin chops, boneless
½ cup sugar-free BBQ sauce
1 tbsp erythritol
½ tsp ginger powder
½ tsp garlic powder
2 tsp smoked paprika

Directions and Total Time: approx. 1 hour 50 minutes

In a bowl, mix black pepper, erythritol, ginger powder, ½ tsp garlic powder, and smoked paprika, and rub pork chops on all sides with the mixture. Cover the pork chops with plastic wraps and place in the refrigerator for 90 minutes. Preheat grill. Unwrap the meat, place on the grill grate, and cook for 2 minutes per side. Reduce the heat and brush with BBQ sauce; grill for 5 minutes. Flip and brush again with BBQ sauce. Cook for 5 minutes. Serve.

Per serving: Cal 363, Net Carbs 0g, Fat 26.6g, Protein 34.1g

Pecorino Romano Kohlrabi with Sausage

Ingredients for 4 servings

1 cup grated Pecorino Romano cheese
2 tbsp olive oil
1 cup sliced pork sausage
4 bacon slices, chopped
4 large kohlrabi, spiralized
6 garlic cloves, minced
1 cup cherry tomatoes, halved
7 fresh basil leaves
1 tbsp pine nuts for topping

Directions and Total Time: approx. 15 minutes

Heat olive oil in a skillet and cook sausage and bacon until brown, 5 minutes. Transfer to a plate. Stir in kohlrabi and garlic and cook until tender, 5-7 minutes. Add in cherry tomatoes, salt, and pepper and cook for 2 minutes. Mix in the sausage, bacon, basil, and Pecorino Romano cheese. Garnish with pine nuts and serve warm.

Per serving: Cal 229; Fats 20.2g; Net Carbs 2.4g; Protein 8g

Chorizo Smoky Pizza

Ingredients for 4 servings

2 cups shredded mozzarella
1 cup sliced smoked mozzarella
2 tbsp cream cheese, softened
¾ cup almond flour
2 tbsp almond meal
1 tbsp olive oil
1 cups sliced chorizo
¼ cup marinara sauce
1 jalapeño pepper, sliced
¼ red onion, thinly sliced

Directions and Total Time: approx. 45 minutes

Preheat oven to 390 F and line a pizza pan with parchment paper. Microwave the mozzarella and cream cheeses for 30 seconds. Remove, and mix in almond flour and almond meal. Spread the mixture on the pizza pan and bake for 10 minutes or until crusty. Heat olive oil and cook chorizo until brown, 5 minutes. Spread marinara sauce on the crust, top with smoked mozzarella cheese, chorizo, jalapeño pepper, and onion. Bake until the cheese melts, 15 minutes. Remove, slice and serve warm.

Per serving: Cal 302; Net Carbs 1.4g; Fats 17g; Protein 31g

Monterey Jack & Sausage-Pepper Pizza

Ingredients for 4 servings

1 ½ lb Italian pork sausages, crumbled
½ cup grated Monterey Jack cheese
1 cup chopped bell peppers
4 cups grated mozzarella
¼ cup grated Parmesan
2 tbsp cream cheese, softened
¼ cup coconut flour
1 cup almond flour
2 eggs
1 tbsp olive oil
1 onion, thinly sliced
2 garlic cloves, minced
1 cup baby spinach
½ cup sugar-free pizza sauce

Directions and Total Time: approx. 45 minutes

Preheat oven to 390 F and line a pizza pan with parchment paper. Microwave 2 cups of mozzarella cheese and 2 tbsp of the cream cheese for 1 minute. Mix in sausages, coconut flour, almond flour, Parmesan cheese, and eggs. Spread the mixture on the pizza pan and bake for 15 minutes; set aside.

Heat olive oil in a skillet and sauté onion, garlic, and bell peppers for 5 minutes. Stir in spinach and allow wilting for 3 minutes. Spread the pizza sauce on the crust and top with the bell pepper mixture. Scatter mozzarella and Monterey Jack cheeses on top. Bake for 5 minutes.

Per serving: Cal 460; Net Carbs 3g; Fats 25.6g; Protein 47g

Maple Pork with Spaghetti Squash

Ingredients for 4 servings

3 lb spaghetti squashes, halved and deseeded
2 tbsp minced lemongrass
3 tbsp fresh ginger paste
2 tbsp sugar-free maple syrup
2 tbsp coconut aminos
1 tbsp fish sauce
4 boneless pork chops
3 tbsp peanut oil
1 tbsp olive oil
Salt and black pepper to taste
1 lb baby spinach
½ cup coconut milk
¼ cup peanut butter

Directions and Total Time: approx. 1 hour + marinating

In a bowl, mix lemongrass, 2 tbsp of the ginger paste, maple syrup, aminos, and fish sauce. Place the pork in the liquid and coat well. Marinate for 45 minutes. Heat 2 tbsp of peanut oil in a skillet, remove pork from the marinade and sear on both sides for 10-15 minutes. Transfer to a plate and cover with foil. Preheat oven to 380 F. Place the spaghetti squashes on a baking sheet, brush with olive oil and season with salt and pepper. Bake for 45 minutes. Remove the squash and shred with two forks into spaghetti-like strands. Keep warm. Heat the remaining peanut oil in the same skillet and sauté the remaining ginger paste. Add in spinach and cook for 2 minutes; set aside. In a bowl, whisk coconut milk with peanut butter until well combined. Divide the pork into four bowls, add the spaghetti squash to the side, then the spinach and drizzle the peanut sauce on top. Serve immediately.

Per serving: Cal 694; Fats 34g; Net Carbs 7.6g; Protein 53g

Spicy Grilled Pork Spareribs

Ingredients for 4 servings

4 tbsp sugar-free BBQ sauce + extra for serving
2 tbsp erythritol
1 tbsp olive oil
3 tsp cayenne powder
1 tsp garlic powder
1 lb pork spareribs

Directions and Total Time: approx. 2 hours

Mix erythritol, salt, pepper, oil, cayenne, and garlic. Brush on the meaty sides of the ribs and wrap in foil. Sit for 30 minutes to marinate. Preheat oven to 400 F, place wrapped ribs on a baking sheet, and cook for 40 minutes. Remove foil, brush with BBQ sauce, and brown under the broiler for 10 minutes on both sides. Slice and serve.

Per serving: Cal 395, Net Carbs 3g, Fat 33g, Protein 21g

Asian-Style Pork and Celeriac Noodles

Ingredients for 4 servings

3 tbsp sugar-free maple syrup
3 tbsp coconut aminos
1 tbsp fresh ginger paste
¼ tsp Chinese five spice
Salt and black pepper to taste
1 lb pork tenderloin, cubed
2 tbsp butter
4 large celeriac, spiralized
1 tbsp sesame oil
24 oz bok choy, chopped
2 green onions, chopped
2 tbsp sesame seeds

Directions and Total Time: approx. 1 hour 20 minutes

Preheat oven to 400 F and line a baking sheet with foil. In a bowl, mix maple syrup, coconut aminos, ginger paste, Chinese five-spice powder, salt, and pepper. Spoon 3 tablespoons of the mixture into a bowl and reserve for topping. Mix pork cubes into the remaining marinade and marinate for 25 minutes. Melt butter in a skillet and sauté celeriac for 7 minutes; set aside. Remove the pork from the marinade onto the baking

sheet and bake for 40 minutes. Heat sesame oil in a skillet and sauté bok choy and celeriac pasta for 3 minutes. Transfer to serving bowls and top with pork. Garnish with green onions and sesame seeds. Drizzle with the reserved marinade and serve.

Per serving: Cal 409; Fats 17.8g; Net Carbs 3g; Protein 44g

Pulled Pork Tenderloin with Avocado

Ingredients for 8 servings

4 pounds pork tenderloin
1 tbsp avocado oil
½ cup chicken stock
¼ cup jerk seasoning
6 avocado, sliced
Salt and black pepper to taste

Directions and Total Time: approx. 2 hours

Rub the pork shoulder with jerk seasoning, and set in a greased baking dish. Pour in the stock, and cook for 1 hour 30 minutes in your oven at 350 F covered with aluminium foil. Discard the foil and cook for another 20 minutes. Leave to rest for 10-15 minutes, and shred it with 2 forks. Serve topped with avocado slices.

Per serving: Cal 567, Net Carbs 4.1g, Fat 42.6g, Protein 42g

Broccoli Tips with Lemon Pork Chops

Ingredients for 6 servings

1 lb fresh broccoli tips, halved
3 tbsp lemon juice
3 cloves garlic, pureed
1 tbsp olive oil
6 pork loin chops
1 tbsp butter
2 tbsp white wine

Directions and Total Time: approx. 30 minutes

Preheat broiler to 400 F and mix the lemon juice, garlic, salt, pepper, and oil in a bowl. Brush the pork with the mixture, place in a baking sheet, and cook for 6 minutes on each side until browned. Share into 6 plates. Melt butter in a small wok or pan and cook broccoli tips for 5 minutes until tender. Drizzle with white wine, sprinkle with salt and pepper and cook for another 5 minutes. Ladle broccoli to the side of the chops and serve with hot sauce.

Per serving: Cal 549, Net Carbs 2g, Fat 48g, Protein 26g

Jerk Pork Pot Roast

Ingredients for 8 servings
4-pound pork roast
1 tbsp olive oil
¼ cup Jerk spice blend
½ cup beef stock

Directions and Total Time: approx. 4 hours 20 minutes
Rub the pork with olive oil and the spice blend. Heat a dutch oven over medium heat and sear the meat well on all sides. Add the beef broth. Cover the pot, reduce the heat, and let cook for 4 hours.

Per serving: Cal 282; Net Carbs 0g; Fat 24g; Protein 23g

Swiss Pork Patties with Salad

Ingredients for 4 servings
1 lb ground pork
3 tbsp olive oil
2 hearts romaine lettuce, torn
2 firm tomatoes, sliced
¼ red onion, sliced
3 oz Swiss cheese, shredded

Directions and Total Time: approx. 30 minutes
Season pork with salt and pepper, mix, and shape several medium-sized patties. Heat 2 tbsp oil in a skillet and fry the patties on both sides for 10 minutes. Transfer to a wire rack to drain oil. When cooled, cut into quarters. Mix lettuce, tomatoes, and onion in a bowl, season with oil, salt and pepper. Toss and add the patties on top. Microwave the cheese for 90 seconds, drizzle it over the salad.

Per serving: Cal 310, Net Carbs 2g, Fat 23g, Protein 22g

Maple Scallion Pork Bites

Ingredients for 4 servings
½ cup + 1 tbsp red wine
1 tbsp + 1/3 cup tamari sauce
1 pork tenderloin, cubed
½ cup sugar-free maple syrup
½ cup sesame seeds
1 tbsp sesame oil

1 tsp freshly pureed garlic
½ tsp freshly grated ginger
1 scallion, finely chopped

Directions and Total Time: approx. 50 minutes
Preheat oven to 350 F. In a zipper bag, combine ½ cup of red wine with 1 tbsp of tamari sauce. Add in pork cubes, seal the bag, and marinate the meat in the fridge overnight. Remove from the fridge and drain. Pour maple syrup and sesame seeds into two separate bowls; roll the pork in maple syrup and then in the sesame seeds. Place on a greased baking sheet and bake for 35 minutes. In a bowl, mix the remaining wine, tamari sauce, sesame oil, garlic, and ginger. Pour the sauce into a bowl. Transfer pork to a platter and garnish with scallions. Serve with sauce.

Per serving: Cal 352; Net Carbs 6.4g; Fat 18g; Protein 39g

Pork Medallions with Pancetta

Ingredients for 4 servings
1 lb pork loin, cut into medallions
2 onions, chopped
6 pancetta slices, chopped
½ cup vegetable stock
Salt and black pepper, to taste

Directions and Total Time: approx. 55 minutes
Set a pan over medium heat, and cook the pancetta until crispy; remove to a plate. Add onions and stir-fry for 5 minutes; set aside to the same plate as pancetta. Add pork medallions to the pan, season with pepper and salt, brown for 3 minutes on each side, turn, reduce heat, and cook for 7 minutes. Stir in the stock, and cook for 2 minutes. Return the pancetta and onions and cook for 1 minute.

Per serving: Cal 325, Net Carbs 6g, Fat 18g, Protein 36g

Golden Pork Chops with Mushrooms

Ingredients for 6 servings
2 (14-oz) cans Mushroom soup
1 onion, chopped
6 pork chops
½ cup sliced mushrooms
Salt and black pepper to taste

Directions and Total Time: approx. 1 hour 15 minutes

Preheat the oven to 375 F. Season the pork chops with salt and pepper, and place them in a baking dish. Combine the soup, mushrooms, and onions in a bowl. Pour this mixture over the pork chops. Bake for 45 minutes.

Per serving: Cal 403; Net Carbs 8g; Fat 32.6g; Protein 19g

Cumin Pork Chops

Ingredients for 4 servings

4 pork chops

¾ cup cumin powder

1 tsp chili powder

Salt and black pepper to taste

Directions and Total Time: approx. 25 minutes

In a bowl, combine the cumin with black pepper, salt, and chili. Place in the pork chops and rub them well. Heat a grill over medium temperature, add in the pork chops, cook for 5 minutes, flip, and cook for 5 minutes.

Per serving: Cal 349; Net Carbs 4g; Fat 18.6g; Protein 42g

SEAFOOD

Tasty Shrimp in Creamy Butter Sauce

Ingredients for 2 servings
½ oz grated Parmesan cheese
1 egg, beaten in a bowl
¼ tsp curry powder
2 tsp almond flour
12 shrimp, shelled
3 tbsp coconut oil
2 tbsp curry leaves
2 tbsp butter
½ onion, diced
½ cup heavy cream
½ ounce cheddar cheese
Salt and black pepper to taste

Directions and Total Time: approx. 30 minutes
Combine Parmesan, curry powder, and almond flour in a bowl. Melt the coconut oil in a skillet over medium heat. Dip the shrimp in the egg first, and then coat with the dry mixture. Fry until golden and crispy. In another skillet, melt the butter. Add onion and cook for 3 minutes. Add in curry leaves and cook for 30 seconds. Stir in heavy cream and cheddar cheese and cook until thickened. Add the shrimp and coat well. Adjust the seasoning, and serve.

Per serving: Cal 560; Net Carbs 4.3g; Fat 56g; Protein 18g

Cheesy Baked Trout with Zucchini

Ingredients for 4 servings
4 deboned trout fillets
2 zucchinis, sliced
1 tbsp butter, melted
1 cup Greek yogurt
¼ cup cheddar cheese, grated
Grated Parmesan for topping

Directions and Total Time: approx. 40 minutes
Preheat oven to 390 F and brush the fish and zucchini slices with melted butter. Season with salt and black pepper and spread in a greased baking dish. Mix the Greek yogurt with cheddar cheese in a bowl. Pour and smear the mixture on the fish, and sprinkle with Parmesan cheese. Bake for 30 minutes until golden brown on top.

Per serving: Cal 362; Net Carbs 5.8g; Fat 23g; Protein 25.6g

Chimichurri Shrimp

Ingredients for 4 servings
1 pound shrimp, deveined
2 tbsp olive oil
Juice of 1 lime
Salt and black pepper to taste
Chimichurri sauce:
¼ cup olive oil
2 garlic cloves
¼ cup red onion, chopped
¼ cup red wine vinegar
2 cups parsley
¼ tsp red pepper flakes

Directions and Total Time: approx. 45 minutes
Place all chimichurri ingredients in the blender. Process until smooth. Combine shrimp, olive oil, and lime juice in a bowl and marinate in the fridge for 30 minutes. Preheat grill to medium heat. Add shrimp and cook for 2 minutes per side. Serve drizzled with the sauce.

Per serving: Cal 283; Net Carbs 3.5g; Fat 20g; Protein 16g

Baked Salmon with Pistachio Crust

Ingredients for 4 servings
4 salmon fillets
¼ cup mayonnaise
½ cup ground pistachios
1 chopped shallot
2 tsp lemon zest
1 tbsp olive oil
A pinch of pepper
1 cup heavy cream

Directions and Total Time: approx. 35 minutes
Preheat oven to 375 F. Brush salmon with mayo and season with salt and pepper. Coat with pistachios. Place in a lined baking dish and bake for 15 minutes. Heat the olive oil in a saucepan and sauté shallot for 3 minutes. Stir in heavy cream and lemon zest. Bring to a boil and cook until thickened. Serve salmon with the sauce.

Per serving: Cal 563; Net Carbs 6g; Fat 47g; Protein 34g

Curried Homemade Shrimp

Ingredients for 4 servings
2 tbsp Parmesan, grated
1 egg, beaten
½ tsp curry powder
2 tsp coconut flour
1 pound shrimp, shelled
3 tbsp coconut oil
2 tbsp curry leaves
2 tbsp butter
1 onion, chopped
½ cup coconut cream
2 tbsp mozzarella, shredded
Directions and Total Time: approx. 25 minutes
In a bowl, combine all dry Ingredients for the batter. Melt coconut oil in a skillet over medium heat. Dip the shrimp in the egg first, and then coat with the dry mixture. Fry until golden and crispy. In another skillet, melt butter, and sauté onion for 3 minutes. Add curry leaves, cook for 30 seconds and stir in coconut cream and mozzarella cheese until thickened. Add the shrimp to coat thoroughly. Serve.
Per serving: Cal 422; Net Carbs 4.8g; Fat 32.2g; Protein 29g

Speedy Fish Tacos

Ingredients for 4 servings
1 tbsp olive oil
1 red chili pepper, minced
1 tsp coriander seeds
4 cod fillets, roughly chopped
1 tsp smoked paprika
4 low carb tortillas
Salt and black pepper to taste
1 lemon, juiced
Directions and Total Time: approx. 20 minutes
Season the fish with salt, pepper, and paprika. Heat olive oil in a skillet over medium heat. Add cod and chili pepper and stir-fry for 6 minutes. Pour in lemon juice and cook for another 2 minutes. Divide the fish between the tortillas.
Per serving: Cal 447; Net Carbs 4.3g; Fat 21g; Protein 24.3g

Asian-Style Steamed Mussels

Ingredients for 6 servings
5 tbsp sesame oil
1 onion, chopped
3 lb mussels, cleaned
2 garlic cloves, minced
12 oz coconut milk
16 oz white wine
1 lime, juiced
2 tsp red curry powder
2 tbsp cilantro, chopped
Directions and Total Time: approx. 25 minutes
Warm the sesame oil in a saucepan over medium heat and cook onion and garlic cloves for 3 minutes. Pour in wine, coconut milk, and curry powder and cook for 5 minutes. Add mussels, turn off the heat, cover the saucepan, and steam the mussels until the shells open up, 5 minutes. Discard any closed mussels. Top with cilantro and serve.
Per serving: Cal 323; Net Carbs 5.4g; Fat 16g; Protein 28.2g

Easy Coconut Cocktail Crab Balls

Ingredients for 4 servings
1 lime, juiced
2 tbsp coconut oil
8 oz lump crab meat
2 tsp wasabi sauce
1 egg, beaten
1 tbsp coconut flour
Directions and Total Time: approx. 15 minutes
Mix together the crab meat, wasabi sauce, lime juice, and egg in a bowl. Season with salt and black pepper. Make balls out of the mixture. Fry in melted coconut oil over medium heat for 5-6 minutes in total; serve.
Per serving: Cal 277; Net Carbs 5.1g; Fat 11g; Protein 24.2g

Party Smoked Salmon Balls

Ingredients for 6 servings
12 oz sliced smoked salmon, finely chopped
1 parsnip, cooked and mashed
Salt and chili pepper to taste
4 tbsp olive oil
3 eggs, beaten
2 tbsp pesto sauce
1 tbsp pork rinds, crushed
Directions and Total Time: approx. 30 minutes

In a bowl, add the salmon, eggs, pesto sauce, pork rinds, salt, and chili pepper. With your hands, mix and make 6 compact balls. Heat olive oil in a skillet over medium heat and fry the balls for 3 minutes on each side until golden brown. Remove to a wire rack to cool.
Per serving: Cal 254; Net Carbs 4.3g; Fat 18g; Protein 17g

Tuna Stuffed Avocado

Ingredients for 4 servings
2 avocados, halved and pitted
4 ounces Colby Jack, grated
2 ounces canned tuna, flaked
2 tbsp chives, chopped
Salt and black pepper, to taste
½ cup curly endive, chopped
Directions and Total Time: approx. 20 minutes
Set oven to 360 F. Set avocado halves in an ovenproof dish. In a bowl, mix colby jack cheese, chives, pepper, salt, and tuna. Stuff the cheese/tuna mixture in avocado halves. Bake for 15 minutes or until the top is golden brown. Sprinkle with cilantro and serve with curly endive.
Per serving: Cal: 286; Net Carbs 9g; Fat 23.9g; Protein 11g

Mediterranean Tilapia

Ingredients for 4 servings
4 Tilapia fillets
2 garlic cloves, minced
2 tsp oregano
14 ounces diced tomatoes
1 tbsp olive oil
½ red onion, chopped
2 tbsp parsley
¼ cup kalamata olives
Directions and Total Time: approx. 30 minutes
Heat oil in a skillet over medium heat and cook onion for 3 minutes. Add garlic and oregano and cook for 30 seconds. Stir in tomatoes and bring the mixture to a boil. Reduce the heat and simmer for 5 minutes. Add olives and tilapia. Cook for 8 minutes. Serve the fish with tomato sauce!
Per serving: Cal 182; Net Carbs 6g; Fat 15g; Protein 23g

Pomodoro Zoodles with Sardines

Ingredients for 2 servings
½ cup canned chopped tomatoes
4 cups zoodles
2 ounces cubed bacon
4 oz canned sardines, chopped
1 tbsp capers
1 tbsp parsley
1 tsp minced garlic
Directions and Total Time: approx. 10 minutes
Pour some of the sardine oil in a pan. Add garlic and cook for 1 minute. Add the bacon and cook for 2 more minutes. Stir in the tomatoes and let simmer for 5 minutes. Add zoodles and sardines and cook for 3 minutes.
Per serving: Cal 230; Net Carbs 6g; Fat 31g; Protein 20g

Tuna Salad Pickle Boats

Ingredients for 12 servings
18 oz canned and drained tuna
6 large dill pickles
¼ tsp garlic powder
¼ cup sugar-free mayonnaise
1 tsp onion powder
Directions and Total Time: approx. 40 minutes
Mix the mayo, tuna, onion and garlic powders in a bowl. Cut the pickles in half, lengthwise. Top each half with tuna mixture. Place in the fridge for 30 minutes and serve.
Per serving: Cal 118; Net Carbs 1.5g; Fat 10g; Protein 11g

Nutty Sea Bass

Ingredients for 2 servings
2 sea bass fillets
2 tbsp butter
⅓ cup roasted hazelnuts
A pinch of cayenne pepper
Directions and Total Time: approx. 30 minutes
Preheat oven to 420 F. Line a baking dish with waxed paper. Melt butter and brush it over the fillets. In a food processor, combine the remaining ingredients. Coat the fish with the hazelnut mixture. Bake for 15 minutes.
Per serving: Cal 467; Net Carbs 2.8g; Fat 31g; Protein 40g

Blackened Fish Tacos with Slaw

Ingredients for 4 servings

2 tbsp olive oil
1 tsp chili powder
2 tilapia fillets
1 tsp paprika
4 zero carb tortillas
½ cup red cabbage, shredded
1 tbsp lemon juice
1 tsp apple cider vinegar
1 tbsp olive oil
Salt and black pepper to taste

Directions and Total Time: approx. 20 minutes

Season tilapia with chili powder, paprika, salt, and pepper. Heat half of olive oil in a skillet over medium heat. Add tilapia and cook until blackened, about 6 minutes. Cut into strips. Divide tilapia between the tortillas. Combine cabbage, lemon juice, vinegar, and remaining olive oil in a bowl; toss to combine. Add to the tortillas and serve.

Per serving: Cal 260; Net Carbs 3.5g; Fat 20g; Protein 13.8g

Crab Cakes

Ingredients for 8 servings
2 tbsp coconut oil
1 tbsp lemon juice
1 cup lump crab meat
2 tbsp parsley
2 tsp Dijon mustard
1 egg, beaten
1 ½ tbsp coconut flour
Salt and black pepper to taste

Directions and Total Time: approx. 15 minutes

Place crab meat in a bowl. Add the remaining ingredients, except for coconut oil. Mix well to combine. Make 8 crab cakes out of the mixture. Melt the oil in a skillet. Add the crab cakes and cook for 2-3 minutes per side.

Per serving: Cal 65; Net Carbs 3.6g; Fat 5g; Protein 5.3g

Saucy Salmon in Tarragon Sauce

Ingredients for 2 servings
2 salmon fillets
1 tbsp duck fat
Salt and black pepper to taste
2 tbsp butter
½ tsp tarragon
¼ cup heavy cream

Directions and Total Time: approx. 20 minutes

Season the salmon with salt and pepper. Melt the duck fat in a pan over medium heat. Add salmon and cook for 4 minutes on both sides; set aside. In the same pan, melt the butter and add the tarragon. Cook for 30 seconds to infuse the flavors. Whisk in heavy cream and cook for 1 minute. Serve salmon topped with the sauce.

Per serving: Cal 468; Net Carbs 1.5g; Fat 40g; Protein 22g

Garlic-Lime Shrimp Pasta

Ingredients for 4 servings
1 lb jumbo shrimp, deveined
2 tbsp butter
4 garlic cloves, minced
1 pinch red chili flakes
¼ cup white wine
1 lime, zested and juiced
3 zucchinis, spiralized
2 tbsp chopped parsley
1 cup grated Parmesan cheese
Salt and black pepper to taste

Directions and Total Time: approx. 20 minutes

Melt butter in a skillet and cook the shrimp for 3-4 minutes. Flip and stir in garlic and red chili flakes. Cook further for 1 minute; set aside. Pour wine and lime juice into the skillet, and cook until reduced by a third. Stir to deglaze the bottom. Mix in zucchinis, lime zest, shrimp, and parsley. Season with salt and pepper, and toss well. Cook for 2 minutes. Top with Parmesan cheese and serve.

Per serving: Cal 255; Net Carbs 9.8g; Fats 8g; Protein 32g

Angel Hair Shirataki with Creamy Shrimp

Ingredients for 4 servings
2 (8 oz) packs angel hair shirataki noodles
1 tbsp olive oil
1 lb shrimp, deveined
2 tbsp unsalted butter
6 garlic cloves, minced
½ cup dry white wine
1 ½ cups heavy cream
½ cup grated Asiago cheese
2 tbsp chopped fresh parsley

Directions and Total Time: approx. 25 minutes

Heat olive oil in a skillet, season the shrimp with salt and pepper, and cook on both sides, 2 minutes; set aside. Melt butter in the skillet and sauté garlic. Stir in wine and cook until reduced by half, scraping the bottom of the pan to deglaze. Stir in heavy cream. Let simmer for 1 minute and stir in Asiago cheese to melt. Return the shrimp to the sauce and sprinkle the parsley on top. Bring 2 cups of water to a boi. Strain shirataki pasta and rinse under hot running water. Allow proper draining and pour the shirataki pasta into the boiling water. Cook for 3 minutes and strain again. Place a dry skillet and stir-fry the pasta until dry, 1-2 minutes. Season with salt and plate. Top with the shrimp sauce and serve.
Per serving: Cal 493; Net Carbs 6.3g; Fats 32g; Protein 33g

Tuna & Zucchini Traybake

Ingredients for 4 servings
1 bunch asparagus, trimmed and cut into 1-inch pieces
1 (15 oz) can tuna in water, drained and flaked
1 tbsp butter
1 cup green beans, chopped
2 tbsp arrowroot starch
2 cups coconut milk
4 zucchinis, spiralized
1 cup grated Parmesan cheese
Directions and Total Time: approx. 40 minutes

Preheat the oven to 380 F. Melt butter in a skillet and sauté green beans and asparagus until softened, about 5 minutes; set aside. In a saucepan, mix in arrowroot starch with coconut milk. Bring to a boil over medium heat with frequent stirring until thickened, 3 minutes. Stir in half of Parmesan cheese until melted. Mix in the green beans, asparagus, zucchinis, and tuna. Season with salt and pepper. Transfer the mixture to a baking dish and cover with the remaining Parmesan cheese. Bake until the cheese is melted and golden, 20 minutes. Serve.
Per serving: Cal 389; Net Carbs 8.1g; Fats 34g; Protein 11g

Garlic & Parsley Shrimp

Ingredients for 6 servings
½ cup ghee, divided
2 lb shrimp, deveined
Salt and black pepper to taste
¼ tsp sweet paprika
1 tbsp minced garlic
3 tbsp water
1 lemon, zested and juiced
2 tbsp chopped parsley
Directions and Total Time: approx. 30 minutes

Melt half of the ghee in a skillet, season the shrimp with salt, pepper, paprika, and add to the ghee. Stir in garlic and cook for 4 minutes on both sides. Remove to a bowl. Put remaining ghee in the skillet; add lemon zest, juice, and water. Add shrimp, parsley, and adjust taste with salt and black pepper. Cook for 2 minutes on low heat. Serve the shrimp, drizzled with sauce and some squash pasta.
Per serving: Cal 258; Net Carbs 2g; Fat 22g; Protein 13g

Haddock in Garlic Butter Sauce

Ingredients for 6 servings
2 tsp olive oil
6 haddock fillets
Salt and black pepper to taste
4 tbsp salted butter
4 cloves garlic, minced
¼ cup lemon juice
3 tbsp white wine
2 tbsp chopped chives
Directions and Total Time: approx. 20 minutes

Heat oil in a skillet and season the haddock with salt and black pepper. Fry the fillets for 4 minutes on one side, flip and cook for 1 minute; set aside. In another skillet, melt butter and sauté garlic for 2 minutes. Add in lemon juice, wine, and chives. Season with salt, pepper, and cook for 3 minutes. Put the fish in the skillet, spoon sauce over, cook for 30 seconds and turn the heat off. Top with sauce and serve with buttered green beans.
Per serving: Cal 264; Net Carbs 2.3g; Fat 17.3g; Protein 20g

Traditional Salmon Panzanella

Ingredients for 4 servings
1 lb skinned salmon, cut into 4 steaks each
1 cucumber, cubed

Salt and black pepper to taste
8 black olives, chopped
1 tbsp capers, rinsed
2 large tomatoes, diced
3 tbsp white wine vinegar
¼ cup thinly sliced red onion
3 tbsp olive oil
2 slices zero carb bread, cubed
¼ cup sliced basil leaves

Directions and Total Time: approx. 25 minutes

Preheat grill to 360 F. In a bowl, mix cucumbers, olives, pepper, capers, tomatoes, wine vinegar, onion, olive oil, bread, and basil leaves. Let sit for the flavors to incorporate.Season the salmon with salt and pepper; grill them on both sides for 8 minutes. Serve the salmon steaks warm on a bed of the veggies salad.

Per serving: Cal 338; Net Carbs 3.1g; Fat 21g; Protein 28.5g

White Wine Salmon Shirataki Fettucine

Ingredients for 4 servings
2 (8 oz) packs shirataki fettuccine
5 tbsp butter
4 salmon fillets, cubed
Salt and black pepper to taste
3 garlic cloves, minced
1 ¼ cups heavy cream
½ cup dry white wine
1 tsp grated lemon zest
1 cup baby spinach

Directions and Total Time: approx. 35 minutes

Boil 2 cups of water in a pot. Strain the shirataki pasta t and rinse well under hot running water. Allow proper draining and pour the shirataki pasta into the boiling water. Cook for 3 minutes and strain again. Place a dry skillet and stir-fry the shirataki pasta until visibly dry, 1-2 minutes; set aside. Melt half of the butter in a skillet; season the salmon with salt and pepper and cook for 8 minutes; set aside. Add the remaining butter to the skillet and stir in garlic. Cook for 30 seconds. Mix in heavy cream, white wine, lemon zest, salt, and pepper. Boil over low heat for 5 minutes. Stir in spinach, let wilt for

2 minutes and stir in shirataki fettuccine and salmon. Serve warm.

Per serving: Cal 795; Net Carbs 9g; Fats 46g; Protein 72g

Creamy Salmon with Lemon

Ingredients for 4 servings
½ cup grated Pecorino Romano cheese
1 cup sour cream
½ tbsp minced dill
½ lemon, zested and juiced
4 salmon steaks

Directions and Total Time: approx. 30 minutes

Preheat oven to 400 F and line a baking sheet with parchment paper; set aside. In a bowl, mix sour cream, dill, lemon zest, juice, salt, and pepper; set aside. Season the fish with salt and pepper, drizzle with lemon juice and arrange in the baking sheet. Spread sour cream mixture on each fish steak and sprinkle with Pecorino Romano cheese. Bake for 15 minutes. Broil the top for 2 minutes until nicely brown. Serve with buttery green beans.

Per serving: Cal 288; Net Carbs 1.2g; Fat 23.4g; Protein 16g

Coconut Crab Cakes

Ingredients for 8 servings
2 tbsp coconut oil
1 tbsp lime juice
1 cup lump crab meat
2 tsp Dijon mustard
1 egg, beaten
1 ½ tbsp coconut flour

Directions and Total Time: approx. 15 minutes

In a bowl, to the crab meat add all ingredients, except for the oil; mix well to combine. Make patties out of the mixture. Melt coconut oil in a skillet over medium heat. Cook the crabmeat patties for about 3-4 minutes per side.

Per serving: Cal 215; Net Carbs 3.6g; Fat 11g; Protein 15g

Spicy Smoked Mackerel Cakes

Ingredients for 6 servings
4 smoked mackerel steaks, bones removed, flaked
1 rutabaga, peeled and diced

Salt and chili pepper to taste
3 tbsp olive oil + for rubbing
3 eggs, beaten
2 tbsp mayonnaise
1 tbsp pork rinds, crushed

Directions and Total Time: approx. 30 minutes

Bring rutabaga to boil in salted water for 8 minutes. Drain, transfer to a mixing bowl, and mash the lumps. Add mackerel, eggs, mayonnaise, pork rinds, salt, and chili pepper. Make 6 compact patties. Heat olive oil in a skillet and fry the patties for 3 minutes on each side. Remove onto a wire rack to cool. Serve cakes with sesame sauce.

Per serving: Cal 324; Net Carbs 2.2g; Fat 27g; Protein 16g

Stuffed Avocado with Yogurt & Crabmeat

Ingredients for 4 servings
3 oz plain yogurt, strained overnight in a cheesecloth
1 tsp olive oil
1 cup crabmeat
2 avocados, halved and pitted
¼ cup almonds, chopped
1 tsp smoked paprika
Salt and black pepper, to taste

Directions and Total Time: approx. 25 minutes

Set oven to 425 F. Grease oil on a baking pan. In a bowl, mix crabmeat, yogurt, salt, and pepper. Fill avocado halves with almonds and crabmeat/cheese mixture and bake for 18 minutes. Decorate with paprika to serve.

Per serving: Cal 264; Net Carbs 11g; Fat 24.4g; Protein 4g

Hazelnut Cod Fillets

Ingredients for 2 servings
2 cod fillets
2 tbsp ghee
¼ cup roasted hazelnuts
A pinch of cayenne pepper

Directions and Total Time: approx. 30 minutes

Preheat your oven to 425 F. Line a baking dish with waxed paper. Melt the ghee and brush it over the fish. In a food processor, combine the rest of the ingredients. Coat the cod with the hazelnut mixture. Place in the oven and bake for about 15 minutes. Serve.

Per serving: Cal 467; Net Carbs 2.8g; Fat 31g; Protein 40g

Wine Shrimp Scampi Pizza

Ingredients for 4 servings
½ cup almond flour
¼ tsp salt
2 tbsp ground psyllium husk
3 tbsp olive oil
2 tbsp butter
2 garlic cloves, minced
¼ cup white wine
½ tsp dried basil
½ tsp dried parsley
½ lemon, juiced
½ lb shrimp, deveined
2 cups grated cheese blend
½ tsp Italian seasoning
¼ cup grated Parmesan

Directions and Total Time: approx. 35 minutes

Preheat oven to 390 F and line a baking sheet with parchment paper. In a bowl, mix almond flour, salt, psyllium powder, 1 tbsp of olive oil, and 1 cup of lukewarm water until dough forms. Spread the mixture on the pizza pan and bake for 10 minutes. Heat butter and the remaining olive oil in a skillet. Sauté garlic for 30 seconds. Mix in white wine, reduce by half, and stir in basil, parsley and lemon juice. Stir in shrimp and cook for 3 minutes. Mix in the cheese blend and Italian seasoning. Let the cheese melt, 3 minutes. Spread the shrimp mixture on the crust and top with Parmesan cheese. Bake for 5 minutes or until Parmesan melts. Slice and serve warm.

Per serving: Cal 423; Net Carbs 3.9g; Fats 34g; Protein 23g

Shallot Mussel with Shirataki

Ingredients for 4 servings
2 (8 oz) packs angel hair shirataki
1 lb mussels
1 cup white wine
4 tbsp olive oil
3 shallots, finely chopped
6 garlic cloves, minced
2 tsp red chili flakes
½ cup fish stock
1 ½ cups heavy cream

2 tbsp chopped fresh parsley
Salt and black pepper to taste
Directions and Total Time: approx. 25 minutes
Bring 2 cups of water to a boil in a pot. Strain the shirataki pasta and rinse well under hot running water. Drain and transfer to the boiling water. Cook for 3 minutes and strain again. Place a large dry skillet and stir-fry the shirataki pasta until visibly dry, 1-2 minutes; set aside. Pour mussels and white wine into a pot, cover, and cook for 3-4 minutes. Strain mussels and reserve the cooking liquid. Let cool, discard any closed mussels, and remove the meat out of ¾ of the mussel shells. Set aside with the remaining mussels in the shells. Heat olive oil in a skillet and sauté shallots, garlic, and chili flakes for 3 minutes. Mix in reduced wine and fish stock. Allow boiling and whisk in remaining butter and then the heavy cream. Season with salt, and pepper, and mix in parsley. Pour in shirataki pasta, mussels and toss well in the sauce. Serve.
Per serving: Cal 471; Net Carbs 6.9g; Fats 34g; Protein 18g

Nori Shrimp Rolls

Ingredients for 5 servings
2 cups cooked shrimp
1 tbsp Sriracha sauce
¼ cucumber, julienned
5 hand roll nori sheets
¼ cup mayonnaise
1 tbsp dill
Directions and Total Time: approx. 10 minutes
Chop the shrimp and combine with mayo, dill, and sriracha sauce in a bowl. Place a single nori sheet on a flat surface and spread about a fifth of the shrimp mixture. Roll the nori sheet as desired. Repeat with the other ingredients.
Per serving: Cal 130; Net Carbs 1g; Fat 10g; Protein 8.7g

Hazelnut-Crusted Salmon

Ingredients for 4 servings
4 salmon fillets
Salt and black pepper to taste
¼ cup mayonnaise
½ cup chopped hazelnuts

1 chopped shallot
2 tsp lemon zest
1 tbsp olive oil
1 cup heavy cream
Directions and Total Time: approx. 35 minutes
Preheat oven to 360 F. Brush the salmon with mayonnaise and coat with hazelnuts. Place in a lined baking dish and bake for 15 minutes. Heat olive oil in a saucepan and sauté shallot for 3 minutes. Stir in lemon zest and heavy cream and bring to a boil; cook until thickened, 5 minutes. Adjust seasoning and drizzle the sauce over the fish to serve.
Per serving: Cal 563; Net Carbs 6g; Fat 47g; Protein 34g

Fish & Cauliflower Parmesan Gratin

Ingredients for 4 servings
1 head cauliflower, cut into florets
2 cod fillets, cubed
3 white fish fillets, cubed
1 tbsp butter, melted
1 cup crème fraiche
¼ cup grated Parmesan
Grated Parmesan for topping
Directions and Total Time: approx. 40 minutes
Preheat oven to 400 F. Coat fish cubes and broccoli with butter. Spread in a greased baking dish. Mix crème fraiche with Parmesan cheese, pour and smear the cream on the fish, and sprinkle with some more Parmesan cheese. Bake for 25-30 minutes. Let sit for 5 minutes and serve in plates.
Per serving: Cal 354; Net Carbs 4g; Fat 17g; Protein 28g

Broccoli & Fish Gratin

Ingredients for 4 servings
¼ cup grated Pecorino Romano cheese + some more
2 salmon fillets, cubed
3 white fish, cubed
1 broccoli, cut into florets
1 tbsp butter, melted
Salt and black pepper to taste
1 cup crème fraiche
Directions and Total Time: approx. 45 minutes
Preheat oven to 400 F. Toss the fish cubes and broccoli in butter and season with salt

and pepper. Spread in a greased dish. Mix crème fraiche with Pecorino Romano cheese, pour and smear the cream on the fish. Bake for 30 minutes. Serve with lemon-mustard asparagus.

Per serving: Cal 354; Net Carbs 4g; Fat 17g; Protein 28g

Salmon Caesar Salad with Poached Eggs

Ingredients for 4 servings
½ cup chopped smoked salmon
2 tbsp heinz low carb caesar dressing
3 cups water
8 eggs
2 cups torn romaine lettuce
6 slices pancetta

Directions and Total Time: approx. 15 minutes
Boil water in a pot for 5 minutes. Crack each egg into a small bowl and gently slide into the water. Poach for 2-3 minutes, remove, and transfer to a paper towel to dry. Poach the remaining 7 eggs. Put the pancetta in a skillet and fry for 6 minutes, turning once. Allow cooling, and chop into small pieces. Toss the lettuce, smoked salmon, pancetta, and caesar dressing in a salad bowl. Top with two eggs each, and serve immediately.

Per serving: Cal 260; Net Carbs 5g; Fat 21g; Protein 8g

Avocado & Cauliflower Salad with Prawns

Ingredients for 6 servings
1 cauliflower head, florets only
1 lb medium-sized prawns
¼ cup + 1 tbsp olive oil
1 avocado, chopped

3 tbsp chopped dill
¼ cup lemon juice
2 tbsp lemon zest

Directions and Total Time: approx. 30 minutes
Heat 1 tbsp olive oil in a skillet and cook the prawns for 8-10 minutes. Microwave cauliflower for 5 minutes. Place prawns, cauliflower, and avocado in a large bowl. Whisk together the remaining olive oil, lemon zest, juice, dill, and some salt and pepper, in another bowl. Pour the dressing over, toss to combine and serve immediately.

Per serving: Cal 214; Net Carbs 5g; Fat 17g; Protein 15g

Fish Fritters

Ingredients for 4 servings
1 pound cod fillets, sliced
¼ cup mayonnaise
¼ cup almond flour
2 eggs
Salt and black pepper to taste
1 cup Swiss cheese, grated
1 tbsp chopped dill
3 tbsp olive oil

Directions and Total Time: approx. 40 min + cooling time
Mix the fish, mayo, flour, eggs, salt, pepper, Swiss cheese, and dill, in a bowl. Cover the bowl with plastic wrap and refrigerate for 2 hours. Warm olive oil and fetch 2 tbsp of fish mixture into the skillet, use the back of a spatula to flatten the top. Cook for 4 minutes, flip, and fry for 4 more. Remove onto a wire rack and repeat until the fish batter is over; add more oil if needed.

Per serving: Cal 633; Net Carbs 7g; Fat 46.9g; Protein 39g

VEGAN & VEGETARIAN

Broccoli & Mushrooms with Pasta

Ingredients for 4 servings

1 cup sliced cremini mushrooms
1 cup grated Gruyere cheese
4 large broccoli
2 tbsp olive oil
2 garlic cloves, minced
4 scallions, chopped
2 tbsp almond flour
1 ½ cups almond milk
Salt and black pepper to taste
¼ cup chopped fresh parsley

Directions and Total Time: approx. 20 minutes

Cut off the florets of the broccoli heads, leaving only the stems. Cut the ends of the stem flatly and evenly. Run the stems through a spiralizer to make the noodles. Heat olive oil in a skillet and sauté the broccoli noodles, mushrooms, garlic, and scallions until softened, 5 minutes. In a bowl, combine almond flour and almond milk, and pour the mixture over the vegetables. Stir and allow thickening for 2-3 minutes. Whisk in half of the Gruyere cheese to melt and adjust the taste with salt and black pepper. Garnish with the remaining Gruyere cheese and parsley, and serve.

Per serving: Cal 221; Net Carbs 1.4g; Fats 15g; Protein 9.3g

Spaghetti Bolognese with Tofu

Ingredients for 4 servings

2 tbsp butter
4 large parsnips, spiralized
2 tbsp olive oil
1 cup crumbled firm tofu
1 white onion, chopped
2 celery stalks, chopped
1 garlic clove, minced
2 cups sugar-free passata
¼ cup vegetable broth
Salt and black pepper to taste
1 small bunch basil, chopped
1 cup grated Parmesan cheese

Directions and Total Time: approx. 25 minutes

Melt butter in a skillet and sauté parsnips for 5 minutes. Season with salt and set aside.

Heat olive oil in a pot and cook tofu for 5 minutes. Stir in onion, garlic, and celery and cook for 5 minutes. Mix in passata and vegetable broth and season with salt and pepper. Cover the pot and cook until the sauce thickens, 8-10 minutes. Stir in basil. Divide the pasta between serving plates and top with the sauce. Sprinkle the Parmesan cheese on top and serve warm.

Per serving: Cal 424; Net Carbs 31g; Fats 20g; Protein 22g

Tofu Meatballs with Cauli Mash

Ingredients for 4 servings

1 cup white button mushrooms, chopped
1 lb tofu, pressed and cubed
2 garlic cloves, minced
2 small red onions, chopped
1 red bell pepper, chopped
½ cup golden flaxseed meal
½ almond milk
1 ½ + 1 tbsp olive oil
2 cups tomato sauce
6 fresh basil leaves to garnish
1 lb cauliflower, cut into florets
Salt and black pepper to taste
2 tbsp butter
½ cup heavy cream
¼ cup grated Parmesan

Directions and Total Time: approx. 65 minutes

Preheat oven to 350 F and line a baking tray with parchment paper. In a bowl, add silken tofu, half of garlic, half of onion, mushrooms, salt, and pepper; mix to combine. Mold bite-size balls out of the mixture. Place flaxseed meal and almond milk each in a shallow dish. Dip each ball in almond milk and then in the flaxseed meal. Place on the baking sheet and bake for 10 minutes. Heat 1 ½ tbsp of olive oil in a saucepan and fry in the oil until golden brown on all sides; set aside. Heat the remaining oil in the same saucepan and sauté onion, garlic, and bell pepper for 5 minutes. Pour in tomato sauce and cook for 20 minutes or until stew forms. Add in tofu balls and simmer for 7 minutes. In a pot, add cauliflower, 1 cup of water, and salt. Bring to a boil for 10 minutes. Drain pour into a bowl. Add in butter, salt, and pepper; mash into a puree using a potato mash. Stir in heavy cream and Parmesan until evenly combined. Spoon the cauli mash into bowls, top with tofu balls and sauce, and garnish with basil leaves.

Per serving: Cal 686; Net Carbs 5.6g, Fat 31g, Protein 22g

Chili Vegetables & Pasta Bake

Ingredients for 4 servings
1 cup sliced white button mushrooms
1 cup shredded mozzarella
1 cup chopped bell peppers
1 egg yolk
1 tbsp olive oil
1 yellow squash, chopped
1 red onion, sliced
Salt and black pepper to taste
¼ tsp red chili flakes
1 cup marinara sauce
1 cup grated mozzarella cheese
1 cup grated Parmesan cheese
¼ cup chopped fresh basil

Directions and Total Time: approx. 15 min + chilling time
Microwave mozzarella cheese for 2 minutes. Take out the bowl and allow cooling for 1 minute. Mix in egg yolk until well-combined. Lay a parchment paper on a flat surface, pour the cheese mixture on top and cover with another parchment paper. Flatten the dough into 1/8-inch thickness. Take off the parchment paper and cut the dough into penne-size pieces. Place in a bowl and refrigerate overnight. Bring 2 cups of water to a boil and add in penne. Cook for 1 minute and drain; set aside. Heat olive oil in a pan and sauté bell peppers, garlic, squash, onion, and mushrooms. Cook for 5 minutes. Season with salt, pepper, and red chili flakes. Mix in marinara sauce and cook for 5 minutes. Stir in penne and spread the mozzarella and Parmesan cheeses on top. Bake for 15 minutes. Serve.

Per serving: Cal 248; Net Carbs 4.9g; Fats 12g; Protein 27g

White Egg Tex Mex Pizza

Ingredients for 2 servings
4 eggs
2 tbsp water
1 Jalapeno pepper, diced
2 oz Monterey Jack, shredded
2 tbsp chopped green onions
¼ cup Alfredo sauce
¼ tsp cumin
2 tbsp olive oil

Directions and Total Time: approx. 17 minutes
Preheat the oven to 350 F. Heat olive oil in a skillet. Whisk the eggs along with water and cumin; pour into the skillet and cook until set. Top with alfredo sauce and jalapeno. Sprinkle green onions and cheese over. Place in the oven and bake for 5 minutes. Serve.

Per serving: Cal 591; Net Carbs 2g; Fat 55g; Protein 22g

Baked Cauliflower with Shirataki

Ingredients for 4 servings
2 (8 oz) packs spinach angel hair shirataki
1 medium head cauliflower, cut into florets
1 cup grated Monterey Jack cheese
1 cup heavy cream
1 tsp dried thyme
1 tsp smoked paprika
½ tsp red chili flakes

Directions and Total Time: approx. 45 minutes
To make the shirataki angel hair, boil 2 cups of water in a medium pot over medium heat. Strain the shirataki pasta through a colander and rinse very well under hot running water. Allow proper draining and pour the shirataki pasta into the boiling water. Cook for 3 minutes and strain again. Place a dry skillet over medium heat and stir-fry the shirataki pasta until visibly dry, and makes a squeaky sound when stirred, 1 to 2 minutes. Set aside. Preheat oven to 350 F. Bring 4 cups of water to a boil in a large pot and blanch the cauliflower for 4 minutes. Drain through a colander. In a bowl, mix cauliflower, shirataki, heavy cream, half of Monterey Jack cheese, thyme, paprika, salt, and chili flakes until well combined. Transfer the mixture to a greased baking dish and top with the remaining cheese. Bake for 30 minutes until the cheese melts. Serve.

Per serving: Cal 301; Net Carbs 13g; Fats 21g; Protein 12g

Almond-Flour Pizza with Kale & Artichokes

Ingredients for 4 servings

2 ½ cups grated mozzarella
¼ cup grated Parmesan
6 tbsp cream cheese, softened
1 egg, beaten
1 tsp Italian seasoning
½ tsp garlic powder
½ cup almond flour
½ cup chopped kale
¼ cup chopped artichokes
1 lemon, juiced
½ tsp garlic powder
Salt and black pepper to taste

Directions and Total Time: approx. 45 minutes

Preheat the oven to 390 F and line a round pizza pan with parchment paper. Microwave 2 cups of mozzarella and 2 tbsp of cream cheese for 1 minute. Mix in egg, Italian seasoning, garlic powder, and almond flour. Spread the mixture on the pizza pan and bake for 15 minutes; set aside. In a bowl, mix remaining cream cheese, kale, artichokes, lemon juice, garlic powder, Parmesan cheese, remaining mozzarella cheese, salt, and pepper. Spread the mixture on the crust and bake for 15 minutes. Serve sliced.

Per serving: Cal 223; Net Carbs 3.1g; Fats 10g; Protein 24g

Balsamic Veggie-Pasta Mix

Ingredients for 4 servings

1 cup grated Parmigiano-Reggiano cheese
1 cup shredded mozzarella
1 head broccoli, cut into florets
1 egg yolk
3 tbsp olive oil
1 red onion, thinly sliced
1 lb green beans, halved
1 red bell pepper, sliced
5 garlic cloves, minced
Salt and black pepper to taste
1 tsp dried oregano
3 tbsp balsamic vinegar
2 tbsp chopped walnuts

Directions and Total Time: approx. 25 min + chilling time

Microwave mozzarella cheese for 2 minutes. Let cool for 1 minute and mix in egg yolk until well-combined. Lay a parchment paper on a flat surface, pour the cheese mixture on top and cover with another parchment paper.

Flatten the dough into 1/8-inch thickness. Take off the parchment paper and cut the dough into mimicked penne-size pieces. Place in a bowl and refrigerate overnight. Bring 2 cups water to a boil and add in keto penne. Cook for 1 minute and drain; set aside. Heat olive oil in a skillet and sauté onion, garlic, green beans, broccoli, and bell pepper for 5 minutes. Season with salt, pepper, and oregano. Mix in balsamic vinegar, cook for 1 minute, and toss in the pasta. Garnish with Parmigiano-Reggiano cheese and walnuts.

Per serving: Cal 326; Net Carbs 7.5g; Fats 21g; Protein 20g

Fried Mac & Cheese

Ingredients for 4 servings

1 cauliflower head, riced
1 ½ cups shredded cheese
2 tsp paprika
2 tsp turmeric
3 eggs
4 tbsp olive oil

Directions and Total Time: approx. 45 minutes

Microwave the cauliflower for 5 minutes. Place it in cheesecloth and squeeze the extra juices out. Remove to a bowl. Stir in the rest of the ingredients. Heat olive oil in a deep pan over medium heat. Add the 'mac and cheese' and fry until golden and crispy. Serve.

Per serving: Cal 160; Net Carbs 2g; Fat 12g; Protein 8.6g

Quick Grilled Cheddar Cheese

Ingredients for 2 servings

4 eggs
1 tsp baking powder
3 tbsp butter
3 tbsp almond flour
2 tbsp psyllium husk powder
4 oz cheddar cheese

Directions and Total Time: approx. 15 minutes

Whisk together all ingredients, except for 1 tbsp butter and cheddar cheese. Microwave for 90 seconds. Flip the "bun" over and cut in half. Place the cheddar on one half of the bun and top with the other. Melt the remaining butter in a skillet. Add the sandwich and grill until the cheese is melted and the bun is crispy.

Per serving: Cal 623; Net Carbs 6.1g; Fat 51g; Protein 25g

Vegan Olive and Avocado Zoodles

Ingredients for 4 servings
¼ cup chopped sun-dried tomatoes
4 zucchini, spiralized
½ cup pesto
2 avocados, sliced
1 cup kalamata olives, chopped
¼ cup chopped basil
2 tbsp olive oil

Directions and Total Time: approx. 15 minutes
Heat 1 tbsp olive oil in a pan over medium heat. Add zoodles, and cook for 4 minutes. Transfer to a plate. Stir in 1 tbsp olive oil, pesto, basil, salt, tomatoes, and olives. Top with avocado slices.

Per serving: Cal 449; Net Carbs 8.4g; Fat 42g; Protein 6g

Enchilada Vegetarian Pasta

Ingredients for 4 servings
1 cup shredded mozzarella
1 cup chopped bell peppers
1 egg yolk
1 tsp olive oil
6 garlic cloves, minced
2 cups enchilada sauce
1 tsp cumin powder
½ tsp smoked paprika
1 tsp chili powder
Salt and black pepper to taste
¾ cup chopped green onions
1 avocado, pitted, sliced

Directions and Total Time: approx. 20 min + chilling time
Microwave mozzarella cheese for 2 minutes. Take out the bowl and allow cooling for 1 minute. Mix in egg yolk until well-combined. Lay a parchment paper on a flat surface, pour the cheese mixture on top and cover with another parchment paper. Flatten the dough into 1/8-inch thickness. Take off the parchment paper and cut the dough into penne-size pieces. Place in a bowl and refrigerate overnight. Bring 2 cups water to a boil in medium saucepan and add the keto penne. Cook for 1 minute and drain; set aside. Heat olive oil in a skillet and sauté garlic for 30 seconds. Mix in enchilada sauce, cumin,

paprika, chili powder, bell peppers, salt, and pepper. Cook for 5 minutes. Mix in pasta. Top with green onions and avocado.

Per serving: Cal 151; Net Carbs 3.3g; Fats 8g; Protein 11.9g

Cheesy Roasted Vegetable Spaghetti

Ingredients for 4 servings
2 (8 oz) packs shirataki spaghetti
1 cup chopped mixed bell peppers
½ cup grated Parmesan cheese for topping
1 lb asparagus, chopped
1 cup broccoli florets
1 cup green beans, chopped
3 tbsp olive oil
1 small onion, chopped
2 garlic cloves, minced
1 cup diced tomatoes
½ cup chopped basil

Directions and Total Time: approx. 45 minutes
Boil 2 cups water in a pot. Strain the shirataki pasta and rinse well under hot running water. Allow draining and pour the shirataki pasta into the boiling water. Cook for 3 minutes and strain again. Place a dry skillet and stir-fry the shirataki pasta until visibly dry, 1-2 minutes; set aside. Preheat oven to 425 F. In a bowl, add asparagus, broccoli, bell peppers, and green beans and toss with half of olive oil, salt, and pepper. Spread the vegetables on a baking sheet and roast for 20 minutes. Heat the remaining olive oil in a skillet and sauté onion and garlic for 3 minutes. Stir in tomatoes for 8 minutes. Mix in shirataki and vegetables. Top with Parmesan cheese and serve.

Per serving: Cal 272; Net Carbs 7.2g; Fats 12g; Protein 12g

One-Skillet Green Pasta

Ingredients for 4 servings
1 cup shredded mozzarella cheese
1 cup grated Pecorino Romano cheese for topping
1 egg yolk
2 garlic cloves, minced
1 lemon, juiced
1 cup baby spinach
½ cup almond milk
1 avocado, pitted and peeled
1 tbsp olive oil

Salt to taste

Directions and Total Time: approx. 15 min + chilling time

Microwave mozzarella cheese for 2 minutes. Take out the bowl and allow cooling for 1 minute. Mix in egg yolk until well-combined. Lay a parchment paper on a flat surface, pour the cheese mixture on top and cover with another parchment paper. Flatten the dough into 1/8-inch thickness. Take off the parchment paper and cut the dough into thick fettuccine strands. Place in a bowl and refrigerate overnight. Bring 2 cups water to a boil in a saucepan and add the fettuccine. Cook for 1 minute and drain; set aside. In a blender, combine garlic, lemon juice, spinach, almond milk, avocado, olive oil, and salt. Process until smooth. Pour fettuccine into a bowl, top with sauce, and mix. Top with Pecorino Romano cheese and serve.

Per serving: Cal 290; Net Carbs 5.3g; Fats 19g; Protein 18g

Tempeh Taco Cups

Ingredients for 4 servings

8 iceberg lettuce leaves
4 zero carb tortilla wraps
2 tsp melted butter
1 tbsp olive oil
1 yellow onion, chopped
½ cup tempeh, crumbled
1 tsp smoked paprika
½ tsp cumin powder
1 red bell pepper, chopped
1 avocado, halved and pitted
1 small lemon, juiced
¼ cup sour cream

Directions and Total Time: approx. 30 minutes

Preheat oven to 400 F. Divide each tortilla wrap into 2, lay on a chopping board, and brush with butter. Line 8 muffin tins with the tortilla and bake for 9 minutes; set aside. Heat olive oil in a skillet and sauté onion for 3 minutes. Crumble tempeh into the pan and cook for 8 minutes. Stir in paprika and cumin and cook for 1 minute. To assemble, fit lettuce leaves into the tortilla cups, share tempeh mixture on top, top with bell pepper, avocado, and drizzle with lemon juice. Add sour cream and serve.

Per serving: Cal 220; Net Carbs 3.8g, Fat 17g, Protein 6.7g

Bell Pepper & Broccoli Spaghetti

Ingredients for 4 servings

1 head broccoli, cut into florets
1 cup sliced mixed bell peppers
2 tbsp olive oil
4 zucchinis, spiralized
4 shallots, finely chopped
Salt and black pepper to taste
2 garlic cloves, minced
¼ tsp red pepper flakes
1 cup chopped kale
2 tbsp balsamic vinegar
½ lemon, juiced
1 cup grated Parmesan cheese

Directions and Total Time: approx. 20 minutes

Heat oil in a skillet and sauté turnips, broccoli, bell peppers, and shallots until softened, 7 minutes. Mix in garlic, and pepper flakes and cook until fragrant, 30 seconds. Stir in kale and zucchinis; cook until tender, 3 minutes. Mix in vinegar and lemon juice and adjust the taste with salt and pepper. Garnish with Parmesan cheese and serve.

Per serving: Cal 199; Net Carbs 5.9g; Fats 13g; Protein 9g

Rich Veggie Pasta Primavera

Ingredients for 4 servings

2 cups cauliflower florets, cut into matchsticks
½ cup grated Pecorino Romano cheese
1 cup shredded mozzarella
½ cup chopped green onions
1 egg yolk
¼ cup olive oil
1 red bell pepper, sliced
4 garlic cloves, minced
1 cup grape tomatoes, halved
2 tsp dried Italian seasoning
½ lemon, juiced
2 tbsp chopped fresh parsley

Directions and Total Time: approx. 25 min + chilling time

Microwave mozzarella cheese for 2 minutes. Take out the bowl and let cool for 1 minute. Mix in egg yolk until well-combined. Lay a parchment paper on a flat surface, pour the cheese mixture on top and cover with another parchment paper. Flatten the dough into 1/8-inch thickness. Take off the parchment paper and cut the dough into penne-size pieces. Place in a bowl and refrigerate overnight. Bring 2 cups water to a boil and add in penne. Cook for 1 minute and drain; set aside. Heat olive oil in a skillet and sauté onion, garlic cauliflower, and bell pepper for 7 minutes. Stir in tomatoes and Italian seasoning and cook for 5 minutes. Mix in lemon juice, penne, salt, and pepper. Top with Pecorino Romano cheese

Per serving: Cal 283; Net Carbs 5.2g; Fats 18g; Protein 15g

Herby Mushroom Pizza

Ingredients for 4 servings
2 medium cremini mushrooms, sliced
2 ½ cups grated mozzarella
½ cup grated Parmesan cheese
2 tbsp cream cheese, softened
½ cup almond flour
1 egg, beaten
1 tsp olive oil
1 garlic clove, minced
½ cup tomato sauce
1 tsp erythritol
1 tsp dried oregano
1 tsp dried basil
½ tsp paprika
Salt and black pepper to taste
6 black olives, sliced

Directions and Total Time: approx. 45 minutes
Preheat oven to 390 F. Line a pizza pan with parchment paper. Microwave 2 cups mozzarella cheese and 2 tbsp cream cheese for 1 minute. Mix in almond meal and egg. Spread the mixture on the pizza pan and bake for 5 minutes; set aside. Heat olive oil in a skillet and sauté mushrooms and garlic until softened, 5 minutes. Mix in tomato sauce, erythritol, oregano, basil, paprika, salt, and pepper. Cook for 2 minutes. Spread the sauce on the crust, top with the remaining mozzarella and Parmesan cheeses and olives. Bake for 15 minutes. Slice and serve.

Per serving: Cal 203; Net Carbs 2.6g; Fats 8g; Protein 24.3g

Cheesy Broccoli Nachos with Salsa

Ingredients for 4 servings

2 heads broccoli, chopped
3 tbsp coconut flour
1 tsp smoked paprika
½ tsp coriander powder
1 tsp cumin powder
½ tsp garlic powder
2 eggs, beaten
¼ cup grated Monterey jack
4 plum tomatoes, chopped
½ lime, juiced
4 sprigs cilantro, chopped
1 avocado, chopped

Directions and Total Time: approx. 30 minutes
Preheat oven to 350 F. Pour broccoli in a food processor and blend into a rice-like consistency. Heat a skillet over low heat, pour in broccoli, and fry for 10 minutes. Transfer to a bowl. Line 2 baking sheets with parchment papers. Onto the broccoli, add coconut flour, paprika, coriander, cumin, garlic, and eggs. Mix and form into a ball. Divide into halves, place each half on each baking sheet, and press down into a rough circle. Bake for 10 minutes. Take out of the oven, cut into triangles, and sprinkle with cheese; let cool. In a bowl, combine tomatoes, lime, cilantro, and avocado. Serve nachos with salsa.

Per serving: Cal 208; Net Carbs 4.5g, Fat 12.4g, Protein 7g

Cheesy Bell Pepper Pizza

Ingredients for 2 servings
6 oz mozzarella, grated
2 tbsp cream cheese
2 tbsp Parmesan cheese
1 tsp oregano
½ cup almond flour
2 tbsp psyllium husk
4 oz grated cheddar cheese
¼ cup marinara sauce
⅔ bell pepper, sliced
1 tomato, sliced
2 tbsp chopped basil
6 black olives

Directions and Total Time: approx. 40 minutes
Preheat the oven to 400 F. Combine all crust ingredients in a bowl, except for the mozzarella. Melt mozzarella in a microwave. Stir it into the bowl and mix to combine.

Divide the dough in 2. Roll out the crusts in circles and place on a lined baking sheet. Bake for 10 minutes. Top with cheddar, marinara, bell pepper, tomato, and basil. Return to oven and bake for 10 minutes. Serve with olives.

Per serving: Cal 510; Net Carbs 3.7g; Fat 39g; Protein 31g

Thyme and Collard Green Waffles

Ingredients for 4 servings
2 green onions
1 tbsp olive oil
2 eggs
⅓ cup Parmesan cheese
1 cup collard greens
1 cup mozzarella, grated
½ cauliflower head, chopped
1 tsp garlic powder
1 tbsp sesame seeds
2 tsp chopped thyme

Directions and Total Time: approx. 45 minutes
Place the cauliflower in a food processor and process until a rice-like mixture is formed. Add collard greens, spring onions, and thyme. Pulse until smooth. Transfer to a bowl. Stir in the rest of the ingredients and mix to combine. Heat waffle iron and spread the mixture onto the iron, evenly. Cook following the manufacturer's instructions.

Per serving: Cal 283; Net Carbs 3.5g; Fat 20g; Protein 16g

Stuffed Portobello Mushrooms

Ingredients for 2 servings
4 Portobello mushrooms
2 tbsp olive oil
2 cups lettuce
1 cup crumbled blue cheese

Directions and Total Time: approx. 30 minutes
Preheat oven to 350 F. Remove the stems from the mushrooms. Fill the mushrooms with blue cheese and place on a lined baking sheet. Bake for about 20 minutes. Serve with lettuce drizzled with olive oil.

Per serving: Cal 334; Net Carbs 5.5g; Fat 29g; Protein 14g

Spinach-Olive Pizza

Ingredients for 4 servings
1 cup grated mozzarella
½ cup almond flour
¼ tsp salt
2 tbsp ground psyllium husk
1 tbsp olive oil
1 cup lukewarm water
½ cup tomato sauce
½ cup baby spinach
1 tsp dried oregano
3 tbsp sliced black olives

Directions and Total Time: approx. 40 minutes
Preheat oven to 390 F and line a baking sheet with parchment paper. In a bowl, mix almond flour, salt, psyllium powder, olive oil, and water until dough forms. Spread the mixture on the sheet and bake for 10 minutes. Remove the crust and spread the tomato sauce on top. Add spinach, mozzarella cheese, oregano, and olives. Bake for 15 minutes. Take out of the oven, slice and serve warm.

Per serving: Cal 195; Net Carbs 1.8g; Fats 8g; Protein 11g

Fake Mushroom Risotto

Ingredients for 4 servings
2 shallots, diced
3 tbsp olive oil
¼ cup veggie broth
⅓ cup Parmesan cheese
4 tbsp butter
3 tbsp chopped chives
2 pounds mushrooms, sliced
4 ½ cups riced cauliflower

Directions and Total Time: approx. 15 minutes
Heat 2 tbsp. oil in a saucepan. Add the mushrooms and cook over medium heat for 3 minutes. Remove and set aside. Heat the remaining oil and cook the shallots for 2 minutes. Stir in the cauliflower and broth, and cook until the liquid is absorbed. Stir in the rest of the ingredients.

Per serving: Cal 264; Net Carbs 8.4g; Fat 18g; Protein 11g

Vegetarian Ketogenic Burgers

Ingredients for 2 servings
1 garlic cloves, minced
2 Portobello mushrooms
1 tbsp coconut oil, melted
1 tbsp chopped basil

1 tbsp oregano
2 eggs, fried
2 zero carb buns
2 tbsp mayonnaise
2 lettuce leaves
Salt to taste

Directions and Total Time: approx. 20 minutes

Combine the melted coconut oil, garlic, herbs, and salt in a bowl. Place the mushrooms in the bowl and coat well. Preheat the grill to medium. Grill the mushrooms about 2 minutes per side. Slice them and grill for 2 minutes per side. Cut the buns in half. Add the lettuce leaves, mushrooms, eggs, and mayo. Top with the other bun.

Per serving: Cal 637; Net Carbs 8.5g; Fat 53g; Protein 23g

Mediterranean Pasta

Ingredients for 4 servings
¼ cup sun-dried tomatoes
5 garlic cloves, minced
2 tbsp butter
1 cup spinach
2 Large zucchini, spiralized
¼ cup crumbled feta
¼ cup Parmesan
10 kalamata olives, halved
2 tbsp olive oil
2 tbsp chopped parsley

Directions and Total Time: approx. 15 minutes

Heat the olive oil in a pan over medium heat. Add zoodles, butter, garlic, and spinach; stir-fry for 5 minutes. Stir in the olives, tomatoes, and parsley. Cook for 2 more minutes. Stir in the cheeses and serve.

Per serving: Cal 231; Net Carbs 6.5g; Fat 21g; Protein 6g

Mint Ice Cream

Ingredients for 4 servings
2 avocados, pitted
1 ¼ cups coconut cream
½ tsp vanilla extract
2 tbsp erythritol
2 tsp chopped mint leaves

Directions and Total Time: approx. 10 min+ chilling time

Into a blender, spoon avocado pulps, pour in coconut cream, vanilla extract, erythritol, and mint leaves. Process until smooth. Pour the mixture into your ice cream maker and freeze according to the manufacturer's instructions. When ready, remove and scoop the ice cream into bowls.

Per serving: Cal 370; Net Carbs 4g; Fat 38g; Protein 4g

Eggplant & Goat Cheese Pizza

Ingredients for 4 servings
4 tbsp olive oil
2 eggplants, sliced lengthwise
1 cup tomato sauce
2 garlic cloves, minced
1 red onion, sliced
12 oz goat cheese, crumbled
Salt and black pepper to taste
½ tsp cinnamon powder
1 cup mozzarella, shredded
2 tbsp oregano, chopped

Directions and Total Time: approx. 45 minutes

Line a baking sheet with parchment paper. Lay the eggplant slices in a baking dish and drizzle with some olive oil. Bake for 20 minutes at 390 F. Heat the remaining olive oil in a skillet and sauté garlic and onion for 3 minutes. Stir in goat cheese and tomato sauce and season with salt and pepper. Simmer for 10 minutes. Remove eggplant from the oven and spread the cheese sauce on top. Sprinkle with mozzarella cheese and oregano. Bake further for 10 minutes until the cheese melts. Slice to serve.

Per serving: Cal 557; Net Carbs 8.3g; Fat 44g; Protein 33.7g

Charred Asparagus with Creamy Sauce

Ingredients for 4 servings
½ lb asparagus, no hard stalks
Salt and chili pepper to taste
4 tbsp flax seed powder
½ cup coconut cream
1 cup butter, melted
⅓ cup mozzarella, grated
2 tbsp olive oil
Juice of half lemon

Directions and Total Time: approx. 12 minutes

Heat olive oil in a saucepan and roast the asparagus until lightly charred. Season with salt and pepper; set aside. Melt half of butter in a pan until nutty and golden brown. Stir in lemon juice and pour the mixture over the asparagus. In a safe microwave bowl, mix flax seed powder with ½ cup water and let sit for 5 minutes. Microwave flax egg 1-2 minutes, then pour into a blender. Add the remaining butter, mozzarella cheese, coconut cream, salt, and chili pepper. Puree until well combined and smooth. Serve.

Per serving: Cal 442; Net Carbs 5.4g; Fat 45g; Protein 5.9g

Tomato & Mozzarella Caprese Bake

Ingredients for 4 servings
4 tbsp olive oil
4 tomatoes, sliced
1 cup fresh mozzarella, sliced
2 tbsp basil pesto
1 cup mayonnaise
2 oz Parmesan cheese, grated

Directions and Total Time: approx. 25 minutes

In a baking dish, arrange tomatoes and mozzarella slices. In a bowl, mix pesto, mayonnaise, 1 oz of Parmesan cheese, salt, and pepper; mix to combine. Spread this mixture over tomatoes and mozzarella cheese, and top with remaining Parmesan cheese. Bake for 20 minutes at 360 F. Remove, allow cooling slightly, and slice to serve.

Per serving: Cal 420; Net Carbs 4.9g; Fat 36.6g; Protein 17g

Sweet Onion & Goat Cheese Pizza

Ingredients for 4 servings
2 cups grated mozzarella
2 tbsp cream cheese, softened
2 large eggs, beaten
⅓ cup almond flour
1 tsp dried Italian seasoning
2 tbsp butter
2 red onions, thinly sliced
1 cup crumbled goat cheese
1 tbs almond milk
1 cup curly endive, chopped

Directions and Total Time: approx. 35 minutes

Preheat oven to 390 F and line a round pizza pan with parchment paper. Microwave the mozzarella and cream cheeses for 1 minute. Remove and mix in eggs, almond flour, and Italian seasoning. Spread the dough on the pizza pan and bake for 6 minutes. Melt butter in a skillet and stir in onions, salt, and pepper and cook on low heat with frequent stirring until caramelized, 15- 20 minutes. In a bowl, mix goat cheese with almond milk and spread on the crust. Top with the caramelized onions. Bake for 10 minutes. Scatter curly endive on top, slice and serve.

Per serving: Cal 317; Net Carbs 3.1g; Fats 20g; Protein 28g

Vegan BBQ Tofu Kabobs with Green Dip

Ingredients for 4 servings
½ tbsp BBQ sauce
1 lb extra firm tofu, cubed
1 tbsp vegan butter, melted
1 cup canola oil
5 tbsp fresh cilantro, chopped
3 tbsp fresh basil, chopped
2 garlic cloves
Juice of ½ a lime
4 tbsp capers
Salt and black pepper to taste

Directions and Total Time: approx. 20 minutes

In a blender, add cilantro, basil, garlic, lemon juice, capers, 2/3 cup of canola oil, salt and pepper. Process until smooth. Set aside. Thread the tofu cubes on wooden skewers to fit into your grill pan. Season with salt and brush with the BBQ sauce. Brush the grill pan with remaining canola oil and cook the tofu until browned on both sides. Serve.

Per serving: Cal 471; Net Carbs 3.8g; Fat 47g; Protein 11.9g

One-Pot Spicy Brussel Sprouts with Carrots

Ingredients for 4 servings
1 pound Brussels sprouts
¼ cup olive oil
4 green onions, chopped
1 carrot, grated
Salt and black pepper to taste
Hot chili sauce

Directions and Total Time: approx. 15 minutes

Sauté green onions in warm olive oil for 2 minutes. Stir in salt and pepper; transfer to a plate. Trim the Brussel sprouts and cut in halves. Leave the small ones as wholes. Pour the Brussel sprouts with and carrot into the same saucepan and stir-fry until softened but al dente. Season with salt and pepper, stir in onions, and heat for a few seconds. Top with the hot chili sauce. Serve.

Per serving: Cal 198; Net Carbs 6.5g; Fat 14g; Protein 4.9g

Tofu Nuggets with Cilantro Dip

Ingredients for 4 servings
1 lime, ½ juiced and ½ cut into wedges
1 ½ cups olive oil
28 oz tofu, pressed and cubed
1 egg, lightly beaten
1 cup golden flaxseed meal
1 ripe avocado, chopped
½ tbsp chopped cilantro
Salt and black pepper to taste
½ tbsp olive oil

Directions and Total Time: approx. 25 minutes
Heat olive oil in a deep skillet. Coat tofu cubes in the egg and then in the flaxseed meal. Fry until golden brown. Transfer to a plate. Place avocado, cilantro, salt, pepper, and lime juice in a blender; puree until smooth. Spoon into a bowl, add tofu nuggets, and lime wedges to serve.

Per serving: Cal 665; Net Carbs 6.2g, Fat 54g, Protein 32g

Zucchini-Cranberry Cake Squares

Ingredients for 6 servings
1 ¼ cups chopped zucchinis
2 tbsp olive oil
½ cup dried cranberries
1 lemon, zested
3 eggs
1 ½ cups almond flour
½ tsp baking powder
1 tsp cinnamon powder
A pinch of salt

Directions and Total Time: approx. 45 minutes
Preheat oven to 350 F and line a square cake tin with parchment paper. Combine zucchinis, olive oil, cranberries, lemon zest, and eggs in a bowl until evenly combined. Sift flour, baking powder, and cinnamon powder into the mixture and fold with the salt. Pour the

mixture into the cake tin and bake for 30 minutes. Remove; allow cooling in the tin for 10 minutes and transfer the cake to a wire rack to cool completely. Cut into squares and serve.

Per serving: Cal 121; Net Carbs 2.5g, Fat 10g, Protein 4g

Egg Cauli Fried Rice with Grilled Cheese

Ingredients for 4 servings
2 cups cauliflower rice, steamed
½ lb halloumi, cut into ¼ to ½ inch slabs
1 tbsp ghee
4 eggs, beaten
1 green bell pepper, chopped
¼ cup green beans, chopped
1 tsp soy sauce
2 tbsp chopped parsley

Directions and Total Time: approx. 10 minutes
Melt ghee in a skillet and pour in the eggs. Swirl the pan to spread the eggs around and cook for 1 minute. Move the scrambled eggs to the side of the skillet, add bell pepper and green beans, and sauté for 3 minutes. Pour in the cauli rice and cook for 2 minutes. Top with soy sauce; combine evenly, and cook for 2 minutes. Dish into plates, garnish with the parsley, and set aside. Preheat a grill pan and grill halloumi cheese on both sides until the cheese lightly browns. Place on the side of the rice and serve warm.

Per serving: Cal 275; Net Carbs 4.5g, Fat 19g, Protein 15g

Strawberry Faux Oats

Ingredients for 2 servings
2 tbsp coconut flour
2 tbsp golden flaxseed meal
2 tbsp chia seeds
2 tbsp heavy cream
½ cup almond milk
3 tbsp sugar-free maple syrup
1 tsp vanilla extract
1 cup strawberries, halved
¼ cup desiccated coconut

Directions and Total Time: approx. 20 minutes
Combine coconut flour, flaxseed meal, and chia seeds in a saucepan. Stir in heavy cream, almond milk, maple syrup, and vanilla extract.

Place the pan over medium heat, whisk the Ingredients for 10 minutes. Pour the mixture into 2 serving bowls and top with strawberries and desiccated coconut. Drizzle with some more maple syrup and serve.

Per serving: Cal 289; Net Carbs 6g, Fat 18.5g, Protein 5g

Cheese Quesadillas with Fruit Salad

Ingredients for 2 servings
2 large zero carb tortillas
1 cup grated cheddar cheese
2 green onions, chopped
1 cup mixed berries
½ tsp cinnamon powder
½ lemon, juiced
1 cup Greek yogurt
Sugar-free maple syrup to taste
Directions and Total Time: approx. 10 minutes
Divide the tortillas into two, top half each with the cheddar cheese and spring onions, and cover with the halves. Place in a skillet and heat until golden and the cheese melted. Remove onto a plate, allow cooling, and cut into four wedges. Combine berries, cinnamon powder, lemon juice, Greek yogurt, and maple syrup in a bowl. Divide into 2 bowls and serve with the quesadillas.
Per serving: Cal 135; Net Carbs 3g, Fat 13.5g, Protein 3.5g

Mushroom & Broccoli Pizza

Ingredients for 4 servings
½ cup almond flour
¼ tsp salt
2 tbsp ground psyllium husk
2 tbsp olive oil
1 cup sliced fresh mushrooms
1 white onion, thinly sliced
3 cups broccoli florets
4 garlic cloves, minced
½ cup sugar-free pizza sauce
4 tomatoes, sliced
1 ½ cups grated mozzarella
⅓ cup grated Parmesan
Directions and Total Time: approx. 25 minutes
Preheat oven to 390 F and line a baking sheet with parchment paper. In a bowl, mix almond flour, salt, psyllium powder, 1 tbsp of olive oil, and 1 cup of lukewarm water until dough

forms. Spread the mixture on the pizza pan and bake for 10 minutes. Heat the remaining olive oil in a skillet and sauté mushrooms, onion, garlic, and broccoli for 5 minutes. Spread the pizza sauce on the crust and top with the broccoli mixture, tomato, and mozzarella and Parmesan cheeses. Bake for 5 minutes. Serve sliced.

Per serving: Cal 180; Net Carbs 3.6g; Fats 9.4g; Protein 17g

Tofu Radish Bowls

Ingredients for 4 servings
¼ cup chopped baby bella mushrooms
2 yellow bell peppers, chopped
1 (14 oz) block tofu, cubed
1 tbsp + 1 tbsp olive oil
1 ½ cups shredded radishes
½ cup chopped white onions
4 eggs
1/3 cup tomato salsa
A handful chopped parsley
1 avocado, and chopped
Directions and Total Time: approx. 35 minutes
Heat 1 tbsp olive oil in a skillet and add the tofu, radishes, onions, mushrooms, and bell peppers. Season with salt and pepper; cook for 10 minutes. Share into 4 bowls. Heat the remaining oil in the skillet, crack an egg into the pan, and cook until the white sets, but the yolk quite runny. Transfer to the top of one tofu-radish hash bowl and make the remaining eggs. Top the bowls with tomato salsa, parsley, and avocado. Serve.
Per serving: Cal 353; Net Carbs 5.9g, Fat 25g, Protein 19g

Mascarpone and Kale Asian Casserole

Ingredients for 4 servings
2 cups tofu, grilled and cubed
1 cup smoked seitan, chopped
1 cup mascarpone cheese
1 tbsp mustard powder
1 tbsp plain vinegar
1 ¼ cups cheddar, shredded
½ cup kale, chopped
2 tbsp olive oil
Directions and Total Time: approx. 30 minutes

Mix the mascarpone cheese, mustard powder, plain vinegar, kale, and cheddar cheese in a greased baking dish. Top with the tofu, seitan, and season with salt and black pepper. Bake in the oven until the casserole is golden brown on top, for about 15 to 20 minutes, at 400 F. Serve.

Per serving: Cal 612; Net Carbs 9.1g; Fat 51g; Protein 30.5g

Cauliflower Couscous & Halloumi Packets

Ingredients for 4 servings
2 heads cauliflower, chopped
¼ cup vegetable broth
1 lemon, juiced
2 tbsp sugar-free maple syrup
1 red bell pepper, chopped
1 orange bell pepper, chopped
¼ cup cubed halloumi
Olive oil to drizzle

Directions and Total Time: approx. 25 minutes
Preheat oven to 350 F. Put cauliflower in a food processor and pulse until a coarse consistency is achieved. Pour the couscous and vegetable stock into a pot and cook for 2-3 minutes. Drain and set aside. In a bowl, whisk lemon juice and maple syrup, and set aside. Cut out two 2 x 15 inches parchment papers onto a flat surface spoon the couscous in the middle of each, top with bell peppers, halloumi cheese, and drizzle the dressing on top. Wrap papers into parcels and place on a baking tray; cook for 15 minutes. Remove and carefully open the pouches. Serve warm.

Per serving: Cal 240; Net Carbs 4.7g, Fat 19g, Protein 5.1g

Mushroom White Pizza

Ingredients for 4 servings
2 tbsp flax egg + 6 tbsp water
½ cup mayonnaise
¾ cup almond flour
1 tbsp psyllium husk powder
1 tsp baking soda
½ tsp salt
¼ cup mushrooms, sliced
1 tbsp oregano
1 tbsp basil pesto
2 tbsp olive oil
Salt and black pepper

½ cup coconut cream
¾ cup Parmesan, shredded
6 black olives

Directions and Total Time: approx. 35 minutes
Combine the flax seed powder with water and allow sitting to thicken for 5 minutes. Whisk in mayonnaise, almond flour, psyllium husk powder, baking soda, and salt. Allow sitting for 5 minutes. Pour the batter into a greased baking sheet. Bake for 10 minutes at 350 F. In a bowl, mix mushrooms with pesto, olive oil, salt, and pepper. Remove the crust from the oven and spread the coconut cream on top. Add the mushroom mixture and Parmesan cheese. Bake the pizza further until the cheese melts, for 10 minutes. Spread the olives on top and serve.

Per serving: Cal 346; Net Carbs 5.5g; Fat 32.7g; Protein 8g

Garam Masala Traybake

Ingredients for 4 servings
3 tbsp butter
3 cups tempeh slices
1 turnip, sliced
Salt to taste
2 tbsp garam masala
1 cup mushrooms, sliced
1 ¼ cups coconut cream
1 tbsp fresh cilantro, chopped

Directions and Total Time: approx. 30 minutes
Place a skillet and melt butter. Fry tempeh for 4 minutes. Stir half of the garam masala into the tempeh until evenly mixed and turn the heat off. Transfer the tempeh with the spice into a baking dish and set aside. In a bowl, mix the mushrooms, turnip, coconut cream, cilantro, and remaining garam masala. Pour the mixture over tempeh and bake for 20 minutes at 400 F. Garnish with cilantro.

Per serving: Cal 591; Net Carbs 9.4g; Fat 48.4g; Protein 28g

Walnut Chocolate Squares

Ingredients for 6 servings
3½ oz dairy-free dark chocolate
4 tbsp vegan butter
1 pinch salt
¼ cup walnut butter
½ tsp vanilla extract

¼ cup chopped walnuts
Directions and Total Time: approx. 10 minutes
Microwave chocolate and vegan butter for 2 minutes. Remove and mix in salt, walnut butter, and vanilla extract. Grease a small baking sheet with cooking spray and line with parchment paper. Pour in the batter and top with walnuts and chill in the refrigerator. Cut into squares.
Per serving: Cal 125; Net Carbs 3g; Fat 10g; Protein 2g

Cauliflower & Broccoli Gratin with Seitan

Ingredients for 4 servings
4 tbsp avocado oil
2 shallots, chopped
2 cups broccoli florets
1 cup cauliflower florets
2 cups seitan, crumbled
1 cup heavy cream
2 tbsp mustard powder
5 oz Pecorino, shredded
4 tbsp rosemary, chopped
Salt and black pepper to taste
Directions and Total Time: approx. 40 minutes
Heat half of the avocado oil in a pot and add shallots, broccoli, and cauliflower and cook for 6 minutes. Transfer the vegetables to a baking dish. Warm the remaining avocado oil in a skillet and cook the seitan until browned. Mix heavy cream and mustard powder in a bowl. Then, pour the mixture over the vegetables. Scatter seitan and Pecorino cheese on top and sprinkle with rosemary, salt ,and pepper. Bake for 15 minutes at 400 F. Serve.
Per serving: Cal 753; Net Carbs 12g; Fat 37g; Protein 86g

Baked Creamy Brussels Sprouts

Ingredients for 4 servings
3 tbsp ghee
1 cup tempeh, cubed
1 lb Brussels sprouts, halved
5 garlic cloves, minced
1 ¼ cups crème fraîche
1 ⅓ cups cheddar, shredded
¼ cup Gruyère, shredded
Salt and black pepper to taste

Directions and Total Time: approx. 25 minutes
Melt ghee in a large skillet and fry tempeh for 6 minutes; set aside. Pour Brussels sprouts and garlic into the skillet and sauté until nice color forms. Stir in crème fraîche and simmer for 4 minutes. Add tempeh cubes and mix well. Pour the sautéed ingredients into a baking dish, sprinkle with cheddar cheese and Gruyère cheese. Bake for 10 minutes at 400 F or until golden brown on top. Serve.
Per serving: Cal 563; Net Carbs 8.7g; Fat 44g; Protein 25.2g

Mom's Cheesy Pizza

Ingredients for 4 servings
1 cup sliced mozzarella
1 cup grated mozzarella
3 tbsp grated Parmesan
½ cup almond flour
¼ tsp salt
2 tbsp ground psyllium husk
1 tbsp olive oil
½ cup sugar-free pizza sauce
2 tsp Italian seasoning
1 cup lukewarm water
Directions and Total Time: approx. 35 minutes
Preheat oven to 390 F and line a pizza pan with parchment paper. In a bowl, mix almond flour, salt, psyllium powder, olive oil, and water until dough forms. Spread the mixture on the pizza pan and bake for 10 minutes. Remove the crust and spread the pizza sauce on top. Add the sliced mozzarella, grated mozzarella, Parmesan cheese, and Italian seasoning. Bake for 18 minutes. Slice and serve.
Per serving: Cal 193; Net Carbs 3.2g; Fats 10g; Protein 19g

Easy Cheesy Green Pizza

Ingredients for 4 servings
¼ cup canned artichokes, cut into wedges
2 tbsp flax seed powder + 6 tbsp water
1 cup broccoli, grated
1 red bell pepper, sliced
1 cup Parmesan, shredded
½ tsp salt
2 tbsp marinara sauce
¼ cup mozzarella cheese
1 garlic clove, thinly sliced

1 tbsp dried oregano

Directions and Total Time: approx. 40 minutes

In a bowl, mix flax seed powder and water and allow thickening for 5 minutes. Add broccoli, ¾ cup of Parmesan cheese, salt, and stir to combine well. Pour the mixture into a baking sheet and spread out with a spatula. Bake for about 20 minutes at 350 F. Remove from the oven and spread the marinara sauce on top, sprinkle with the remaining Parmesan and mozzarella cheeses, artichokes, red bell pepper slices, and garlic. Spread the oregano on top. Bake for 10 minutes at 420 F. Slice to serve.

Per serving: Cal 108; Net Carbs 4.8g; Fat 5.4g; Protein 9.2g

Keto Brownies

Ingredients for 4 servings
2 tbsp flax seed powder
¼ cup cocoa powder
½ cup almond flour
½ tsp baking powder
½ cup erythritol
10 tbsp vegan butter
2 oz dairy-free dark chocolate
½ tsp vanilla extract

Directions and Total Time: approx. 30 min+ chilling time

Preheat oven to 375 F and line a baking sheet with parchment paper. Mix the flax seed powder with 6 tbsp water in a bowl and allow thickening for 5 minutes. In a separate bowl, mix cocoa powder, almond flour, baking powder, and erythritol until no lumps from the erythritol remain. In another bowl, add butter and dark chocolate and microwave both for 30 seconds. Whisk flax egg and vanilla into the chocolate mixture, then pour the mixture into the dry ingredients; mix well. Pour the batter onto the paper-lined sheet and bake for 20 minutes. Let cool completely and refrigerate for 2 hours. Slice into squares.

Per serving: Cal 227; Net Carbs 3g; Fat 19g; Protein 4g

Mixed Berry Yogurt Ice Pops

Ingredients for 6 servings
2/3 cup frozen strawberries & blueberries, thawed
2/3 cup avocado, halved, pitted
1 cup dairy-free yogurt
½ cup coconut cream
1 tsp vanilla extract

Directions and Total Time: approx. 2 min+ chilling time

Pour avocado pulp, berries, dairy-free yogurt, coconut cream, and vanilla extract. Process until smooth. Pour into ice pop sleeves and freeze for 8 hours. Serve when ready.

Per serving: Cal 80; Net Carbs 4g; Fat 5g; Protein 2g

Speedy Custard Tart

Ingredients for 4 servings
¼ cup butter, cold and crumbled
¼ cup almond flour
3 tbsp coconut flour
½ tsp salt
3 tbsp erythritol
1 ½ tsp vanilla extract
4 whole eggs
2 whole eggs + 3 egg yolks
½ cup swerve sugar
1 tsp vanilla bean paste
2 tbsp coconut flour
1 ¼ cup almond milk
1 ¼ cup heavy cream
2 tbsp sugar-free maple syrup
¼ cup chopped almonds

Directions and Total Time: approx. 75 minutes

Preheat oven to 350 F and grease a pie pan with cooking spray. In a bowl, mix almond flour, coconut flour, and salt. Add in butter and mix with an electric mixer until crumbly. Add in erythritol and vanilla extract and mix. Pour in the four eggs one after another while mixing until formed into a ball. Dust a clean flat surface with almond flour, unwrap the dough, and roll out the dough into a large rectangle, fit into the pie pan; prick the base of the crust. Bake until golden. Remove after and allow cooling.

In a mixing bowl, whisk the 2 whole eggs, 3 egg yolks, swerve sugar, vanilla bean paste, and coconut flour. Put almond milk, heavy cream, and maple syrup into a pot and bring to a boil. Pour the mixture into the egg mix and whisk while pouring. Run batter through a fine strainer into a bowl and skim off any froth. Remove the parchment paper, and transfer the egg batter into the pie. Bake for

45 minutes. Garnish with almonds, slice, and serve.

Per serving: Cal 459; Net Carbs 1.2g, Fat 40g, Protein 12g

Vegan Cheesecake with Blueberries

Ingredients for 6 servings

2 oz vegan butter
1 ¼ cups almond flour
3 tbsp Swerve sugar
½ tsp vanilla extract
3 tbsp flax seed powder
2 cups dairy-free cream cheese
½ cup coconut cream
1 tsp lemon zest
½ tsp vanilla extract
2 oz fresh blueberries

Directions and Total Time: approx. 70 min+ chilling time

Preheat oven to 350 F. Line a springform pan with parchment paper. Melt vegan butter in a skillet until nutty in flavor. Turn the heat off and stir in almond flour, 2 tbsp swerve, and vanilla until a dough forms. Press the mixture into the springform pan and bake for 8 minutes. Mix the flax seed powder with 9 tbsp water and allow sitting for 5 minutes. In a bowl, combine cream cheese, coconut cream, remaining swerve, lemon zest, vanilla extract, and flax egg. Remove the crust from oven and pour the mixture on top. Bake the cake for 15 minutes at 400 F. Reduce the heat 230 F and bake further for 50 minutes. Refrigerate overnight and scatter the blueberries on top.

Per serving: Cal 330; Net Carbs 4g; Fat 31g; Protein 8g

Pistachio Heart Biscuits

Ingredients for 4 servings

1 cup butter, softened
2/3 cup swerve sugar
1 large egg, beaten
2 tsp pistachio extract
2 cups almond flour
½ cup dark chocolate
Chopped pistachios

Directions and Total Time: approx. 30 min + cooling time

Add butter and swerve to a bowl; beat until smooth and creamy. Whisk in egg until combined. Mix in pistachio extract and flour

until a smooth dough forms. Wrap the dough in plastic wrap and chill for 10 minutes. Preheat oven to 350 F and lightly dust a chopping board with some almond flour. Unwrap the dough and roll out to 2-inch thickness. Cut out as many biscuits as you can get while rerolling the trimming and making more biscuits. Arrange the biscuits on the parchment paper-lined baking sheet and bake for 15 minutes. Transfer to a wire rack to cool completely. In 2 separate bowls, melt chocolate in a microwave while adding some maple syrup for taste. Dip one side of each biscuit in the dark chocolate and then in the white chocolate. Garnish dark chocolate's side with the pistachios and cool on the wire rack.

Per serving: Cal 470; Net Carbs 3.4g, Fat 45g, Protein 6.2g

Lime Avocado Ice Cream

Ingredients for 4 servings

2 large avocados, pitted
Juice and zest of 3 limes
1/3 cup erythritol
1¾ cups coconut cream
¼ tsp vanilla extract

Directions and Total Time: approx. 10 minutes

In a blender, combine avocado pulp, lime juice and zest, erythritol, coconut cream, and vanilla extract. Process until smooth. Pour the mixture into an ice cream maker and freeze. When ready, remove and scoop the ice cream into bowls. Serve immediately.

Per serving: Cal 260; Net Carbs 4g; Fat 25g; Protein 4g

Red Berries Fat Bombs

Ingredients for 4 servings

1 cup strawberries
1 cup raspberries
1 cup cranberries
1 tsp vanilla extract
16 oz cream cheese, softened
4 tbsp unsalted butter
2 tbsp sugar-free maple syrup

Directions and Total Time: approx. 20 minutes

Line a muffin tray with liners and set aside. Puree the fruits in a blender with the vanilla. In a saucepan, melt cream cheese and butter together over medium heat until mixed. In a bowl, combine the fruit, cheese mixtures, and maple syrup evenly and fill the muffin tray with the mix. Refrigerate for 40 minutes and serve.

Per serving: Cal 227, Net Carbs 3.1g, Fat 15g, Protein 4g

Cardamom Coconut Fat Bombs

Ingredients for 6 servings
½ cup grated coconut
3 oz vegan butter, softened
¼ tsp cardamom powder
½ tsp vanilla extract
¼ tsp cinnamon powder

Directions and Total Time: approx. 5 minutes
Pour grated coconut into a skillet and roast until lightly brown. Set aside to cool. In a bowl, combine butter, half of the coconut, cardamom, vanilla, and cinnamon. Form balls from the mixture and roll each in the remaining coconut. Refrigerate until ready to serve.

Per serving: Cal 85; Net Carbs 1g; Fat 9g; Protein 1g

Chocolate Peppermint Mousse

Ingredients for 4 servings
¼ cup swerve sugar, divided
4 oz dairy-free cream cheese,
3 tbsp cocoa powder
¾ tsp peppermint extract
½ tsp vanilla extract
1/3 cup coconut cream

Directions and Total Time: approx. 10 min+ chilling time
Put 2 tbsp of swerve, cream cheese, and cocoa powder in a blender. Add in peppermint extract, and ¼ cup warm water; process until smooth. In a bowl, whip vanilla extract, coconut cream, and remaining swerve using a whisk. Fetch out 5 tbsp for garnishing. Fold in cocoa mixture until thoroughly combined. Spoon the mousse into cups and refrigerate. Garnish with whipped cream.

Per serving: Cal 170; Net Carbs 2g; Fat 16g; Protein 3g

Raspberries Turmeric Panna Cotta

Ingredients for 6 servings

½ tbsp unflavored powdered vegetarian gelatin
2 cups coconut cream
¼ tsp vanilla extract
1 pinch turmeric powder
1 tbsp erythritol
1 tbsp chopped toasted pecans
12 fresh raspberries

Directions and Total Time: approx. 10 min+ chilling time
Mix gelatin and ½ tsp water and allow sitting to dissolve. Pour coconut cream, vanilla extract, turmeric, and erythritol into a saucepan and bring to a boil, then, simmer for 2 minutes. Turn the heat off. Stir in gelatin. Pour into 6 glasses, cover with a plastic wrap, and refrigerate for 2 hours. Top with pecans and raspberries, and serve.

Per serving: Cal 270; Net Carbs 3g; Fat 27g; Protein 4g

Dark Chocolate Cake

Ingredients for 4 servings
½ cup olive oil
1 cup almond flour
½ cup dark chocolate, melted
1 cup swerve sugar
2 tsp vanilla bean paste
½ tsp salt
2 tsp cinnamon powder
½ cup boiling water
3 large eggs

Directions and Total Time: approx. 5 minutes
Preheat oven to 350 F and grease a springform pan and line with parchment paper. In a bowl, combine olive oil, almond flour, chocolate, swerve, vanilla bean paste, salt, cinnamon, and boiling water. Crack the eggs one after the other, beating until smooth. Pour batter into the springform pan and bake for 45 minutes. Remove from oven; allow cooling in the pan for 10 minutes; turn over onto a wire rack. Dust with confectioner's sugar, and serve.

Per serving: Cal 417; Net Carbs 1.7g, Fat 41g, Protein 16g

Mint Chocolate Cheesecake

Ingredients for 4 servings
1 cup raw almonds
½ cup salted butter, melted

2 tbsp + ½ cup swerve sugar
1 cup dark chocolate, chopped
2 gelatin sheets
2 tbsp lime juice
1 ½ cups cream cheese
1 cup Greek yogurt
1 tbsp mint extract

Directions and Total Time: approx. 15 minutes

Preheat oven to 350 F. In a blender, process the almonds until finely ground. Add in butter and 2 tbsp of swerve, and mix until combined. Press the crust mixture into the bottom of the cake pan until firm. Bake for 5 minutes. Place in the fridge to chill. In a pot, combine gelatin with lime juice, and a tbsp of water. Let set for 5 minutes and, place the pot over medium heat to dissolve the gelatin. Pour dark chocolate in a bowl and melt in the microwave for 1 minute; set aside. In another bowl, beat cream cheese and remaining swerve sugar using an electric mixer until smooth. Stir in yogurt and gelatin until combined. Fold in melted chocolate and then the mint extract. Remove the pan from the fridge and pour the cream mixture on top. Tap the side gently to release any trapped air bubbles and transfer to the fridge to chip for 3 hours or more. Remove and release the pan's locker, top with more dark chocolate.

Per serving: Cal 235g, Net Carbs 3.8g, Fat 14g, Protein 7g

Dark Chocolate Fudge

Ingredients for 4 servings
1 cup dark chocolate, melted
4 large eggs
1 cup swerve sugar
½ cup melted butter
1/3 cup coconut flour

Directions and Total Time: approx. 30 minutes

Preheat oven to 350 F and line a rectangular baking tray with parchment paper. In a bowl, cream the eggs with swerve sugar until smooth. Add in melted chocolate, butter, and whisk until evenly combined. Carefully fold in the coconut flour to incorporate and pour the mixture into the baking tray. Bake for 20 minutes or until a toothpick inserted comes out clean. Remove from the oven and allow cooling in the tray. Cut into squares and serve.

Per serving: Cal 491; Net Carbs 2.8g, Fat 45g, Protein 13g

Key Lime Truffles

Ingredients for 6 servings
¼ cup cocoa powder mixed with 2 tbsp swerve sugar
1 cup dark chocolate, chopped
2/3 cup heavy cream
2 tsp lime extract

Directions and Total Time: approx. 5 min + cooling time

Heat heavy cream in a pan over low heat until tiny bubbles form around the edges of the pan. Turn the heat off. Pour dark chocolate into the pan, swirl the pan to allow the hot cream to spread over the chocolate, and then gently stir the mixture until smooth. Mix in lime extract and transfer to a bowl. Refrigerate for 4 hours. Line 2 baking trays with parchment papers; set one aside and pour cocoa powder mixture onto the other. Take out the chocolate mixture; form bite-size balls out of the mix and roll all round in the cocoa powder to completely coat. Place the truffles on the baking tray and refrigerate for 30 minutes before serving.

Per serving: Cal 143; Net Carbs 0.6g, Fat 12g, Protein 2.4g

Lemon Sponge Cake with Cream

Ingredients for 4 servings
1 tbsp swerve confectioner's sugar, for dusting
4 large lemons, chopped
¼ cup sugar-free maple syrup
½ cup butter, softened
½ cup erythritol
1 tsp vanilla extract
½ cup almond flour, sifted
3 large eggs, lightly beaten
½ cup heavy cream

Directions and Total Time: approx. 40 minutes

Place the chopped lemons in a saucepan. Add in sugar-free maple syrup and simmer over low heat for 30 minutes. Pour the mixture into a blender and process until smooth. Pour into a jar and set aside. Preheat oven to 350 F, grease two (8-inch) springform pans with cooking spray, and line with parchment paper. In a bowl, cream the butter, erythritol, and vanilla extract with an electric whisk until light and fluffy. Pour in the eggs gradually while beating until fully mixed. Carefully fold in the almond flour and share the mixture into the cake pans. Bake for 30 minutes or until springy when touched and a toothpick inserted comes out clean. Remove and let cool for 5 minutes before turning out onto a wire rack. In a bowl, whip heavy cream until a soft peak forms. Spoon onto the bottom sides of the cake and spread the lemon puree on top. Sandwich both cakes and sift confectioner's sugar on top. Slice and serve.

Per serving: Cal 266; Net Carbs 4.6g; Fat 25g; Protein 6g

Zucchini Cake Slices

Ingredients for 4 servings
1 cup butter, softened
1 cup erythritol
4 eggs
2/3 cup coconut flour
2 tsp baking powder
2/3 cup ground almonds
1 lemon, zested and juiced
1 cup finely grated zucchini
1 cup crème fraiche
1 tbsp chopped walnuts

Directions and Total Time: approx. 30 min + cooling time
Preheat oven to 375 F, grease a springform pan with and line with parchment paper. In a bowl, beat butter and erythritol until creamy and pale. Add eggs one after another while whisking. Sift coconut flour and baking powder into the mixture and stir along with ground almonds, lemon zest, juice, and zucchini. Spoon the mixture into the pan and bake for 40 minutes or until risen and a toothpick inserted into the cake comes out clean. Let cool inside the pan for 10 minutes, and transfer to a wire rack. Spread crème fraiche on top and sprinkle with walnuts to serve.

Per serving: Cal 778; Net Carbs 3.7g, Fat 71g, Protein 32g

Blackberry Lemon Tarte Tatin

Ingredients for 4 servings
¼ cup butter, cold and crumbled
¼ cup almond flour

3 tbsp coconut flour
½ tsp salt
3 tbsp erythritol
1 ½ tsp vanilla extract
4 whole eggs
4 tbsp melted butter
3 tsp swerve brown sugar
1 cup fresh blackberries
1 tsp vanilla extract
1 lemon, juiced
1 cup ricotta cheese
4 fresh basil leaves to garnish
1 egg, lightly beaten

Directions and Total Time: approx. 50 minutes
Preheat oven to 350 F. In a bowl, mix almond and coconut flour, and salt. Add in butter and mix until crumbly. Mix in erythritol and vanilla extract. Pour in the 4 eggs and mix until formed into a ball. Flatten the dough on a clean flat surface, cover in plastic wrap, and refrigerate for 1 hour. Dust a clean flat surface with almond flour, unwrap the dough, and roll out the dough into a circle. In a greased baking pan, mix butter, swerve brown sugar, blackberries, vanilla extract, and lemon juice. Arrange blackberries uniformly across the pan. Lay the pastry over the fruit filling and tuck the sides into the pan. Brush with beaten egg and bake for 40 minutes. Turn the pie onto a plate, crumble ricotta cheese on top, and garnish with basil.

Per serving: Cal 465; Net Carbs 5.8g, Fat 41g, Protein 16g

Avocado Truffles with Chocolate Coating

Ingredients for 6 servings
1 ripe avocado, pitted
½ tsp vanilla extract
½ tsp lemon zest
5 oz dark chocolate
1 tbsp coconut oil
1 tbsp cocoa powder

Directions and Total Time: approx. 5 minutes
Scoop pulp of the avocado into a bowl and mix with vanilla using an immersion blender. Stir in lemon zest and a pinch of salt. Microwave chocolate and coconut oil for 1 minute. Add to the avocado mixture and stir.

124

Allow cooling to firm up a bit. Form balls out of the mix. Roll each ball in the cocoa powder and serve immediately.

Per serving: Cal 70; Net Carbs 2g; Fat 6g; Protein 2g

Strawberry Blackberry Pie

Ingredients for 4 servings
¼ cup butter, cold and crumbled
2 ¼ cup strawberries and blackberries
1 vanilla pod, bean paste extracted
¼ cup almond flour
3 tbsp coconut flour
½ tsp salt
3 tbsp + 1 cup erythritol
1 ½ tsp vanilla extract
4 whole eggs
1 egg, beaten

Directions and Total Time: approx. 30 min + cooling time
Preheat oven to 350 F. In a bowl, mix almond and coconut flours, and salt. Add in butter and mix until crumbly. Stir in 3 tbsp of erythritol and vanilla extract. Pour in the 4 eggs one after another while mixing until formed into a ball. Cover the dough with plastic wrap, and refrigerate for 1 hour. Dust a clean flat surface with almond flour, unwrap the dough, and roll out into a large rectangle to fit into a greased pie pan; prick the base of the crust. Bake until golden. In a bowl, mix berries, remaining erythritol, and vanilla paste. Spoon mixture into the pie and use the pastry strips to create a lattice over the berries. Brush with beaten egg and bake for 30 minutes. Slice and serve.

Per serving: Cal 262; Net Carbs 3g, Fat 21.7g, Protein 9g

Berry Hazelnut Trifle

Ingredients for 4 servings
1 ½ ripe avocados
¾ cup coconut cream
Zest and juice of ½ a lemon
1 tbsp vanilla extract
3 oz fresh strawberries
2 oz toasted hazelnuts

Directions and Total Time: approx. 5 minutes
In a bowl, add avocado pulp, coconut cream, lemon zest and juice, and half of the vanilla extract. Mix with an immersion blender. Put

the strawberries and remaining vanilla in another bowl and use a fork to mash the fruits. In a tall glass, alternate layering the cream and strawberry mixtures. Drop a few hazelnuts on each and serve.

Per serving: Cal 360; Net Carbs 7g; Fat 34g; Protein 4g

Coconut Chocolate Fudge

Ingredients for 6 servings
2 cups coconut cream
1 tsp vanilla extract
3 oz vegan butter
3 oz dark chocolate, chopped
Swerve sugar for sprinkling

Directions and Total Time: approx. 20 min+ chilling time
Pour coconut cream and vanilla into a saucepan and bring to a boil over medium heat, then simmer until reduced by half, about 15 minutes. Stir in vegan butter until the batter is smooth. Add in dark chocolate and stir until melted. Pour the mixture into a baking sheet; chill in the fridge. Cut into squares, sprinkle with swerve sugar, and serve.

Per serving: Cal 116; Net Carbs 3g; Fat 11g; Protein 2g

Raspberry & Red Wine Crumble

Ingredients for 6 servings
2 cups raspberries
¼ cup red wine
1 teaspoon cinnamon
1 ¼ cup erythritol, divided
1 tsp vanilla extract
1 cup salted butter, cubed
1 ½ cups almond flour
¾ cup coconut flour

Directions and Total Time: approx. 55 minutes
Preheat oven 375 F. In a baking dish, add raspberries, red wine, half of erythritol, vanilla extract, and stir. In a bowl, rub butter with almond and coconut flours, and erythritol until it resembles large breadcrumbs. Spoon the mixture to cover the raspberries, place in the oven, and bake for 45 minutes until the top is golden brown. Cool and serve.

Per serving: Cal 318; Net Carbs 4.8g, Fat 31g, Protein 1.5g

Avocado Fries

Ingredients for 2 servings
½ cup olive oil
3 avocados, sliced
1 ½ tbsp almond flour
Salt and black pepper to taste
1 cup grated Parmesan cheese
2 large eggs, beaten in a bowl
Directions and Total Time: approx. 10 minutes
In a bowl, combine flour, salt, pepper, and Parmesan. Toss avocado slices in eggs and then dredge in the Parmesan mixture. Heat olive oil in a deep pan. Fry avocado slices until golden brown, 2 minutes, and transfer to a wire rack.
Per serving: Cal 849; Net Carbs 7.2g; Fat 77g; Protein 21g

Cacao Nut Bites

Ingredients for 4 servings
3 ½ oz dark chocolate
½ cup mixed nuts
2 tbsp roasted coconut chips
1 tbsp sunflower seeds
Directions and Total Time: approx. 5 minutes
Microwave chocolate for 2 minutes. Into 10 small cupcake liners, share the chocolate. Drop in nuts, coconut chips, sunflower seeds and sprinkle with salt. Chill until firm.
Per serving: Cal 72; Net Carbs 3g; Fat 5g; Protein 2g

Cranberry Coconut Parfait

Ingredients for 4 servings
2 cups coconut yogurt
¼ cup fresh cranberries
½ lemon, zested
3 mint sprigs, chopped
2 tbsp hemp seeds
Sugar-free maple syrup to taste
Directions and Total Time: approx. 5 minutes
In serving glasses, add half of coconut yogurt, cranberries, lemon zest, mint, hemp seeds, and drizzle with maple syrup. Repeat a second layer. Serve with maple syrup.
Per serving: Cal 105; Net Carbs 2.9g, Fat 7.8g, Protein 5g

SNACKS & SIDE DISHES

Jalapeño Nacho Wings

Ingredients for 4 servings
2 cups shredded Mexican cheese blend
16 chicken wings, halved
½ cup butter, melted
1 cup golden flaxseed meal
2 tbsp chopped green chilies
1 cup chopped scallions
1 jalapeño pepper, sliced

Directions and Total Time: approx. 45 minutes
Preheat oven to 350 F. Toss chicken with butter, salt, pepper to coat. Spread the flaxseed meal in a wide plate and roll in each chicken wing. Place on a baking sheet and bake for 30-35 minutes or until golden brown and cooked within. Sprinkle with the cheese blend, green chilies, scallions, and jalapeño pepper on top. Serve immediately.
Per serving: Cal 798; Net Carbs 1.5g; Fat 61g; Protein 48g

Easy Bacon & Cheese Balls

Ingredients for 4 servings
7 bacon slices, chopped
6 oz cream cheese
6 oz shredded Gruyere cheese
2 tbsp butter, softened
½ tsp red chili flakes

Directions and Total Time: approx. 30 minutes
Put bacon in a skillet and fry over medium heat until crispy, 5 minutes. Transfer to a plate, crumble after. Pour the bacon grease into a bowl and mix in cream cheese, Gruyere cheese, butter, and red chili flakes. Refrigerate to set for 15 minutes. Remove and mold into walnut-sized balls. Roll in the crumbled bacon. Plate and serve.
Per serving: Cal 538; Net Carbs 0.5g; Fat 50g; Protein 22g

Chili Turnip Fries

Ingredients for 4 servings
6 large parsnips, sliced
3 tbsp ground pork rinds
3 tbsp olive oil
¼ tsp red chili flakes

Directions and Total Time: approx. 50 minutes
Preheat oven to 425 F. Pour parsnips into a bowl and add in pork rinds, salt, and pepper. Toss and divide the parsnips between 2 baking sheets. Drizzle with olive oil and sprinkle with chili flakes. Bake in the oven until crispy, 40 to 45 minutes, tossing halfway. Serve.
Per serving: Cal 260; Net Carbs 22.6g; Fat 11g; Protein 3g

Baked Toast Strips with Prosciutto Butter

Ingredients for 4 servings
4 slices prosciutto, chopped
2 shallots
½ cup butter, softened
1 tbsp fresh basil
1 tsp tomato paste
4 slices zero carb bread
2 tbsp extra-virgin olive oil

Directions and Total Time: approx. 0 minutes
Add prosciutto, 1 tbsp of butter, and shallots to a skillet. Cook with frequent stirring for 5 minutes; let cool. Mix in the remaining butter, basil, and tomato paste. Season with salt and pepper. Spoon into a bowl and chill for 30 minutes to solidify slightly. Brush zero carb bread with olive oil, cut into strips, place on a baking sheet and toast for 3-5 minutes in a preheated at 400 F oven or until brown and crispy. Sprinkle with salt, and serve with prosciutto butter.
Per serving: Cal 315; Net Carbs 8.8g; Fat 28g; Protein 5g

Wrapped Halloumi in Bacon

Ingredients for 4 servings
16 bacon strips
½ lb halloumi cheese, cut into 16 cubes
½ cup swerve brown sugar
½ cup mayonnaise
¼ cup hot sauce

Directions and Total Time: approx. 30 minutes
Lay bacon in a skillet and cook over medium heat on both sides until crisp, 5 minutes; transfer to a plate. Wrap each halloumi

cheese with a bacon strip and secure with a toothpick each. Place on a baking sheet. In a bowl, combine brown sugar, mayonnaise, and hot sauce. Pour the mixture all over the bacon-halloumi pieces and bake in the oven at 350 F for 10 minutes. Let cool and serve.

Per serving: Cal 346; Net Carbs 4.6g; Fat 25g; Protein 13g

Sweet Mustard Mini Sausages

Ingredients for 4 servings
1 cup swerve brown sugar
3 tbsp almond flour
2 tsp mustard powder
¼ cup lemon juice
¼ cup white vinegar
1 tsp tamari sauce
2 lb mini smoked sausages

Directions and Total Time: approx. 15 minutes
In a pot, combine swerve, flour, and mustard. Gradually stir in lemon juice, vinegar, and tamari sauce. Bring to a boil over medium heat while stirring until thickened, 2 minutes. Mix in sausages until properly coated. Cook them for 5 minutes. Dish the food into plates and serve.

Per serving: Cal 744; Net Carbs 7.2g; Fat 45g; Protein 24g

Chili Broccoli & Pancetta Roast

Ingredients for 4 servings
1 lb broccoli rabe, halved
6 pancetta slices, chopped
2 tbsp olive oil
¼ tsp red chili flakes

Directions and Total Time: approx. 40 minutes
Preheat oven to 425 F. Scatter broccoli rabe in a baking sheet, top with pancetta, drizzle with olive oil, season to taste, and with sprinkle chili flakes. Roast for 30 minutes.

Per serving: Cal 125; Net Carbs 0.2g; Fat 10g; Protein 7g

Cheesy Bacon & Eggplant Gratin

Ingredients for 4 servings
6 bacon slices, chopped
3 large eggplants, sliced
1 tbsp dried oregano
1/3 cup chopped parsley
Salt and black pepper to taste

½ cup crumbled feta cheese
¾ cup heavy cream
½ cup shredded Parmesan

Directions and Total Time: approx. 50 minutes
Preheat oven to 400 F. Put bacon in a skillet and fry over medium heat until brown and crispy, 6 minutes; transfer to a plate. Arrange half of eggplants in a greased baking sheet, season with oregano, parsley, salt, and pepper. Scatter half of bacon and half of feta cheese on top and repeat the layering process using the remaining ingredients. In a bowl, combine heavy cream with half of Parmesan, and spread on top of the layered ingredients. Sprinkle with the remaining Parmesan. Bake until the cream is bubbly and the gratin golden, 20 minutes. Serve.

Per serving: Cal 433; Net Carbs 1.7g; Fat 29g; Protein 16g

Buttery Radish & Minute Steak Sauté

Ingredients for 4 servings
10 oz minute steak, cut into small pieces
3 tbsp butter
1½ lb radishes, quartered
1 garlic clove, minced
2 tbsp freshly chopped thyme

Directions and Total Time: approx. 30 minutes
Melt in a skillet over, season the meat with salt and pepper, and fry until brown on all sides, 12 minutes; transfer to a plate. Add and sauté radishes, garlic, and thyme until the radishes cook within, 10 minutes. Plate and serve warm.

Per serving: Cal 252; Net Carbs 0.4g; Fat 16g; Protein 21g

Delicious Pancetta Strawberries

Ingredients for 4 servings
2 tbsp swerve confectioner's sugar
1 cup mascarpone cheese
1/8 tsp white pepper
12 fresh strawberries
12 thin slices pancetta

Directions and Total Time: approx. 30 minutes
In a bowl, combine mascarpone, swerve, and white pepper. Coat strawberries in the cheese mixture, wrap each strawberry in a pancetta slice, and place on an ungreased baking sheet.

Bake in the oven for 425 F for 15-20 minutes until pancetta browns and is crispy. Serve warm.

Per serving: Cal 171; Net Carbs 1.2g; Fat 11g; Protein 12g

Salami & Cheddar Skewers

Ingredients for 4 servings

¼ cup olive oil
1 tbsp plain vinegar
2 garlic cloves, minced
1 tsp dried Italian herb blend
4 oz hard salami, cubed
¼ cup pitted Kalamata olives
12 oz cheddar cheese, cubed
1 tsp chopped parsley

Directions and Total Time: approx. 4 hours

In a bowl, mix olive oil, vinegar, garlic, and herb blend. Add in salami, olives, and cheddar cheese. Mix until well coated. Cover the bowl with plastic wrap and marinate in the refrigerator for 4 hours. Remove, drain the marinade and skewer one salami cube, one olive, and one cheese cube. Repeat making more skewers with the remaining ingredients. Plate and garnish with the parsley to serve.

Per serving: Cal 585; Net Carbs 1.8g; Fat 52g; Protein 27g

Chives & Green Beans Ham Rolls

Ingredients for 4 servings

8 oz Havarti cheese, cut into 16 strips
16 thin slices deli ham, cut in half lengthwise
1 medium sweet red pepper, cut into 16 strips
1 ½ cups water
16 fresh green beans
2 tbsp salted butter
16 whole chives

Directions and Total Time: approx. 50 minutes

Bring the water to a boil in a skillet over medium heat. Add in green beans, cover, and cook for 3 minutes or until softened; drain. Melt butter in a skillet and sauté green beans for 2 minutes; transfer to a plate. Assemble 1 green bean, 1 strip of red pepper, 1 cheese strip, and wrap with a ham slice. Tie with one chive. Repeat the assembling process with the remaining ingredients and refrigerate.

Per serving: Cal 399; Net Carbs 8.7g; Fat 24g; Protein 35g

Savory Pan-Fried Cauliflower & Bacon

Ingredients for 4 servings

1 large head cauliflower, cut into florets
10 oz bacon, chopped
1 garlic clove, minced
Salt and black pepper to taste
2 tbsp parsley, finely chopped

Directions and Total Time: approx. 15 minutes

Pour cauliflower in salted boiling water over medium heat and cook for 5 minutes or until soft; drain and set aside. In a skillet, fry bacon until brown and crispy. Add cauliflower and garlic. Sauté until the cauli browns slightly. Season with salt and pepper. Garnish with parsley and serve.

Per serving: Cal 243; Net Carbs 3.9g; Fat 21g; Protein 9g

Roasted Ham with Radishes

Ingredients for 4 servings

1 lb radishes, halved
Salt and black pepper to taste
1 tbsp cold butter
3 slices deli ham, chopped

Directions and Total Time: approx. 30 minutes

Preheat oven to 375 F. Arrange the radishes on a greased baking sheet. Season with salt and pepper; divide butter and ham on top. Bake for 25 minutes. Serve.

Per serving: Cal 68; Net Carbs 0.5g; Fat 4g; Protein 4g

Green Bean & Mozzarella Roast with Bacon

Ingredients for 4 servings

2 tbsp olive oil
1 tsp onion powder
1 egg, beaten
15 oz fresh green beans
5 tbsp grated mozzarella
4 bacon slices, chopped

Directions and Total Time: approx. 30 minutes

Preheat oven to 350 F and line a baking sheet with parchment paper. In a bowl, mix olive oil, onion and garlic powders, salt, pepper, and egg. Add in green beans and mozzarella; toss to coat. Pour the mixture onto the baking sheet and bake until the green beans brown slightly and cheese melts, 20 minutes. Fry bacon in a skillet until crispy and brown. Remove green beans and divide between serving plates. Top with bacon and serve.

Per serving: Cal 208; Net Carbs 2.6g; Fat 19g; Protein 6g

Cheddar Bacon & Celeriac Bake

Ingredients for 4 servings
6 bacon slices, chopped
3 tbsp butter
3 garlic cloves, minced
3 tbsp almond flour
2 cups coconut cream
1 cup chicken broth
Salt and black pepper to taste
2 lb celeriac, peeled and sliced
2 cups shredded cheddar
¼ cup chopped scallions

Directions and Total Time: approx. 1 hour 30 minutes
Preheat oven to 400 F. Add bacon to a skillet and fry over medium heat until brown and crispy. Spoon onto a plate. Melt butter in the same skillet and sauté garlic for 1 minute. Mix in almond flour and cook for another minute. Whisk in coconut cream, broth, and season with salt and pepper. Simmer for 5 minutes. Spread a layer of the sauce in a greased casserole dish, arrange a layer celeriac on top, cover with more sauce, top with some bacon and cheddar cheese, and scatter scallions on top. Repeat the layering process until the ingredients are exhausted. Bake for 75 minutes. Let rest and serve.

Per serving: Cal 981; Net Carbs 20.5g; Fat 86g; Protein 28g

Chicken Ham with Mini Bell Peppers

Ingredients for 4 servings
12 mini green bell peppers, halved and deseeded
4 slices chicken ham, chopped
1 tbsp chopped parsley
8 oz cream cheese
½ tbsp hot sauce
2 tbsp melted butter
1 cup shredded Gruyere

Directions and Total Time: approx. 30 minutes
Preheat oven to 400 F. Place peppers in a greased baking dish and set aside. In a bowl, combine chicken ham, parsley, cream cheese, hot sauce, and butter. Spoon the mixture into the peppers and sprinkle Gruyere cheese on top. Bake until the cheese melts, 15 minutes. Serve.

Per serving: Cal 408; Net Carbs 4g; Fat 32g; Protein 19g

Crispy Baked Cheese Asparagus

Ingredients for 4 servings
1 cup grated Pecorino Romano cheese
4 slices Serrano ham, chopped
2 lb asparagus, stalks trimmed
¾ cup coconut cream
3 garlic cloves, minced
1 cup crushed pork rinds
1 cup grated mozzarella
½ tsp sweet paprika

Directions and Total Time: approx. 40 minutes
Preheat oven to 400 F. Arrange asparagus on a greased baking dish and pour coconut cream on top. Scatter the garlic on top, season with salt and pepper, top with pork rinds, serrano ham, and sprinkle with Pecorino cheese, mozzarella, and paprika. Bake until the cheese melts and is golden and asparagus tender, 30 minutes. Serve.

Per serving: Cal 361; Net Carbs 15g; Fat 21g; Protein 32g

Creamy Ham & Parsnip Puree

Ingredients for 4 servings
2 lb parsnips, diced
3 tbsp olive oil, divided
2 tsp garlic powder
¾ cup almond milk
4 tbsp heavy cream
4 tbsp butter
6 slices deli ham, chopped
2 tsp freshly chopped oregano

Directions and Total Time: approx. 45 minutes
Preheat oven to 400 F. Spread parsnips on a greased baking sheet, drizzle with 2 tbsp olive oil, and season with salt and pepper. Cover tightly with aluminum foil and bake until the parsnips are tender, 40 minutes.

Remove from the oven, take off the foil, and transfer to a bowl. Add in garlic powder, almond milk, heavy cream, and butter. Using an immersion blender, puree the ingredients until smooth. Fold in the ham and sprinkle with oregano.

Per serving: Cal 477; Net Carbs 20g; Fat 30g; Protein 10g

Chili Baked Zucchini Sticks with Aioli

Ingredients for 4 servings
¼ cup Pecorino Romano cheese, shredded
¼ cup pork rind crumbs
1 tsp sweet paprika
Salt and chili pepper to taste
1 cup mayonnaise
Juice from half lemon
2 garlic cloves, minced
3 fresh eggs
2 zucchinis, cut into strips
Directions and Total Time: approx. 25 minutes
Preheat oven to 425 F and line a baking sheet with foil. In a bowl, mix pork rinds, paprika, Pecorino Romano cheese, salt, and chili pepper. Beat the eggs in another bowl. Coat zucchini strips in egg, then in the cheese mixture, and arrange on the sheet. Grease lightly with cooking spray and bake for 15 minutes. Combine in a bowl mayonnaise, lemon juice, and garlic, and gently stir until everything is well incorporated. Serve the strips with aioli.

Per serving: Cal 180; Net Carbs 2g; Fat 14g; Protein 6g

Cauliflower Rice & Bacon Gratin

Ingredients for 4 servings
1 cup canned artichoke hearts, drained and chopped
6 bacon slices, chopped
2 cups cauliflower rice
3 cups baby spinach, chopped
1 garlic clove, minced
1 tbsp olive oil
Salt and black pepper to taste
¼ cup sour cream
8 oz cream cheese, softened
¼ cup grated Parmesan
1 ½ cups grated mozzarella
Directions and Total Time: approx. 30 minutes

Preheat oven to 350 F. Cook bacon in a skillet over medium heat until brown and crispy, 5 minutes. Spoon onto a plate. In a bowl, mix cauli rice, artichokes, spinach, garlic, olive oil, salt, pepper, sour cream, cream cheese, bacon, and half of Parmesan cheese. Spread the mixture into a baking dish and top with the remaining Parmesan and mozzarella cheeses. Bake 15 minutes. Serve.

Per serving: Cal 500; Net Carbs 5.3g; Fat 37g; Protein 28g

Crunchy Rutabaga Puffs

Ingredients for 4 servings
1 rutabaga, peeled and diced
2 tbsp melted butter
½ oz goat cheese
¼ cup ground pork rinds
Directions and Total Time: approx. 35 minutes
Preheat oven to 400 F and spread rutabaga on a baking sheet. Season with salt, pepper, and drizzle with the butter. Bake until tender, 15 minutes. Transfer to a bowl. Allow cooling and add in goat cheese. Using a fork, mash and mix the ingredients. Pour the pork rinds onto a plate. Mold 1-inch balls out of the rutabaga mixture and roll properly in the rinds while pressing gently to stick. Place in the same baking sheet and bake for 10 minutes until golden.

Per serving: Cal 129; Net Carbs 5.9g; Fat 8g; Protein 3g

Crispy Pancetta & Butternut Squash Roast

Ingredients for 4 servings
2 butternut squash, cubed
1 tsp turmeric powder
½ tsp garlic powder
8 pancetta slices, chopped
2 tbsp olive oil
1 tbsp chopped cilantro,
Directions and Total Time: approx. 30 minutes
Preheat oven to 425 F. In a bowl, add butternut squash, salt, pepper, turmeric, garlic powder, pancetta, and olive oil. Toss until well-coated. Spread the mixture onto a greased baking sheet and roast for 10-15 minutes. Transfer the veggies to a bowl and garnish with cilantro to serve.

Per serving: Cal 148; Net Carbs 6.4g; Fat 10g; Protein 6g

Simple Stuffed Eggs with Mayonnaise

Ingredients for 6 servings
6 eggs
1 tbsp green tabasco
¼ cup mayonnaise
2 tbsp black olives, sliced

Directions and Total Time: approx. 30 minutes
Place eggs in a saucepan and cover with salted water. Boil for 10 minutes. Place the eggs in an ice bath and let cool. Peel and slice in half lengthwise. Scoop out the yolks to a bowl; mash with a fork. Whisk together the tabasco, mayonnaise, mashed yolks, and salt, in a bowl. Spoon this mixture into egg white. Garnish with olive slices to serve.
Per serving: Cal 178; Net Carbs: 5g; Fat: 17g; Protein: 6g

Cheesy Pork Rind Bread

Ingredients for 4 servings
¼ cup grated Pecorino Romano cheese
8 oz cream cheese
2 cups grated mozzarella
1 tbsp baking powder
1 cup crushed pork rinds
3 large eggs
1 tbsp Italian mixed herbs

Directions and Total Time: approx. 30 minutes
Preheat oven to 375 F and line a baking sheet with parchment paper. Microwave cream and mozzarella cheeses for 1 minute or until melted. Whisk in baking powder, pork rinds, eggs, Pecorino cheese, and mixed herbs. Spread the mixture in the baking sheet and bake for 20 minutes until lightly brown. Let cool, slice and serve.
Per serving: Cal 437; Net Carbs 3.2g; Fat 23g; Protein 32g

Savory Lime Fried Artichokes

Ingredients for 4 servings
12 fresh baby artichokes
2 tbsp lime juice
2 tbsp olive oil
Salt to taste

Directions and Total Time: approx. 20 minutes

Slice artichokes vertically into narrow wedges. Drain on paper towels before frying. Heat olive oil in a skillet. Fry the artichokes until browned and crispy. Drain excess oil on paper towels. Sprinkle with salt and lime juice.
Per serving: Cal 35; Net Carbs: 2.9g; Fat: 2.4g; Protein: 2g

Rosemary Cheese Chips with Guacamole

Ingredients for 4 servings
1 tbsp rosemary
1 cup Grana Padano, grated
¼ tsp sweet paprika
¼ tsp garlic powder
2 avocados, pitted and scooped
1 tomato, chopped

Directions and Total Time: approx. 20 minutes
Preheat oven to 350 F and line a baking sheet with parchment paper. Mix Grana Padano cheese, paprika, rosemary, and garlic powder evenly. Spoon 6-8 teaspoons on the baking sheet creating spaces between each mound.; flatten mounds. Bake for 5 minutes, cool, and remove to a plate. To make the guacamole, mash avocado, with a fork in a bowl, add in tomato and continue to mash until mostly smooth. Season with salt. Serve crackers with guacamole.
Per serving: Cal 229; Net Carbs 2g; Fat 20g; Protein 10g

Parmesan Green Bean Crisps

Ingredients for 6 servings
¼ cup Parmesan, shredded
¼ cup pork rind crumbs
1 tsp minced garlic
2 eggs
1 lb green beans
Salt and black pepper to taste

Directions and Total Time: approx. 30 minutes
Preheat oven to 425 F and line two baking sheets with foil. Mix Parmesan cheese, pork rinds, garlic, salt, and pepper in a bowl. Beat the eggs in another bowl. Coat green beans in eggs, then cheese mixture and arrange evenly on the baking sheets. Grease lightly with cooking spray and bake for 15 minutes. Transfer to a wire rack to cool. Serve.

Per serving: Cal 210; Net Carbs 3g; Fat 19g; Protein 5g

Paprika & Dill Deviled Eggs

Ingredients for 4 servings
1 tsp dill, chopped
8 large eggs
3 cups water
3 tbsp sriracha sauce
4 tbsp mayonnaise
¼ tsp sweet paprika

Directions and Total Time: approx. 20 minutes
Bring eggs to boil in salted water, reduce the heat, and simmer for 10 minutes. Transfer to an ice water bath, let cool completely and peel the shells. Slice the eggs in half height wise and empty the yolks into a bowl. Smash with a fork and mix in sriracha sauce, mayonnaise, and half of the paprika until smooth. Spoon filling into a piping bag and fill the egg whites to be slightly above the brim. Garnish with remaining paprika and dill and serve immediately.

Per serving: Cal 195; Net Carbs 1g; Fat 19g; Protein 4g

Cheese & Garlic Crackers

Ingredients for 6 servings
1 ¼ cups Pecorino Romano cheese, grated
1 ¼ cups coconut flour
Salt and black pepper to taste
1 tsp garlic powder
¼ cup ghee
¼ tsp sweet paprika
½ cup heavy cream

Directions and Total Time: approx. 30 minutes
Preheat oven to 350 F. Mix flour, Pecorino Romano cheese, salt, pepper, garlic and paprika in a bowl. Add in ghee and mix well. Top with heavy cream and mix again until a thick mixture has formed. Cover the dough with plastic wrap. Use a rolling pin to spread out the dough into a light rectangle. Cut into cracker squares and arrange them on a baking sheet. Bake for 20 minutes.

Per serving: Cal 115; Net Carbs 0.7g; Fat 3g; Protein 5g

Cheesy Chicken Wraps

Ingredients for 8 servings
¼ tsp garlic powder
8 ounces fontina cheese
8 raw chicken tenders
8 prosciutto slices

Directions and Total Time: approx. 20 minutes
Pound chicken until half an inch thick. Season with garlic powder. Cut fontina cheese into 8 strips. Place a slice of prosciutto on a flat surface. Place one chicken tender on top. Top with a fontina strip. Roll the chicken and secure with skewers. Grill the wraps for 3 minutes per side.

Per serving: Cal 174; Net Carbs: 0.7g; Fat: 10g; Protein: 17g

Baked Chorizo with Cottage Cheese

Ingredients for 6 servings
7 oz Spanish chorizo, sliced
4 oz cottage cheese, pureed
¼ cup chopped parsley

Directions and Total Time: approx. 30 minutes
Preheat the oven to 325 F. Line a baking dish with waxed paper. Bake the chorizo for 15 minutes until crispy. Remove from the oven and let cool. Arrange on a serving platter. Top each slice with cottage cheese and parsley.

Per serving: Cal 172; Net Carbs: 0.2g; Fat: 13g; Protein: 5g

Goat Cheese Stuffed Peppers

Ingredients for 8 servings
8 canned roasted piquillo peppers
3 slices prosciutto, cut into thin slices
2 tbsp olive oil
8 ounces goat cheese
3 tbsp heavy cream
3 tbsp chopped parsley
½ tsp minced garlic
1 tbsp chopped mint

Directions and Total Time: approx. 15 minutes
Combine goat cheese, heavy cream, parsley, garlic, and mint in a bowl. Place the mixture in a freezer bag, press down and squeeze, and cut off the bottom. Drain and deseed the peppers. Squeeze about 2 tbsp of the filling into each pepper. Wrap a prosciutto slice onto each pepper. Secure with toothpicks. Arrange them on a serving platter. Sprinkle the olive oil and vinegar over.

Per serving: Cal 110; Net Carbs 2.5g; Fat 9g; Protein 6g

Spinach Cheesy Puff Balls

Ingredients for 8 servings
⅓ cup crumbled ricotta
¼ tsp nutmeg
¼ tsp black pepper
3 tbsp heavy cream
1 tsp garlic powder
1 tbsp onion powder
2 tbsp butter, melted
⅓ cup Parmesan cheese
2 eggs
8 ounces spinach
1 cup almond flour
Directions and Total Time: approx. 30 minutes
Place all ingredients in a food processor. Process until smooth. Place in the freezer for 10 minutes. Make balls out of the mixture and arrange them on a lined baking sheet. Bake at 350 F for about 10-12 minutes.
Per serving: Cal 60; Net Carbs 0.8g; Fat 5g; Protein 8g

Crispy & Cheesy Salami

Ingredients for 6 servings
7 ounces dried salami
4 ounces cream cheese
¼ cup chopped parsley
Directions and Total Time: approx. 30 minutes
Preheat oven to 325 F. Slice the salami into 30 slices. Line a baking dish with waxed paper. Bake the salami for 15 minutes until crispy. Remove from the oven and let cool. Arrange on a serving platter. Top each slice with cream cheese. Serve with sprinkled with chopped parsley.
Per serving: Cal 27; Net Carbs 0g; Fat 3g; Protein 2g

Butter-Drowned Broccoli

Ingredients for 6 servings
1 broccoli head, florets only
¼ cup butter, melted
Salt and black pepper to taste
Directions and Total Time: approx. 10 minutes
Place the broccoli in a pot filled with salted water and bring to a boil. Cook for about 3 minutes, or until tender. Drain the broccoli and transfer to a plate. Drizzle the butter over and season with some salt and pepper.
Per serving: Cal 114; Net Carbs 5.5g; Fat 7.8g; Protein 4g

Basic Cauliflower Fritters

Ingredients for 4 servings
1 pound grated cauliflower
½ cup Parmesan cheese
1 chopped onion
½ tsp baking powder
½ cup almond flour
3 eggs
½ tsp lemon juice
4 tbsp olive oil
Directions and Total Time: approx. 35 minutes
Sprinkle the salt over the cauliflower in a bowl, and let it stand for 10 minutes. Place the other ingredients in the bowl; mix to combine. Place a skillet over medium heat and heat olive oil. Shape fritters out of the cauliflower mixture. Fry for 3 minutes per side. Serve warm or cold.
Per serving: Cal 109; Net Carbs 3g; Fat 8.5g; Protein 4.5g

Fried Artichoke Hearts

Ingredients for 4 servings
12 fresh baby artichokes
2 tbsp lemon juice
3 tbsp olive oil
Salt to taste
Directions and Total Time: approx. 15 minutes
Slice the artichokes vertically into narrow wedges. Drain them on a piece of paper towel before frying. Heat olive oil in a cast-iron skillet over high heat. Fry the artichokes until browned and crispy. Drain excess oil, sprinkle with salt and lemon juice.
Per serving: Cal 35; Net Carbs 2.9g; Fat 2.4g; Protein 2g

Provolone & Prosciutto Chicken Wraps

Ingredients for 8 servings
¼ tsp garlic powder
8 ounces provolone cheese
8 chicken tenders
8 prosciutto slices

Directions and Total Time: approx. 20 minutes
Pound the chicken until half an inch thick. Season with garlic powder. Cut the provolone cheese into 8 strips. Place a slice of prosciutto on a flat surface. Place one chicken tender on top. Top with a provolone strip. Roll the chicken and secure with previously soaked skewers. Grill the wraps for about 3 minutes per side.
Per serving: Cal 174; Net Carbs 0.7g; Fat 10g; Protein 17g

Tuna Topped Pickles

Ingredients for 8 servings
12 oz smoked canned tuna
6 large dill pickles, halved
¼ tsp garlic powder
⅓ cup sugar-free mayonnaise
1 tbsp onion flakes
Directions and Total Time: approx. 40 minutes
Combine the seasonings, mayonnaise, and tuna in a bowl. Top each pickle half with the tuna mixture. Place in the fridge for 30 minutes before serving.
Per serving: Cal 118; Net Carbs 1.5g; Fat 10g; Protein 11g

Keto Deviled Eggs

Ingredients for 6 servings
6 eggs
1 tbsp green tabasco
⅓ cup sugar-free mayonnaise Salt to taste
Directions and Total Time: approx. 30 minutes
Place eggs in a saucepan and cover with salted water. Bring to a boil over medium heat, for 8 minutes. Place in an ice bath to cool. Peel and slice. Whisk tabasco, mayo, and salt, in a bowl. Top every egg with some mayo dressing.
Per serving: Cal 178; Net Carbs 5g; Fat 17g; Protein 6g

Bacon & Pistachio Liverwurst Truffles

Ingredients for 8 servings
8 bacon slices, cooked and chopped
8 ounces liverwurst
¼ cup chopped pistachios
1 tsp Dijon mustard

6 ounces cream cheese
Directions and Total Time: approx. 45 minutes
Combine liverwurst and pistachios in a food processor. Pulse until smooth. Whisk cream cheese and mustard in another bowl. Make 12 balls out of the liverwurst mixture. Make a thin cream cheese layer over. Coat with bacon pieces. Arrange on a plate and refrigerate for 30 minutes.
Per serving: Cal 145; Net Carbs 1.5g; Fat 12g; Protein 7g

Roasted Broccoli & Cauliflower Steaks

Ingredients for 6 servings
1 head broccoli and 1 head cauliflower, sliced
2 tbsp olive oil
Salt and chili pepper to taste
1 tsp ground coriander
Directions and Total Time: approx. 30 minutes
Preheat oven to 400 F and line a baking sheet with foil. Brush the broccoli and cauliflower steaks with olive oil and season with chili pepper, coriander, and salt. Spread on a greased baking sheet in one layer. Roast in the oven for 10 minutes until tender and lightly browned.
Per serving: Cal 62; Net Carbs 1.4g; Fat 4.9g; Protein 2.4g

Gruyere & Ham Waffle Sandwiches

Ingredients for 4 servings
4 slices smoked ham, chopped
4 tbsp butter, softened
½ cup Gruyère cheese, grated
6 eggs
½ tsp baking powder
½ tsp dried thyme
4 tomato slices
Directions and Total Time: approx. 20 minutes
In a bowl, mix eggs, baking powder, thyme, butter and salt. Set a waffle iron over medium heat, add in ¼ cup of the batter and cook for 6 minutes until golden. Do the same with the remaining batter until you have 8 thin waffles. Lay a tomato slice on top of one waffle, followed by a ham slice, then top with ¼ of the grated cheese. Cover with another waffle, place the sandwich in the waffle iron and

cook until the cheese melts. Do the same with all remaining ingredients. Serve.
Per serving: Cal 276; Net Carbs 3.1g; Fat 22g; Protein 16g

No Bake Cheesy Walnut Balls

Ingredients for 4 servings
1 ½ cups feta cheese, crumbled
1 cup ground walnuts
½ cream cheese
2 tbsp butter, softened
1 habanero pepper, chopped
¼ tsp parsley flakes
½ tsp hot paprika
Directions and Total Time: approx. 15 minutes
In a bowl, mix all ingredients, except for the walnuts, to combine. Cover with foil and refrigerate for 30 minutes to firm up. Remove from the fridge and form balls from the mixture. Place the ground walnuts in a plate and roll the balls to coat on all sides. Serve.
Per serving: Cal 398; Net Carbs 5.4g; Fat 37g; Protein 12.4g

Smoked Bacon & Poached Egg Cups

Ingredients for 6 servings
4 oz smoked bacon, sliced
6 eggs
2 tbsp chives, chopped
½ cup mozzarella, shredded
4 tbsp sour cream
Salt and black pepper, to taste
Directions and Total Time: approx. 20 minutes
Fry bacon slices in a pan over medium heat for 4 minutes on both sides. With the bacon fat, grease 6 ramekins, then line 2 bacon slices on the inside of each cup. Share the sour cream, mozzarella, and crack an egg in each cup. Sprinkle with salt, pepper and chives. Bake for 15 minutes in a preheated oven at 400 F, until the eggs are set. Serve.
Per serving: Cal 149; Net Carbs 2.4g; Fat 16g; Protein 10g

Cauliflower Popcorn with Walnuts & Parsley

Ingredients for 4 servings
1 head cauliflower, broken into florets
1 tbsp olive oil
1 cup walnuts, halved

¼ cup Parmesan cheese, grated
1 tsp garlic, smashed
1 tsp turmeric
1 tsp fresh parsley, chopped
1 tsp chili pepper powder
Salt to taste
Directions and Total Time: approx. 30 minutes
Preheat oven to 390 F. Coat the florets with olive oil, salt, chili pepper powder, garlic, and turmeric. Pour in a baking dish and add in walnuts and parsley. Bake for 25 minutes until crisp. Sprinkle with Parmesan cheese and bake for another 2-3 minutes until the cheese melts. Serve.
Per serving: Cal 211; Net Carbs 5.7g; Fat 18g; Protein 6.4g

No-Bake & Egg Balls

Ingredients for 6 servings
Salt and crushed red pepper flakes, to taste
3 tbsp mayonnaise
2 eggs, cooked and chopped
½ cup butter, softened
8 black olives, chopped
1 oz salami, chopped
2 tbsp flax seeds
Directions and Total Time: approx. 35 minutes
Throw the eggs, olives, flakes, mayonnaise, butter, and salt in a food processor, and blitz until everything is combined. Stir in the chopped salami. Refrigerate for 20 minutes. Make balls from the mixture. Pour the flax seeds on a large plate; roll the balls through to coat. Serve.
Per serving: Cal 233; Net Carbs 1.3g; Fat 23g; Protein 4.4g

Baked Spicy Eggplants

Ingredients for 4 servings
2 large eggplants
2 tbsp butter
1 tsp red chili flakes
4 oz raw ground almonds
Directions and Total Time: approx. 30 minutes
Preheat oven to 400 F. Cut off the head of the eggplants and slice the body into rounds. Arrange on a parchment paper-lined baking sheet. Drop thin slices of butter on each eggplant slice, sprinkle with chili flakes, and

bake for 20 minutes. Slide out and sprinkle with almonds. Roast further for 5 minutes. Serve with arugula salad.

Per serving: Cal 230; Net Carbs 4g; Fat 16g; Protein 14g

Mashed Broccoli with Roasted Garlic

Ingredients for 4 servings

1 large head broccoli, cut into florets
½ head garlic
2 tbsp olive oil
4 oz butter
¼ tsp dried thyme
Juice and zest of half a lemon
4 tbsp coconut cream
4 tbsp olive oil

Directions and Total Time: approx. 45 minutes

Preheat oven to 400 F. Wrap garlic in aluminum foil and roast for 30 minutes; set aside. Pour broccoli into a pot and cover with salted water. Bring to a boil over high heat until tender, about 7 minutes. Drain and transfer to a bowl. Add in butter, thyme, lemon juice and zest, coconut cream, and olive oil. Use an immersion blender to puree the ingredients until smooth. Serve drizzled with olive oil.

Per serving: Cal 376; Net Carbs 6g; Fat 33g; Protein 11g

Spicy Pistachio Dip

Ingredients for 4 servings

3 oz toasted pistachios
3 tbsp coconut cream
¼ cup water
Juice of half a lemon
½ tsp smoked paprika
Cayenne pepper to taste
½ tsp salt
½ cup olive oil

Directions and Total Time: approx. 5 minutes

Pour pistachios, cream, water, lemon juice, paprika, cayenne, and salt in a food processor. Puree until smooth. Add in olive oil and puree again. Spoon into bowls, garnish with pistachios, and serve with celery and carrots.

Per serving: Cal 220; Net Carbs 5g; Fat 19g; Protein 6g

Prosciutto Appetizer with Blackberries

Ingredients for 4 servings

4 zero carb bread slices
¾ cup balsamic vinegar
2 tbsp erythritol
1 cup fresh blackberries
1 cup crumbled goat cheese
¼ tsp dry Italian seasoning
1 tbsp almond milk
4 thin prosciutto slices

Directions and Total Time: approx. 25 minutes

Cut the bread into 3 pieces each and arrange on a baking sheet. Place under the broiler and toast for 1-2 minutes on each side or until golden brown; set aside. In a saucepan, add balsamic vinegar and stir in erythritol until dissolved. Boil the mixture over medium heat until reduced by half, 5 minutes. Turn the heat off and carefully stir in the blackberries. Make sure they do not break open. Set aside.In a bowl, add goat cheese, Italian seasoning, and almond milk. Mix until smooth. Brush one side of the toasted bread with the balsamic reduction and top with the cheese mixture. Cut each prosciutto slice into 3 pieces and place on the bread. Top with some of the whole blackberries from the balsamic mixture. Serve immediately.

Per serving: Cal 175; Net Carbs 8.7g; Fat 7g; Protein 18g

Onion Rings & Kale Dip

Ingredients for 4 servings

1 onion, sliced in rings
1 tbsp flax seed meal
1 cup almond flour
½ cup grated Parmesan
1 tsp garlic powder
½ tbsp sweet paprika powder
2 oz chopped kale
2 tbsp olive oil
2 tbsp dried cilantro
1 tbsp dried oregano
Salt and black pepper to taste
1 cup mayonnaise
4 tbsp coconut cream
Juice of ½ lemon

Directions and Total Time: approx. 35 minutes

Preheat oven to 400 F. In a bowl, mix flax seed meal and 3 tbsp water and leave the mixture to thicken and fully absorb for 5 minutes. In another bowl, combine almond flour, Parmesan cheese, garlic powder, paprika, and salt. Line a baking sheet with parchment paper. When the flax egg is ready, dip in the onion rings one after another, and then into the almond flour mixture. Place the rings on the sheet and spray with cooking spray. Bake for 20 minutes. Remove to a bowl. Put kale in a bowl. Add in olive oil, cilantro, oregano, salt, pepper, mayonnaise, coconut cream, and lemon juice; mix well. Let sit for 10 minutes. Serve the dip with the crispy onion rings.

Per serving: Cal 410; Net Carbs 7g; Fat 35g; Protein 14g

Paprika Roasted Nuts

Ingredients for 4 servings
8 oz walnuts and pecans
1 tbsp coconut oil
1 tsp cumin powder
1 tsp paprika powder

Directions and Total Time: approx. 10 minutes
In a bowl, mix walnuts, pecans, salt, coconut oil, cumin powder, and paprika powder until the nuts are well coated.Pour the mixture into a frying pan and toast over medium heat while stirring continually until fragrant and brown.

Per serving: Cal 290; Net Carbs 3g; Fat 27g; Protein 6g

Mediterranean Deviled Eggs

Ingredients for 6 servings
6 large eggs
Ice water bath
1 tsp Dijon mustard
3 tbsp mayonnaise
1 tsp white wine vinegar
2 tbsp crumbled feta cheese
¼ tsp turmeric powder
1 red chili, minced
1 tbsp chopped parsley
Smoked paprika to garnish

Directions and Total Time: approx. 30 minutes
Boil eggs in salted water for 10 minutes. Transfer to an ice water bath. Let cool for 5

minutes, peel and slice in half. Remove the yolks to a bowl and put the whites on a plate. Mash yolks with a fork and mix in mustard, mayonnaise, vinegar, feta, turmeric, and chili until evenly combined. Spoon the mixture into a piping bag and fill into the egg whites. Garnish with parsley and paprika. Serve.

Per serving: Cal 139; Net Carbs 1.2g; Fat 8.2g; Protein 7g

Mushroom Broccoli Faux Risotto

Ingredients for 4 servings
1 cup cremini mushrooms, chopped
4 oz butter
2 garlic cloves, minced
1 red onion, finely chopped
1 head broccoli, grated
1 cup water
¾ cup white wine
Salt and black pepper to taste
1 cup coconut cream
¾ cup grated Parmesan
Freshly chopped thyme

Directions and Total Time: approx. 25 minutes
Place a pot over medium heat and melt butter. Sauté mushrooms until golden, 5 minutes. Add in garlic and onions and cook for 3 minutes until fragrant and soft. Mix in broccoli, water, and half of white wine. Season with salt and pepper and simmer for 10 minutes. Mix in coconut cream and simmer until most of the cream evaporates. Turn heat off and stir in Parmesan and thyme. Serve warm.

Per serving: Cal 520; Net Carbs 12g; Fat 43g; Protein 15g

Spinach Chips with Guacamole Hummus

Ingredients for 4 servings
½ cup baby spinach
1 tbsp olive oil
½ tsp plain vinegar
3 avocados, chopped
½ cup chopped parsley
½ cup butter
¼ cup pumpkin seeds
¼ cup sesame paste
Juice from ½ lemon
1 garlic clove, minced
½ tsp coriander powder

Salt and black pepper to taste

Directions and Total Time: approx. 30 minutes

Preheat oven to 300 F. Put spinach in a bowl and toss with olive oil, plain vinegar, and salt. Arrange on a parchment paper-lined baking sheet and bake until the leaves are crispy but not burned, 15 minutes. Place avocado to a food processor. Add in butter, pumpkin seeds, sesame paste, lemon juice, garlic, coriander, salt, and pepper; puree until smooth. Spoon into a bowl and garnish with parsley. Serve with the spinach chips.

Per serving: Cal 473; Net Carbs 3g; Fat 45g; Protein 8g

Tofu Stuffed Peppers

Ingredients for 4 servings

2 red bell peppers
1 cup grated Parmesan
1 oz tofu, chopped
1 tbsp fresh parsley, chopped
1 cup cream cheese
1 tbsp chili paste, mild
2 tbsp melted butter

Directions and Total Time: approx. 25 minutes

Preheat oven to 400 F. Cut bell peppers into two, lengthwise and remove the core and seeds. In a bowl, mix tofu with parsley, cream cheese, chili paste, and melted butter until smooth. Spoon the cheese mixture into the bell peppers. Arrange peppers on a greased sheet. Sprinkle Parmesan on top and bake for 20 minutes.

Per serving: Cal 412; Net Carbs 5g; Fat 36g; Protein 14g

Soy Chorizo Stuffed Cabbage Rolls

Ingredients for 4 servings

¼ cup coconut oil
1 onion, chopped
3 cloves garlic, minced
1 cup crumbled soy chorizo
1 cup cauliflower rice
1 can tomato sauce
1 tsp dried oregano
1 tsp dried basil
Salt and black pepper to taste
8 full green cabbage leaves

Directions and Total Time: approx. 35 minutes

Heat coconut oil in a saucepan and add onion, garlic, and soy chorizo; sauté for 5 minutes. Stir in cauli rice, season with salt and pepper, and cook for 4 minutes; set aside. In the saucepan, pour tomato sauce, season with salt, pepper, oregano, and basil. Add ¼ cup of water and simmer the sauce for 10 minutes. Lay cabbage leaves on a flat surface and spoon the soy chorizo mixture into the middle of each leaf. Roll the leaves to secure the filling. Place the cabbage rolls in the tomato sauce and cook for 10 minutes.

Per serving: Cal 285; Net Carbs 7g; Fat 26g; Protein 5g

Cauliflower Chips with Cheese Dip

Ingredients for 6 servings

1 head cauliflower, cut into florets
¾ cup dried cranberries, chopped
½ cup toasted pecans, chopped
1 ½ tbsp almond flour
1 tbsp flax seeds
4 tbsp chia seeds
8 oz cream cheese, softened
2 tbsp sugar-free maple syrup
1 tbsp lemon zest

Directions and Total Time: approx. 35 minutes

Preheat oven to 350 F. Pour cauliflower and 2 cups salted water in a pot and bring to a boil for 5 minutes. Drain and transfer to a food processor; puree until very smooth. Pour into a bowl and stir in flour until evenly combined. Mix in flax seeds and 1 tbsp chia seeds. Line a large baking sheet with parchment paper and spread in the batter. Cover with a plastic wrap and use a rolling pin to flatten and level the mixture evenly and lightly. Take off the plastic wrap and use cut our chip-size squares on the batter. Bake for 20 minutes or until the chips are golden brown and crispy. Let cool for 5 minutes and transfer to a serving bowl. In a bowl, mix cream cheese with maple syrup until properly mixed. Add in cranberries, pecans, remaining chia seeds, and lemon juice; mix well. Serve the dip with cauli chips.

Mixed Seed Crackers

Ingredients for 6 servings

1/3 cup sesame seed flour
1/3 cup pumpkin seeds

1/3 cup sunflower seeds
1/3 cup sesame seeds
1/3 cup chia seeds
1 tbsp psyllium husk powder
1 tsp salt
¼ cup butter, melted

Directions and Total Time: approx. 60 minutes

Preheat oven to 300 F. Combine sesame seed flour with pumpkin, chia and sunflower seeds, psyllium husk powder, and salt. Pour in butter and 1 cup boiling water and mix until a dough forms with a gel-like consistency. Line a baking sheet with parchment paper and place the dough on the sheet. Cover with another parchment paper and with a rolling pin to flatten into the baking sheet. Remove the parchment paper on top. Bake for 45 minutes. Turn off and allow the crackers to cool and dry in the oven, 10 minutes. Break and serve.

Per serving: Cal 65; Net Carbs 2g; Fat 5g; Protein 3g

Cheddar and Halloumi Sticks

Ingredients for 6 servings
1/3 cup almond flour
2 tsp smoked paprika
1 lb halloumi, cut into strips
½ cup grated cheddar cheese
2 tbsp chopped parsley
½ tsp cayenne powder

Directions and Total Time: approx. 15 minutes

Preheat oven to 350 F. In a bowl, mix flour with paprika and lightly dredge the halloumi cheese in the mixture. Arrange on a greased baking sheet. In a smaller bowl, combine parsley, cheddar cheese, and cayenne. Sprinkle the mixture on the cheese and lightly grease with cooking spray. Bake for 10 minutes until golden brown. Serve.

Per serving: Cal 886; Net Carbs 6.1g; Fat 77g; Protein 14g

Pesto Mushroom Pinwheels

Ingredients for 4 servings
¼ cup almond flour
3 tbsp coconut flour
½ tsp xanthan gum
4 tbsp cream cheese, softened
1/4 teaspoon yogurt

¼ cup butter, cold
3 whole eggs
3 tbsp erythritol
1 ½ tsp vanilla extract
1 whole egg, beaten
1 cup mushrooms, chopped
1 cup basil pesto
2 cups baby spinach
Salt and black pepper to taste
1 cup grated cheddar cheese
1 egg, beaten for brushing

Directions and Total Time: approx. 40 minutes

In a bowl, mix almond and coconut flours, xanthan gum, and ½ tsp salt. Add in yogurt, cream cheese, and butter; mix until crumbly. Add in erythritol and vanilla extract until mixed. Pour in 3 eggs one after another while mixing until formed into a ball. Flatten the dough on a clean flat surface, cover in plastic wrap, and refrigerate for 1 hour. Dust a clean flat surface with almond flour, unwrap the dough, and roll out into 15x12 inches. Spread pesto on top with a spatula, leaving a 2-inch border on one end. In a bowl, combine baby spinach and mushrooms, season with salt and pepper, and spread the mixture over pesto. Sprinkle with cheddar cheese and roll up as tightly as possible from the shorter end. Refrigerate for 10 minutes. Preheat oven to 380 F. Remove the pastry onto a flat surface and use a sharp knife to into 24 slim discs. Arrange on the baking sheet, brush with the remaining egg, and bake for 25 minutes until golden. Let cool for 5 minutes.

Per serving: Cal 535; Net Carbs 4g; Fat 41g; Protein 34.6g

Hemp Seed Zucchini Chips

Ingredients for 4 servings
4 large zucchinis, sliced
4 tbsp olive oil
1 tsp smoked paprika
2 tbsp hemp seeds
2 tbsp poppy seeds
1 tsp red chili flakes

Directions and Total Time: approx. 15 minutes

Preheat oven to 350 F. Drizzle zucchini with olive oil and sprinkle with paprika. Scatter with the hemp seeds, poppy seeds, and chili flakes. Season with salt, pepper, and roast for

20 minutes or until crispy and golden brown. Serve.

Per serving: Cal 173; Net Carbs 1.3g; Fat 18g; Protein 2.2g

All Seeds Flapjacks

Ingredients for 4 servings
4 tbsp dried goji berries, chopped
6 tbsp salted butter
8 tbsp sugar-free maple syrup
8 tbsp swerve brown sugar
3 tbsp sesame seeds
3 tbsp chia seeds
3 tbsp hemp seeds
3 tbsp sunflower seeds
1 tbsp poppy seeds

Directions and Total Time: approx. 30 minutes
Preheat oven to 350 F and line a baking sheet with parchment paper. Place butter, maple syrup, and swerve brown sugar in a saucepan over low heat, stir in swerve brown sugar until dissolved.

Remove and stir all seeds along with goji berries until evenly combined. Spread into the baking sheet and bake for 20 minutes or until golden brown. Slice flapjacks into the 16 strips. Serve.

Per serving: Cal 300; Net Carbs 3g; Fat 28g; Protein 6.8g

Tasty Keto Snickerdoodles

Ingredients for 4 servings
2 cups almond flour
½ tsp baking soda
¾ cup sweetener
½ cup butter, softened
2 tbsp erythritol sweetener
1 tsp cinnamon

Directions and Total Time: approx. 25 minutes
Preheat oven to 350 F. Combine almond flour, baking soda, sweetener, and butter in a bowl. Make 16 balls out of the mixture. Flatten them with your hands. Combine the cinnamon and erythritol in a bowl. Dip in the cookies and arrange on a lined cookie sheet. Bake for 15 minutes.

Per serving: Cal 131; Net Carbs 1.5g; Fat 13g; Protein 3g

Basil-Chili Mozzarella Bites

Ingredients for 4 servings
1 cup olive oil, for frying
1 cup almond flour
½ tsp chili powder
1 tsp onion powder
1 tsp garlic powder
1 tsp dried basil leaves
1 large egg, beaten in a bowl
1 cup golden flaxseed meal
1 cup mozzarella cheese cubes
¼ cup small tomatoes, halved
A handful of basil leaves

Directions and Total Time: approx. 10 minutes
In a bowl, combine flour, chili, onion and garlic powders, and basil; set aside. Pour flaxseed meal in a plate. Coat each cheese cube in the flour mixture, then in the egg, and then lightly in the golden flaxseed meal. Heat olive oil in a deep pan. Fry the cheese until golden brown on both sides. Transfer to a wire rack to drain grease. On each tomato half, place 1 basil leaf, top with a cheese cube, and insert a toothpick at the middle of the sandwich to hold. Serve.

Per serving: Cal 769; Net Carbs 2.4g; Fat 73g; Protein 18g

DESSERTS

Coconut Cake with Raspberries

Ingredients for 8 servings
2 cups fresh raspberries
2 cups flaxseed meal
1 cup almond meal
½ cup melted butter
1 lemon, juiced
1 cup coconut cream
1 cup coconut flakes
1 cup whipping cream

Directions and Total Time: approx. 30 min + chilling time
Preheat oven to 400 F. In a bowl, mix flaxseed meal, almond meal, and butter. Spread the mixture on the bottom of a baking dish. Bake for 20 minutes until the mixture is crusty. Allow cooling. In another bowl, mash 1 ½ cups of the raspberries and mix with the lemon juice. Spread the mixture on the crust. Carefully, spread the coconut cream on top, scatter with the coconut flakes and add the whipped cream all over. Garnish with the remaining raspberries and chill in the refrigerator for at least 2 hours.
Per serving: Cal 413; Net Carbs 5.4g; Fats 41g; Protein 7g

Lemon Panna Cotta

Ingredients for 4 servings
½ cup coconut milk
1 cup heavy cream
¼ cup swerve sugar
5 tbsp sugar-free maple syrup
3 tsp agar agar
¼ cup warm water
3 tbsp water
½ lemon, juiced

Directions and Total Time: approx. 30 min + chilling time
Heat coconut milk and heavy cream in a pot over low heat. Stir in swerve sugar, 3 tbsp maple syrup, and 2 tsp agar agar. Continue cooking for 3 minutes. Divide the mixture between 4 dessert cups and chill in the refrigerator for 5 hours. In a bowl, soak the remaining agar agar with warm water. Allow blooming for 5 minutes. In a small pot, heat 3 tbsp water with lemon juice. Mix in the remaining maple syrup and add agar agar mixture. Whisking while cooking until no lumps form; let cool for 2 minutes. Remove the cups, pour in the mixture and refrigerate for 2 hours. When ready, remove the cups, let sit for 15 minutes, and serve.
Per serving: Cal 208; Net Carbs 2.8g; Fats 18g; Protein 2g

Vanilla & Blackberries Sherbet

Ingredients for 2 servings
¼ tsp vanilla extract
1 packet gelatine
2 tbsp heavy whipping cream
4 tbsp mashed blackberries
2 cups crushed ice
1 cup cold water

Directions and Total Time: approx. 5 minutes
Put the gelatin in boiling water, until dissolved. Place the remaining ingredients in a blender and add in gelatin. Blend until smooth. Serve.
Per serving: Cal 173; Net Carbs 3.7g; Fat 10g; Protein 4g

Strawberry & Ricotta Parfait

Ingredients for 4 servings
2 cups strawberries, chopped
1 cup ricotta cheese
2 tbsp sugar-free maple syrup
2 tbsp balsamic vinegar

Directions and Total Time: approx. 10 minutes
Divide half of the strawberries between 4 small glasses and top with ricotta cheese. Drizzle with maple syrup, balsamic vinegar and finish with the remaining strawberries. Serve.
Per serving: Cal 164; Net Carbs 3.1g; Fats 8.2g; Protein 7g

Speedy Blueberry Sorbet

Ingredients for 4 servings
4 cups frozen blueberries
1 cup swerve sugar
½ lemon, juiced
½ tsp salt

Directions and Total Time: approx. 15 min + chilling time

In a blender, add blueberries, swerve, lemon juice, and salt; process until smooth. Strain through a colander into a bowl. Chill for 3 hours. Pour the chilled juice into an ice cream maker and churn until the mixture resembles ice cream. Spoon into a bowl and chill further for 3 hours.

Per serving: Cal 178; Net Carbs 2.3g; Fats 1g; Protein 0.6g

Creamy Strawberry Mousse

Ingredients for 4 servings
2 cups frozen strawberries
2 tbsp swerve sugar
1 large egg white
2 cups whipped cream

Directions and Total Time: approx. 10 min + chilling time
Pour 1 ½ cups strawberries in a blender and process until smooth. Add swerve and process further. Pour in the egg white and blend until well combined. Pour the mixture into a bowl and use an electric hand mixer to whisk until fluffy. Spoon the mixture into dessert glasses, top with whipped cream and strawberries. Serve chilled.

Per serving: Cal 145; Net Carbs 4.8g; Fats 6.8g; Protein 2g

Berry Clafoutis

Ingredients for 4 servings
4 eggs
2 tsp coconut oil
2 cups berries
1 cup coconut milk
1 cup almond flour
¼ cup sweetener
½ tsp vanilla powder
1 tbsp powdered sweetener

Directions and Total Time: approx. 45 minutes
Preheat oven to 350 F. Place all ingredients except for the oil, berries, and powdered sweetener in a blender; pulse until smooth. Gently fold in the berries. Grease a flan dish with coconut oil. Pour the mixture into the dish; bake for 35 minutes. Sprinkle with powdered sugar and serve.

Per serving: Cal 198; Net Carbs 4.9g; Fat 16g; Protein 15g

Raspberry Coconut Cheesecake

Ingredients for 8 servings
2 egg whites
2 ¼ cups erythritol
3 cups desiccated coconut
1 tsp coconut oil
¼ cup melted butter
3 tbsp lemon juice
6 ounces raspberries
1 cup whipped cream
3 tbsp lemon juice
24 ounces cream cheese

Directions and Total Time: approx. 4 hours 15 minutes
Preheat oven to 350 F. Grease a springform pan with the oil and line with parchment paper. Mix egg whites, ¼ cup of erythritol, coconut, and butter until a crust forms and pour into the pan. Bake for 25 minutes. Let cool. Beat the cream cheese until soft. Add lemon juice and the remaining erythritol. In another bowl, beat the heavy cream with an electric mixer. Fold the whipped cream into the cheese cream mixture; stir in raspberries gently. Spread the filling onto the baked crust. Refrigerate for 4 hours.

Per serving: Cal 215; Net Carbs 3g; Fat 25g; Protein 5g

Peanut Butter & Chocolate Ice Cream Bars

Ingredients for 8 servings
3 ½ tsp THM super sweet blend
¼ cup cocoa butter pieces, chopped
2 cups heavy whipping cream
⅔ cup peanut butter, softened
1 ½ cups almond milk
1 tbsp vegetable glycerin
6 ½ tbsp xylitol
¾ cup coconut oil
2 oz unsweetened chocolate

Directions and Total Time: approx. 4 hours 20 minutes
Blend heavy cream, xanthan gum, peanut butter, almond milk, vegetable glycerin, and 3 tbsp of xylitol until smooth. Place in an ice cream maker and follow the instructions. Spread the ice cream into a lined pan, and freeze for 4 hours. Combine coconut oil, cocoa butter, chocolate, and remaining xylitol in a microwave-safe bowl and microwave until melted; let cool slightly. Slice the ice

cream into bars. Dip into the chocolate mixture.

Per serving: Cal 345 Net Carbs 5 g; Fat 32g; Protein 4g

Lemon-Yogurt Mousse

Ingredients for 4 servings

24 oz plain yogurt, strained overnight in a cheesecloth
2 cups swerve confectioner's sugar
2 lemons, juiced and zested
1 cup whipped cream + extra for garnish

Directions and Total Time: approx. 5 min + cooling time

Whip the plain yogurt in a bowl with a hand mixer until light and fluffy. Mix in the sugar, lemon juice, and salt. Fold in the whipped cream to evenly combine. Spoon the mousse into serving cups and refrigerate for 1 hour. Swirl with extra whipped cream and garnish with lemon zest.

Per serving: Cal 223; Net Carbs 3g; Fat 18g; Protein 12g

Strawberry Chocolate Mousse

Ingredients for 4 servings

1 cup fresh strawberries, sliced
3 eggs
1 cup dark chocolate chips
1 cup heavy cream
1 vanilla extract
1 tbsp swerve

Directions and Total Time: approx. 30 minutes

Melt the chocolate in a microwave-safe bowl in the microwave oven for a minute on high; let cool for 8 minutes. Meanwhile, in a medium-sized bowl, whip the cream until very soft. Add the eggs, vanilla extract, and swerve; whisk to combine. Fold in the cooled chocolate. Divide the mousse between six glasses, top with the strawberry slices and chill in the fridge for 1 hour. Serve.

Per serving: Cal 400; Net Carbs 1.7g; Fat 25g; Protein 8g

Granny Smith Apple Tart

Ingredients for 8 servings

2 cups almond flour
¼ cup + 6 tbsp butter
1 ¼ tsp cinnamon
1 cup sweetener
2 cups sliced Granny Smith
½ tsp lemon juice

Directions and Total Time: approx. 45 minutes

Preheat oven to 375 F. Combine 6 tbsp of butter, almond flour, 1 tsp of cinnamon, and ⅓ cup of sweetener in a bowl. Press this mixture into a greased pan. Bake for 5 minutes. Combine the apples and lemon juice in a bowl and set aside. Arrange on top of the crust. Combine the remaining butter and sweetener, and brush over the apples. Bake for 20 minutes. Press the apples down with a spatula, return to oven, and bake for 10 more minutes. Dust with mixed remaining cinnamon and serve.

Per serving: Cal 302; Net Carbs 6.7g; Fat 26g; Protein 7g

Maple Lemon Cake

Ingredients for 4 servings

4 eggs
1 cup sour cream
2 lemons, zested and juiced
1 tsp vanilla extract
2 cups almond flour
2 tbsp coconut flour
2 tsp baking powder
½ cup xylitol
1 tsp cardamom powder
½ tsp ground ginger
A pinch of salt
¼ cup maple syrup

Directions and Total Time: approx. 30 minutes

Preheat oven to 400 F and grease a cake pan with melted butter. In a bowl, beat eggs, sour cream, lemon juice, and vanilla extract until smooth. In another bowl, whisk almond and coconut flours, baking powder, xylitol, cardamom, ginger, salt, lemon zest, and half of maple syrup. Combine both mixtures until smooth and pour the batter into the pan. Bake for 25 minutes or until a toothpick inserted comes out clean. Transfer to a wire rack, let cool, and drizzle with the remaining maple syrup. Serve sliced.

Per serving: Cal 441; Net Carbs 8.5g; Fat 29g; Protein 33g

Flan with Whipped Cream

Ingredients for 4 servings

⅓ cup erythritol, for caramel
2 cups almond milk
4 eggs
1 tablespoon vanilla
1 tbsp lemon zest
½ cup erythritol, for custard
2 cup heavy whipping cream
Mint leaves, to serve

Directions and Total Time: approx. 10 minutes

Heat erythritol for the caramel in a pan. Add 2-3 tablespoons of water, and bring to a boil. Reduce the heat and cook until the caramel turns golden brown. Carefully divide between 4-6 metal cups. Let them cool. In a bowl, mix eggs, remaining erythritol, lemon zest, and vanilla. Add milk and beat again until combined. Pour the custard into each caramel-lined cup and place them into a baking tin. Pour enough hot water into baking tin to halfway up sides of cups. Bake at 345 F for 45 minutes. Remove the ramekins and refrigerate them for 4 hours. To serve, take a knife and slowly run around the edges to invert onto dishes. Serve with dollops of cream and mint leaves.

Per serving: Cal 169; Net Carbs 1.7g; Fat 10g; Protein 7g

Chocolate Mocha Ice Bombs

Ingredients for 4 servings
½ pound cream cheese
4 tbsp powdered sweetener
2 ounces strong coffee
2 tbsp cocoa powder
1 ounce cocoa butter, melted
2 ½ oz dark chocolate, melted

Directions and Total Time: approx. 2 hours 10 minutes

Combine cream cheese, sweetener, coffee, and cocoa powder in a food processor. Roll 2 tbsp. of the mixture and place on a lined tray. Mix the melted cocoa butter and chocolate, and coat the bombs with it. Freeze for 2 hours.

Per serving: Cal 127; Net Carbs 1.4g; Fat 13g; Protein 2g

Almond & Coconut Bark

Ingredients for 8 servings
½ cup almonds
½ cup coconut butter
10 drops stevia

¼ tsp salt
½ cup coconut flakes
4 ounces dark chocolate

Directions and Total Time: approx. 1 hour 15 minutes

Preheat oven to 350 F. Place almonds in a baking sheet and toast for 5 minutes. Melt together the butter and chocolate. Stir in stevia. Line a cookie sheet with waxed paper and spread the chocolate evenly. Scatter the almonds on top and sprinkle with salt. Refrigerated for 1 hour.

Per serving: Cal 161; Net Carbs 1.9g; Fat 15g; Protein 2g

Coconut Butter Ice Cream

Ingredients for 4 servings
½ cup smooth coconut butter
½ cup swerve
3 cups half and half
1 tsp vanilla extract

Directions and Total Time: approx. 50 min + cooling time

Beat coconut butter and swerve in a bowl with a hand mixer until smooth. Gradually whisk in half and half until thoroughly combined. Mix in vanilla. Pour mixture into a loaf pan and freeze for 45 minutes until firmed up. Scoop into glasses when ready to eat and serve.

Per serving: Cal 290; Net Carbs 6g; Fat 23g; Protein 13g

Saffron & Cardamom Coconut Bars

Ingredients for 4 servings
3 ½ ounces ghee
10 saffron threads
1 ⅓ cups coconut milk
1 ¾ cups shredded coconut
4 tbsp sweetener
1 tsp cardamom powder

Directions and Total Time: approx. 3 hours

Combine the coconut with 1 cup of coconut milk. In another bowl, mix the remaining coconut milk with the sweetener and saffron. Let sit for 30 minutes. Heat the ghee in a wok. Add the coconut mixture as well as the saffron mixture, and cook for 5 minutes on low heat, mixing continuously. Stir in cardamom and cook for 5 more minutes.

Spread the mixture onto a greased baking pan. Freeze for 2 hours. Cut into bars to serve.
Per serving: Cal 130; Net Carbs 1.4g; Fat 12g; Protein 2g

Saffron Coconut Bars

Ingredients for 4 servings
3 ½ ounces ghee
10 saffron threads
1 ¼ cups coconut milk
1 ¾ cups shredded coconut
4 tbsp stevia
1 tsp cardamom powder
Directions and Total Time: approx. 20 min + cooling time
Combine shredded coconut with 1 cup of coconut milk. In another bowl, mix the remaining coconut milk with stevia and saffron. Let sit for 30 minutes. Heat ghee in a wok. Add coconut mixture as well as the saffron mixture, and cook for 5 minutes, mixing continuously. Stir in cardamom and cook for 5 minutes. Spread the mixture onto a small container and freeze for 2 hours. Cut into bars to serve.
Per serving: Cal 215; Net Carbs: 1.4g; Fat: 22g; Protein: 2g

Mom's Walnut Cookies

Ingredients for 12 servings
1 egg
2 cups ground pecans
¼ cup sweetener
½ tsp baking soda
1 tbsp ghee
20 walnuts halves
Directions and Total Time: approx. 25 minutes
Preheat oven to 350 F. In a bowl, mix all the ingredients, except for walnuts, until combined. Make balls out of the mixture and press them with your thumb onto a lined cookie sheet. Top with walnuts. Bake for 12 minutes.
Per serving: Cal 101; Net Carbs: 0.6g; Fat: 11g; Protein: 2g

Almond Ice Cream

Ingredients for 4 servings
2 cups heavy cream
1 tbsp xylitol
½ cup smooth almond butter
1 tbsp olive oil
1 tbsp vanilla extract
½ tsp salt
2 egg yolks
½ cup almonds, chopped
½ cup swerve sweetener confectioners
Directions and Total Time: approx. 3 hours 40 minutes
Warm heavy cream with almond butter, olive oil, xylitol, and salt in a small pan over low heat without boiling, for 3 minutes. Beat the egg yolks until creamy in color. Stir the eggs into the cream mixture. Refrigerate cream mixture for 30 minutes, and stir in swerve sweetener. Pour mixture into ice cream machine and churn it according to the manufacturer's instructions. Stir in almonds and spoon mixture into loaf pan. Refrigerate for at least for 2 hours.
Per serving: Cal 552; Net Carbs 6.2g; Fat 45.4g; Protein 9g

Blueberry Tart

Ingredients for 4 servings
4 eggs
2 tsp coconut oil
2 cups blueberries
1 cup coconut milk
1 cup almond flour
¼ cup sweetener
½ tsp vanilla powder
1 tbsp powdered sweetener
A pinch of salt
Directions and Total Time: approx. 45 minutes
Preheat oven to 350 F. Place all ingredients except coconut oil, berries, and powdered sweetener in a blender, and blend until smooth. Gently fold in the berries. Pour the mixture into a greased dish and bake for 35 minutes. Sprinkle with powdered sweetener.
Per serving: Cal 355; Net Carbs 6.9g; Fat 14.5g; Protein 12g

Matcha Fat Bombs

Ingredients for 4 servings
½ cup coconut oil
1 tbsp vanilla extract
½ cup almond butter
4 tbsp matcha powder powder
½ cup xylitol

Directions and Total Time: approx. 3 min + cooling time
Melt butter and coconut oil in a saucepan over low heat, stirring twice until properly melted and mixed. Mix in matcha powder and xylitol until combined. Pour into muffin moulds and refrigerate for 3 hours to harden.
Per serving: Cal 436; Net Carbs 3.1g; Fat 44.6g; Protein 6g

Coffee Balls

Ingredients for 6 servings
1 ½ cups mascarpone cheese
½ cup melted ghee
3 tbsp cocoa powder
¼ cup erythritol
6 tbsp brewed coffee
Directions and Total Time: approx. 3 min + cooling time
Whisk mascarpone, ghee, cocoa powder, erythritol, and coffee with a hand mixer until creamy and fluffy, for 1 minute. Fill in muffin tins and freeze for 3 hours until firm.
Per serving: Cal 145; Net Carbs 2g; Fat 14g; Protein 4g

Mascarpone Ice Bombs

Ingredients for 4 servings
2 tbsp butter, melted
1 cup mascarpone cheese
4 tbsp xylitol
2 tbsp coffee
2 tbsp cocoa powder
2 ½ oz dark chocolate, melted
Directions and Total Time: approx. 2 hours 10 minutes
Blitz mascarpone cheese, xylitol, coffee, and cocoa powder, in a food processor until mixed. Roll 2 tbsp of the mixture and place on a lined tray. Mix melted butter and chocolate, and coat the bombs with it. Freeze for 2 hours.
Per serving: Cal 286; Net Carbs 7.2g; Fat 23.7g; Protein 10g

Chocolate Mug Cakes

Ingredients for 2 servings
2 tbsp ghee
1 ½ tbsp cocoa powder
2-3 tbsp erythritol
1 egg
2 tbsp almond flour
1 tbsp psyllium husk powder

2 tsp coconut flour
½ tsp baking powder
A pinch of salt
Directions and Total Time: approx. 5 minutes
In a bowl, whisk the butter, cocoa powder, and erythritol until a thick mixture forms. Whisk in the egg until smooth and then the almond flour, psyllium husk, coconut flour, baking powder and salt. Pour the mixture into two medium mugs and microwave for 70 to 90 seconds or until set.
Per serving: Cal 92; Net Carbs 1.8g; Fat 12g; Protein 8.2g

Choco-Coffee Cake

Ingredients for 4 servings
3 tbsp golden flaxseed meal, ground
1 tbsp melted butter
1 cup almond flour
2 tbsp coconut flour
1 tsp baking powder
¼ cup cocoa powder
¼ tsp salt
½ tsp espresso powder
1/3-½ cup coconut sugar
¼ tsp xanthan gum
¼ cup organic coconut oil
2 tbsp heavy cream
2 eggs
Directions and Total Time: approx. 30 minutes
Preheat oven to 400 F and grease a springform pan with melted butter. In a bowl, mix almond flour, flaxseed meal, coconut flour, baking powder, cocoa, salt, espresso, coconut sugar, and xanthan gum. In another bowl, whisk coconut oil, heavy cream, and eggs. Combine both mixtures until smooth batter forms. Pour the batter into the pan and bake until a toothpick comes out clean, 20 minutes. Transfer to a wire rack, let cool, slice and serve.
Per serving: Cal 232; Net Carbs 6.3g; Fat 22g; Protein 5.5g

Keto Caramel Cake

Ingredients for 4 servings
½ cup sugar-free caramel sauce + extra for topping
2 ½ cups almond flour
¼ cup coconut flour

¼ cup whey protein powder
1 tbsp baking powder
½ tsp salt
¾ cup erythritol
4 large eggs
1 tsp vanilla extract
¾ cup almond milk

Directions and Total Time: approx. 30 minutes

Preheat oven to 400 F. In a bowl, mix almond and coconut flours, protein and baking powders, and salt. In another bowl, mix erythritol, eggs, vanilla, milk, and caramel sauce. Combine both mixtures until smooth batter forms. Pour batter into a greased pan; bake for 22 minutes. Let cool and top with caramel sauce to serve.

Per serving: Cal 313; Net Carbs 3.4g; Fat 29g; Protein 8.2g

Gingerbread Cheesecake

Ingredients for 6 servings
For the crust:
1 ¾ cups golden flaxseed meal
6 tbsp melted butter
¼ swerve sugar
A pinch of salt
For the filling
8 oz cream cheese, softened
¾ cup swerve sugar
¼ cup sugar-free maple syrup
3 large eggs
¼ cup sour cream
2 tbsp almond flour
1 tsp pure vanilla extract
2 tsp smooth ginger paste
1 tsp cinnamon powder
¼ tsp nutmeg powder
¼ tsp salt
A pinch of cloves powder

Directions and Total Time: approx. 1 hour 45 minutes

Preheat oven to 325 F and grease a cake pan. In a bowl, mix flaxseed meal, butter, swerve, and salt. Pour and fit the mixture into the pan using a spoon. Bake the crust for 15 minutes or until firm. In a bowl, using an electric mixer, beat cream cheese, swerve sugar, and maple syrup until smooth. Whisk in one after the other, the eggs, sour cream, almond flour, vanilla extract, ginger paste, cinnamon, nutmeg, salt, and cloves powder. Pour the mixture onto the crust while shaking to release any bubbles. Cover with foil and bake for 55 minutes until the center of the cake jiggles slightly. Remove the cake, let cool, and release the cake pan. Garnish with ginger powder, slice and serve.

Per serving: Cal 682; Net Carbs 4.3g; Fat 49g; Protein 31g

Coconut Cake

Ingredients for 4 servings
9 tbsp butter, melted and cooled
6 eggs
2 tsp cream cheese, softened
1 tsp vanilla extract
2 tbsp coconut c¼eam
½ cup swerve sugar
9 tbsp coconut flour
1 ½ tsp baking powder
2 tbsp coconut flakes
½ tsp salt
Coconut flakes for garnishing

Directions and Total Time: approx. 30 minutes

Preheat oven to 400 F and grease cake pan with melted butter. In a bowl, beat the eggs and butter until smooth. Whisk in the cream cheese, vanilla, and coconut cream. In another bowl, mix swerve sugar, coconut flour, baking powder, coconut flakes, and salt. Combine both mixtures until smooth and pour the batter into the pan. Bake for 24 minutes or until a toothpick inserted comes out clean. Transfer to a wire rack and top with coconut flakes.

Per serving: Cal 377; Net Carbs 3.8g; Fat 36g; Protein 9g

Vanilla Berry Mug Cakes

Ingredients for 4 servings
1 tbsp butter, melted
2 tbsp cream cheese
2 tbsp coconut flour
1 tbsp xylitol
1 tsp vanilla extract
¼ tsp baking powder
1 medium egg
6 mixed berries, mashed

Directions and Total Time: approx. 5 minutes

In a bowl, whisk butter, cream cheese, flour, xylitol, baking powder, egg, and mashed berries. Pour the mixture into two mugs and microwave for 80 seconds or until set. Let cool for 1 minute and enjoy.

Per serving: Cal 98; Net Carbs 2.4g; Fat 4g; Protein 3.5g

Chocolate Cake with Raspberry Frosting

Ingredients for 6 servings
2 cups blanched almond flour
1 cup erythritol
½ cup cocoa powder
1 tsp baking powder
½ cup butter, softened
1 tsp vanilla extract
2 eggs
1 cup almond milk

For the frosting:
8 oz cream cheese, softened
½ cup butter, softened
1 cup fresh raspberries, mashed
3 tbsp cocoa powder
2 tbsp heavy whipping cream
1/3 cup powdered erythritol
1 tsp vanilla extract

Directions and Total Time: approx. 40 minutes
Preheat oven to 350 degrees. In a bowl, mix almond flour, erythritol, cocoa, and baking powder until fully combined. Mix in butter and vanilla. Crack open the eggs into the bowl and whisk until completely combined; stir in almond milk. Prepare three 6-inch round cake pans and generously grease with butter. Divide the batter into the 3 cake pans. Place all the pans in the oven and bake for 25 minutes or until the cakes set. Remove them to a wire rack. In a bowl, whip cream cheese, butter, raspberries, cocoa powder, heavy cream, erythritol, and vanilla extract until smooth. To assemble: place the first cake on a flat surface and spread ⅓ of the frosting over top. Place second cake layer, add and smoothen the frosting, and then do the same for the last cake. Slice and serve immediately.

Per serving: Cal 546; Net Carbs 8.4g; Fat 46g; Protein 9g

Chocolate Snowball Cookies

Ingredients for 4 servings
¼ cup swerve confectioner's sugar
1 cup butter, softened
½ cups erythritol, divided
2 cups almond flour
2 tsp cocoa powder
1 tsp vanilla extract
1 cup pecans, finely chopped
½ tsp salt
2 tbsp water

Directions and Total Time: approx. 35 min + chilling time
Preheat oven to 325 F; line a baking sheet with parchment paper. In a bowl and using a hand mixer, cream the butter and erythritol. Fold in almond flour, cocoa powder, vanilla, pecans, salt, and water. Mold 1 tbsp cookie dough from the mixture and place on the sheet. Chill for 1 hour. Transfer to the sheet and bake for 25 minutes or until the cookies look dry and colorless. Remove them from the oven to cool for 10 minutes. Sprinkle with swerve to serve.

Per serving: Cal 584; Net Carbs 3.7g; Fat 61g; Protein 3g

Classic Zucchini Cake

Ingredients for 4 servings
4 egg
4 tbsp butter, melted
½ tsp vanilla extract
¼ cup sugar-free maple syrup
1 ½ cups almond flour
½ cup swerve sugar
1 ½ tsp baking powder
¼ tsp baking soda
½ tsp salt
1 ¼ tsp cinnamon
½ tsp nutmeg
⅛ tsp ground cloves
1 cup grated zucchinis

Directions and Total Time: approx. 30 minutes
Preheat oven to 400 F and grease a cake pan with melted butter. In a bowl, beat the eggs, butter, maple syrup, and vanilla extract until smooth. In another bowl, mix almond flour, swerve, baking powder, baking soda, salt, cinnamon, and ground cloves. Combine both mixtures until smooth, fold in the zucchinis and pour the batter into the cake pan. Bake for 25 minutes or until a toothpick inserted comes out clean. Transfer to a wire rack, let cool, and drizzle the remaining maple syrup. Slice and serve.

Per serving: Cal 235; Net Carbs 6.3g; Fat 21g; Protein 9g

Heart-Shaped Red Velvet Cakes

Ingredients for 6 servings
½ cup butter
6 eggs
1 tsp vanilla extract
1 cup Greek yogurt
1 cup swerve sugar
1 cup almond flour
½ cup coconut flour
2 tbsp cocoa powder
2 tbsp baking powder
¼ tsp salt
1 tbsp red food coloring
For the frosting:
1 cup mascarpone cheese
½ cup erythritol
1 tsp vanilla extract
2 tbsp heavy cream

Directions and Total Time: approx. 30 minutes

Preheat oven to 400 F and grease 2 heart-shaped cake pans with butter. In a bowl, beat butter, eggs, vanilla, Greek yogurt, and swerve sugar until smooth. In another bowl, mix the almond and coconut flours, cocoa, salt, baking powder, and red food coloring. Combine both mixtures until smooth and divide the batter between the two cake pans. Bake in the oven for 25 minutes or until a toothpick inserted comes out clean. Meanwhile, in a bowl, using an electric mixer, whisk the mascarpone cheese and erythritol until smooth. Mix in vanilla and heavy cream until well-combined. Transfer to a wire rack, let cool, and spread the frosting on top. Slice and serve.

Per serving: Cal 643; Net Carbs 9.2g; Fat 46g; Protein 37g

Chocolate Crunch Bars

Ingredients for 4 servings
1 ½ cups chocolate chips
¼ cup almond butter
½ cup sugar-free maple syrup
¼ cup melted butter
2 cups mixed seeds
1 cup chopped walnuts

Directions and Total Time: approx. 5 min + chilling time

Line a baking sheet with parchment paper. In a bowl, mix chips, almond butter, maple syrup, butter, seeds, and walnuts. Spread the mixture onto the sheet and refrigerate until firm, at least 1 hour. Cut into bars and enjoy.

Per serving: Cal 713; Net Carbs 7.1g; Fat 75g; Protein 7.9g

Sticky Maple Cinnamon Cake

Ingredients for 4 servings
9 tbsp butter, melted and cooled
½ cup sugar-free maple syrup + extra for topping
6 eggs
2 tsp cream cheese, softened
1 tsp vanilla extract
2 tbsp heavy cream
¼ cup almond flour
1 ½ tsp baking powder
1 tsp cinnamon powder
½ tsp salt

Directions and Total Time: approx. 30 minutes

Preheat oven to 400 F; grease a cake pan with melted butter. In a bowl, beat the eggs, butter, cream cheese, vanilla, heavy cream, and maple syrup until smooth. In another bowl, mix almond flour, baking powder, cinnamon, and salt. Combine both mixtures until smooth and pour the batter into the cake pan. Bake for 25 minutes or until a toothpick inserted comes out clean. Transfer the cake to a wire rack to cool and drizzle with maple syrup.

Per serving: Cal 362; Net Carbs 1.5g; Fat 35g; Protein 8.9g

Almond Square Cookies

Ingredients for 4 servings
2 ¼ cups almond flour
1 tsp baking powder
½ tsp salt
1 cup butter, softened
1 cup swerve sugar
1 large egg
¾ tsp almond extract

Directions and Total Time: approx. 30 minutes

Preheat oven to 400 F; line a baking sheet with parchment paper. In a bowl, mix almond flour, baking powder, and salt. In another bowl, mix butter, swerve, egg, and almond extract until well smooth. Combine both mixtures until smooth dough forms. Lay a parchment paper on a flat surface, place the dough and cover with another parchment paper. Using a rolling pin, flatten it into ½-inch thickness and cut it into squares. Arrange on the baking sheet with 1-inch intervals and bake in the oven until the edges are set and golden brown, 25 minutes.

Per serving: Cal 426; Net Carbs 0.4g; Fat 46g; Protein 1.4g

White Chocolate Chip Cookies

Ingredients for 4 servings
3 oz unsweetened white chocolate chips
½ cup unsalted butter
¾ cup xylitol
1 tsp vanilla extract
1 large egg
1 ½ cups almond flour
½ tsp baking powder
½ tsp xanthan gum
¼ tsp salt

Directions and Total Time: approx. 25 minutes
Preheat oven to 350 F; line a baking sheet with parchment paper. In a bowl and using an electric mixer, cream the butter and xylitol until light and fluffy. Add vanilla, egg, and beat until smooth. Add almond flour, baking powder, xanthan gum, salt, and whisk the mixture until smooth dough forms. Fold in chocolate chips. Roll the dough into 1 ½-inch balls and arrange on the sheet at 2-inch intervals. Bake for 12 minutes until lightly golden.

Per serving: Cal 163; Net Carbs 0.3g; Fat 16g; Protein 2.6g

Cowboy Cookies

Ingredients for 8 servings
1 cup butter, softened
1 cup swerve white sugar
1 cup swerve brown sugar
1 tbsp vanilla extract
2 large eggs
2 cups almond flour
2 tsp baking powder
1 tsp baking soda
1 tbsp cinnamon powder
1 tsp salt
1 cup sugar-free chocolate chips
1 cup peanut butter chips

2 cups golden flaxseed meal
1 ½ cups coconut flakes
2 cups chopped walnuts

Directions and Total Time: approx. 30 minutes
Preheat oven to 375 F; line a baking sheet with parchment paper. In a large bowl and using a hand mixer, cream the butter and swerve until light and fluffy. Slowly, beat in the vanilla and eggs until smooth. In a separate bowl, mix almond flour, baking powder, baking soda, cinnamon, and salt. Combine both mixtures and fold in the chocolate chips, peanut butter chips, flaxseed meal, coconut flaxes, and walnuts. Roll the dough into 1 ½-inch balls and arrange on the baking sheet at 2-inch intervals. Bake for 10 to 12 minutes, or until lightly golden.

Per serving: Cal 435; Net Carbs 4.6g; Fat 39g; Protein 16g

Danish Butter Cookies

Ingredients for 4 servings
¾ cup swerve confectioner's sugar
2 cups almond flour
½ cup butter, softened
1 large egg
1 tsp vanilla extract
3 oz dark chocolate
½ oz cocoa butter

Directions and Total Time: approx. 35 minutes
Preheat oven to 350 F; line a baking sheet with parchment paper. In a food processor, mix almond flour, swerve, and ¼ tsp salt. Add butter and process until resembling coarse breadcrumbs. Add eggs, vanilla, and process until smooth. Pour the batter into a piping bag and press mounds of the batter onto the baking sheets with 1-inch intervals. Bake for 10 to 12 minutes. Microwave dark chocolate and cocoa butter for 50 seconds, mixing at every 10-seconds interval. When the cookies are ready, transfer to a rack to cool and swirl the chocolate mixture.

Per serving: Cal 253; Net Carbs 0.4g; Fat 27.4g; Protein 2g

Dark Chocolate Cookies

Ingredients for 4 servings
1 ½ cups almond flour
½ cup cocoa powder

1 tsp baking soda
12 tbsp butter, softened
¾ cup swerve sugar
2 eggs
1 tsp vanilla extract
1 cup dark chocolate chips

Directions and Total Time: approx. 35 minutes

Preheat oven to 350 F; line a baking sheet with parchment paper. In a bowl, mix flour, cocoa powder, 1 tsp salt, and baking soda. In a separate bowl, cream the butter and swerve sugar until light and fluffy. Mix in the eggs, vanilla extract and then combine both mixtures. Fold in the chocolate chips until well distributed. Roll the dough into 1 ½-inch balls and arrange on the sheet at 2-inch intervals. Bake for 22 minutes until lightly golden.

Per serving: Cal 270; Net Carbs 6.7g; Fat 29g; Protein 6.2g

Ginger Cookies

Ingredients for 4 servings
4 tbsp coconut oil
2 tbsp sugar-free maple syrup
1 egg
2 tbsp water
2 ½ cups almond flour
1/3 cup swerve sugar
2 tsp ginger powder
1 tsp cinnamon powder
½ tsp nutmeg powder
1 tsp baking soda
¼ tsp salt

Directions and Total Time: approx. 25 minutes

Preheat oven to 350 F; line a baking sheet with parchment paper. In a bowl and using an electric mixer, mix coconut oil, maple syrup, egg, and water. In a separate bowl, mix flour, swerve, ginger, cinnamon, nutmeg, baking soda, and salt. Combine both mixtures until smooth. Roll the dough into 1 ½-inch balls and arrange on the sheet at 2-inch intervals. Bake for 15 minutes until lightly golden.

Per serving: Cal 141; Net Carbs 1.5g; Fat 15g; Protein 2g

Cream Cheese Cookies

Ingredients for 4 servings
¼ cup softened butter

2 oz softened cream cheese
1/3 cup xylitol
1 large egg
2 tsp vanilla extract
¼ tsp salt
1 tbsp sour cream
3 cups blanched almond flour

Directions and Total Time: approx. 25 minutes

Preheat oven to 350 F; line a baking sheet with parchment paper. In a bowl and using an electric mixer, whisk butter, cream cheese, and xylitol until fluffy and light in color. Beat in egg, vanilla, salt, and sour cream until smooth. Add flour and mix until smooth batter forms. With a cookie scoop, arrange 1 ½ tbsp of batter onto the sheet at 2-inch intervals. Bake for 15 minutes until lightly golden.

Per serving: Cal 177; Net Carbs 1.3g; Fat 17g; Protein 3g

Easy No-Bake Cookies

Ingredients for 4 servings
¾ cup coconut oil
¾ cup peanut butter
¼ cup cocoa powder
1 cup swerve brown sugar
1 tsp vanilla extract
1 ½ cup coconut flakes
2 tbsp hulled hemp seeds

Directions and Total Time: approx. 30 minutes

Preheat oven to 350 F; line two baking sheets with parchment paper. Add coconut oil and peanut butter to a pot. Melt the mixture over low heat until smoothly combined. Stir in cocoa powder, swerve sugar, and vanilla until smooth. Slightly increase the heat and simmer the mixture with occasional stirring until slowly boiling. Turn the heat off. Mix in coconut flakes and hemp seeds. Set the mixture aside to cool. Spoon the batter into silicone muffin cups and freeze for 15 minutes or until set. Serve.

Per serving: Cal 364; Net Carbs 5.5g; Fat 37g; Protein 5g

Keto Caramel Shortbread Cookies

Ingredients for 8 servings
¼ cup sugar-free caramel sauce
2 cups butter

1 ½ cups swerve brown sugar
3 cups almond flour
1 cup chopped dark chocolate
Sea salt flakes

Directions and Total Time: approx. 30 minutes

Preheat oven to 350 F; line a baking sheet with parchment paper. In a bowl and using an electric mixer, whisk butter, swerve, and caramel sauce. Mix in flour and chocolate until well combined. Using a scoop, arrange 1 ½ tbsp of the batter onto the sheet at 2-inch intervals and sprinkle salt flakes on top. Bake for 15 minutes until lightly golden.

Per serving: Cal 410; Net Carbs 0.6g; Fat 43g; Protein 5g

Pumpkin Cookies

Ingredients for 4 servings
3 eggs
3 tbsp butter softened
1 oz cream cheese softened
½ cup pumpkin puree
2 tsp pumpkin pie spice
9 tbsp sugar-free maple syrup
1 tsp vanilla extract
¼ tsp salt
¾ tsp baking powder
8 tbsp coconut flour

Directions and Total Time: approx. 30 minutes

Preheat oven to 370 F; line a baking sheet with parchment paper. In a food processor, add eggs and butter and blend until smooth. Top with cream cheese, pumpkin puree, pie spice, maple syrup, and vanilla. Process until smooth. Pour in salt, baking powder, flour, and combine the mixture until smooth thick batter forms. Using a cookie scoop, arrange 1 ½ tbsp of the batter onto the sheet at 2-inch intervals. Refrigerate the dough for 30 minutes and then bake for 23 minutes or until set and lightly golden.

Per serving: Cal 238; Net Carbs 4.2g; Fat 22g; Protein 9.3g

Lemon Glazed Cookies

Ingredients for 4 servings
For the lemon cookies:
¼ cup cream cheese
¼ cup unsalted butter
5 tbsp xylitol

1 egg
2 cups almond flour
1 lemon, zested and juiced
For the lemon glaze:
¼ cup swerve sugar
1 ½ tbsp lemon juice

Directions and Total Time: approx. 40 min + chilling time

Preheat oven to 375 F; line a baking sheet with parchment paper. In a food processor, beat cream cheese, butter, xylitol, and egg until smooth. Pour in almond flour, lemon zest and lemon juice. Miw well until smooth batter forms. With a scoop, arrange 1 ½ tbsp of the batter onto the sheets at 2-inch intervals. Bake for 30 minutes or until set and lightly golden. Transfer them to a wire rack to cool. In a bowl, whisk swerve, lemon juice, and lemon zest until well combined. Drizzle over the cookies and serve.

Per serving: Cal 145; Net Carbs 4.4g; Fat 13g; Protein 3.2g

Magic Bars

Ingredients for 4 servings
1 ½ cups almond flour
2 tbsp erythritol
3 tbsp melted coconut oil
¼ tsp salt
¾ cup mini chocolate chips
¼ cup chopped almonds
2/3 cup coconut flakes
1 ¼ cups coconut cream

Directions and Total Time: approx. 50 minutes

Preheat oven to 350 F; line a baking sheet with parchment paper. In a bowl, mix flour, erythritol, oil, and salt. Spread and press the mixture onto the baking sheet. Scatter chocolate chips, almonds, and coconut flakes on top. Drizzle coconut cream on top. Bake for 33 minutes or until compacted. Let cool for 15 minutes and cut into bars.

Per serving: Cal 436; Net Carbs 7.8g; Fat 44.2g; Protein 4g

Buckeye Fat Bomb Bars

Ingredients for 4 servings
1 ¼ cups peanut butter
½ cup butter, melted
½ cup almond flour
1 tsp vanilla extract

1 tsp swerve sugar
6 oz dark chocolate chips
6 oz heavy cream
1/8 tsp salt

Directions and Total Time: approx. 5 min + chilling time

Line a baking sheet with parchment paper. In a food processor, mix peanut butter, butter, flour, vanilla, and swerve. Spread onto the sheet and refrigerate to firm, 30 minutes. Add the chips, heavy cream and salt to a pot and melt over low heat until bubbles form around the edges. Turn the heat off and let cool for 5 minutes. Whisk until smooth and refrigerate for 1 hour. Cut into bars and serve.

Per serving: Cal 412; Net Carbs 5.5g; Fat 38g; Protein 10g

Samoa Cookie Bars

Ingredients for 4 servings
For the crust:
1 ¼ cups almond flour
¼ cup erythritol
¼ tsp salt
¼ cup butter, melted
For the filling and drizzle:
4 oz dark chocolate
2 tbsp butter
For the coconut caramel topping:
1 ½ cups shredded coconut
3 tbsp butter
¼ cup swerve brown sugar
¾ cup heavy whipping cream
½ tsp vanilla extract
¼ tsp salt

Directions and Total Time: approx. 1 hour 40 minutes

For the crust:
Preheat oven to 325 F; line a baking sheet with parchment paper. In a bowl, mix flour, erythritol, and salt. Stir in melted butter until well-combined. Spread the mixture onto the sheet and bake for 18 minutes until golden brown. Allow complete cooling while you make the filling.

For the filling and drizzle:
In a microwave-safe bowl, melt chocolate and butter for 30 to 40 seconds, mixing the at 10-seconds interval or until fully melted. Spread two-thirds of the mixture over the cooled crust and reserve the rest. Set aside.

For the coconut filling:

Toast shredded coconut in a skillet over medium heat until golden brown; set aside. Add butter and swerve to a pot and melt over low heat until starting to boiling and golden, 3 minutes. Turn the heat off. Whisk in heavy cream, vanilla, and salt until smoothly combined. Pour the mixture all over and refrigerate for 1 hour. Stir in toasted coconut. Spread the mixture over the chocolate-covered crust; let cool completely, and cut into squares. Reheat remaining chocolate mixture and drizzle over the bars.

Per serving: Cal 313; Net Carbs 5.5g; Fat 23g; Protein 3g

Peanut Butter Bars

Ingredients for 8 servings
For the peanut butter filling:
½ cup smooth peanut butter
4 tbsp melted butter
4 tbsp swerve sugar
5 tbsp almond flour
1 tsp vanilla extract
For the coating:
2 ½ oz chopped dark chocolate
A handful peanuts, chopped

Directions and Total Time: approx. 5 min + chilling time

Line a baking sheet with parchment paper. In a bowl, mix peanut butter, butter, swerve, flour, and vanilla. Spread the mixture onto the sheet and top with chocolate and peanuts. Refrigerate until firm, for 1 hour. Cut into bars and enjoy.

Per serving: Cal 155; Net Carbs 5.2g; Fat 12g; Protein 4.9g

All Nuts Bars

Ingredients for 12 servings
1 ½ cups dark chocolate chips
1 cup cashew butter
½ cup sugar-free maple syrup
¼ cup coconut oil
3 cups mixed nuts, chopped

Directions and Total Time: approx. 5 min + chilling time

Line a baking sheet with parchment paper. In a bowl, mix chips, cashew butter, maple syrup, coconut oil, seeds, and nuts. Spread the mixture onto the sheet and refrigerate until firm, at least 1 hour. Cut into bars and enjoy.

Per serving: Cal 323; Net Carbs 3.9g; Fat 29g; Protein 3g

Chocolate Chip Bar

Ingredients for 4 servings
8 oz cream cheese, softened
½ cup butter, softened
2 cups xylitol
5 eggs
2 tsp vanilla extract
1 cup almond flour
1/3 cup of coconut flour
¼ tsp salt
1 ½ tsp baking powder
½ tsp xanthan gum
1 cup dark chocolate chips
1 cup chopped walnuts

Directions and Total Time: approx. 40 minutes
Preheat oven to 350 F; line a baking sheet with parchment paper. In a food processor, blitz cream cheese, butter, and xylitol. Add eggs, vanilla, and mix until smooth. Pour in the flours, salt, baking powder, and xanthan gum; process until smooth. Fold in the chocolate chips and walnuts. Spread the mixture onto the sheet and bake for 30 to 35 minutes or until set and light golden brown. Remove from the oven, let cool completely, and cut into bars.

Per serving: Cal 443; Net Carbs 4.8g; Fat 36g; Protein 22g

Shortbread Lemon Bar

Ingredients for 4 servings
For the shortbread crust:
2 ½ cups almond flour
¼ cup sugar-free maple syrup
¼ tsp salt
¼ cup melted butter
1 large egg
½ tsp vanilla extract
For the lemon filling:
1/3 cup sugar-free maple syrup
¼ cup blanched almond flour
4 large eggs
¾ cup lemon juice

Directions and Total Time: approx. 40 minutes
Preheat oven to 325 F; line a baking sheet with parchment paper. In a bowl, whisk flour, maple syrup, salt, butter, egg, and vanilla

extract until smooth. Spread the mixture onto the sheet and bake for 13 minutes. Allow complete cooling. In a bowl, whisk maple syrup, flour, eggs, and lemon juice until smooth. Spread the mixture over the crust and bake further for 18 minutes or until the filling sets. Remove, let chill for 2 hours and slicing to serve.

Per serving: Cal 139; Net Carbs 4.3g; Fat 13g; Protein 2g

Cinnamon Macadamia Bars

Ingredients for 4 servings
1 ½ cups macadamia nuts
½ cup pepitas
1 cup coconut flakes
1 tsp cinnamon powder
½ cup smooth peanut butter
¼ cup coconut oil, solidified
2 tsp vanilla bean paste

Directions and Total Time: approx. 5 min + chilling time
Line a baking sheet with parchment paper. In a bowl, mix macadamia nuts, pepitas, coconut flakes, cinnamon powder, peanut butter, coconut oil, and vanilla bean paste. Spread the mixture onto the sheet and refrigerate until firm, at least 1 hour. Cut into bars and serve.

Per serving: Cal 417; Net Carbs 5g; Fat 37g; Protein 8g

Cranberry Cheesecake Bars

Ingredients for 4 servings
For the crust:
2 tbsp swerve confectioner's sweetener
8 tbsp melted butter
1 ¼ cups almond flour
For the cheesecake layer:
1/3 cup swerve confectioner's sweetener
8 oz cream cheese
1 egg yolk
2 tsp pure vanilla extract
For the cranberry layer:
1 cup unsweetened cranberry sauce

Directions and Total Time: approx. 40 min + chilling time
Preheat oven to 350 F; line a baking sheet with parchment paper. In a bowl, mix butter, flour and sugar. Spread and press the mixture onto the baking sheet and bake for 13 minutes or until golden brown. Whisk cream

cheese, egg yolk, swerve sugar, and vanilla in a bowl using an electric hand mixer until smooth. Spread the mixture on the crust when ready. Bake further for 15 minutes or until the filling sets. Remove from the oven, spread cranberry sauce on top and refrigerate for 1 hour. Cut into bars and serve.
Per serving: Cal 497; Net Carbs 2.5g; Fat 5.2g; Protein 5g

Avocado Custard

Ingredients for 4 servings
½ cup water
2 tsp agar agar powder
3 soft avocados
½ cup heavy cream
½ lime, juiced
Salt and black pepper to taste
Directions and Total Time: approx. 10 min + chilling time
Pour ¼ cup of water in a bowl and sprinkle agar agar powder on top; set aside to dissolve. Core, peel avocados and add the flesh to a food processor. Top with heavy cream, lime juice, salt, and pepper. Process until smooth and pour in agar agar liquid. Blend further until smooth. Divide the mixture between 4 ramekins and chill overnight.
Per serving: Cal 299; Net Carbs 7.9g; Fat 27g; Protein 3g

Minty Coconut Bars

Ingredients for 4 servings
3 cups shredded coconut flakes
1 cup melted coconut oil
1 tsp mint extract
¼ cup sugar-free maple syrup
Directions and Total Time: approx. 5 min + chilling time
Line loaf pan with parchment paper and set aside. In a bowl, mix coconut flakes, coconut oil, mint, and maple syrup until a thick batter forms. Pour the mixture into the loaf pan and press to fit. Refrigerate for 2 hours or until hardened. Remove from the fridge, cut into bars and serve.
Per serving: Cal 366; Net Carbs 4.3g; Fat 36g; Protein 2g

Keto Snickerdoodle Muffins

Ingredients for 4 servings
For the muffin batter:

2 ½ cups almond flour
½ cup swerve sugar
2 tsp baking powder
1 tsp cinnamon powder
3 large eggs
1/3 cup butter, melted
1/3 cup almond milk
½ cup sour cream
1 tsp vanilla extract
For the topping:
1 tbsp swerve confectioner's sugar
¼ tsp cinnamon powder
Directions and Total Time: approx. 35 minutes
Preheat oven to 350 F; line a 12-cup muffin pan with paper liners. In a bowl, mix almond flour, swerve, baking powder, and cinnamon. In bowl, whisk eggs, butter, milk, sour cream, and vanilla extract. Combine both mixture and fill into the muffin cups, two-thirds way up. For the topping, mix swerve sugar and cinnamon in a bowl and sprinkle the batter. Bake the muffins for 25 minutes or until dark golden brown on top and a toothpick inserted into the muffins comes out clean. Let cool and serve.
Per serving: Cal 221; Net Carbs 3.3g; Fat 17.6g; Protein 7g

Almond Biscuits

Ingredients for 4 servings
¾ cup grated Pecorino Romano cheese
2 ½ cups almond flour
2 tsp baking powder
2 eggs beaten
3 tbsp almond butter
1 tsp vanilla extract
A handful almonds, chopped
Directions and Total Time: approx. 30 minutes
Preheat oven to 350 F; line a baking sheet with parchment paper. In a bowl, mix flour, baking powder, and eggs until smooth. Whisk in almond butter, cheese, and vanilla until well combined. Fold in the almonds until well distributed.Mold 12 balls out of the mixture and arrange on the baking sheet at 2-inch intervals. Bake for 25 minutes or until golden brown. Remove, let cool and serve immediately.
Per serving: Cal 196; Net Carbs 3.1g; Fat 16g; Protein 8.4g

Pillowy Chocolate Donuts

Ingredients for 4 servings
For the donut:
2/3 cup almond flour
3 tbsp coconut flour
1 tbsp flaxseed meal
1 tsp arrowroot starch
1/3 cup water
3 tbsp melted butter
3 tbsp xylitol
¼ tsp salt
3 eggs lightly beaten
1 tsp vanilla extract
1 tsp baking powder
For the chocolate glaze:
¼ cup swerve sugar
2 tbsp cocoa powder
1 tbsp melted butter
1 tsp vanilla extract
2 tbsp coconut milk

Directions and Total Time: approx. 25 minutes
Preheat oven to 350 F; lightly grease an 8-cup donut pan with cooking spray; set aside. In a bowl, mix almond and coconut flours, flaxseed meal, and arrowroot starch. One after another, mix smoothly the water, butter, xylitol, salt, eggs, vanilla, and baking powder. Pour the batter into the donut cups and bake for 18 minutes or until set. Remove from the oven, flip the donut onto a wire rack and let cool.
In a bowl, whisk swerve sugar, cocoa powder, butter, vanilla extract, and coconut milk until smooth. Drizzle the chocolate glaze over the donut and serve.
Per serving: Cal 335; Net Carbs 5.4g; Fat 23g; Protein 24g

Pancake Muffins

Ingredients for 4 servings
½ cup coconut flour
½ cup erythritol
1 ½ tsp baking powder
2 tbsp butter, melted
1 ½ tsp vanilla extract
6 eggs

Directions and Total Time: approx. 35 minutes
Preheat oven to 350 F and line a 12-cup muffin pan with paper liners. In a food processor, blend coconut flour, erythritol, baking powder, butter, vanilla extract, and eggs until smooth. Pour the batter into the muffin cups two-thirds way up and bake for 25 minutes or until a toothpick inserted into the muffins comes out clean. Remove t from the oven, let cool and serve immediately.
Per serving: Cal 156; Net Carbs 1.8g; Fat 12g; Protein 8.6g

Strawberry Scones

Ingredients for 4 servings
1 cup blanched almond flour
¼ cup coconut flour
3 tbsp swerve sugar
½ tsp baking powder
¼ tsp salt
¼ cup almond milk
2 tbsp coconut oil
1 large egg
1 tsp vanilla extract
½ cup chopped strawberries
For the glaze:
1 tsp swerve confectioner's sugar
1 tbsp coconut oil
2 tbsp mashed strawberries

Directions and Total Time: approx. 25 minutes
Preheat oven to 350 F; line a baking sheet with parchment paper. In a bowl, mix almond and coconut flours, swerve, baking powder, and salt. In another bowl, whisk milk, coconut oil, egg, and vanilla. Combine both mixtures and fold in the strawberries. Pour and spread the mixture on the baking sheet. Cut into 8 wedges like a pizza and place the baking sheet in the oven. Bake for 20 minutes or until set and golden brown. Remove and let cool. In a bowl, whisk swerve, oil, and strawberries until smoothly combined. Swirl the glaze over the scones to serve.
Per serving: Cal 121; Net Carbs 2.7g; Fat 11g; Protein 2g

APPENDIX : RECIPES INDEX

Cauliflower Soup with Kielbasa 27
Celery & Beef Stuffed Mushrooms 68
Celery Braised Pork Shanks in Wine Sauce 87
Celery Chicken Sausage Frittata 59
Charred Asparagus with Creamy Sauce 114
Cheddar and Halloumi Sticks 140
Cheddar Bacon & Celeriac Bake 130
Cheddar Biscuits 13
Cheddar Pork Burrito Bowl 81
Cheddar Taco Chicken Bake 56
Cheddar Zucchini & Beef Mugs 70
Cheese & Beef Avocado Boats 67
Cheese & Beef Bake 74
Cheese & Garlic Crackers 133
Cheese Quesadillas with Fruit Salad 117
Cheesy Bacon & Eggplant Gratin 128
Cheesy Baked Trout with Zucchini 98
Cheesy Beef-Asparagus Shirataki Mix 72
Cheesy Bell Pepper Pizza 112
Cheesy Broccoli Nachos with Salsa 112
Cheesy Cauliflower Casserole 43
Cheesy Chicken Tenders 49
Cheesy Chicken with Cauliflower Steaks 50
Cheesy Chicken Wraps 133
Cheesy Mushrooms & Bacon Lettuce Rolls 82
Cheesy Pork Quiche 78
Cheesy Pork Rind Bread 132
Cheesy Roasted Vegetable Spaghetti 110
Cheesy Sausages in Creamy Onion Sauce 87
Cheesy Tomato Beef Tart 66
Cheesy Turkey Sausage Egg Cups 64
Cherry Tomato Salad with Chorizo 20
Chia Pudding with Blackberries 18
Chicken Bake with Onion & Parsnip 55
Chicken Breasts with Jarred Pickle Juice 60
Chicken Ham with Mini Bell Peppers 130
Chicken Stew with Spinach 29
Chicken with Tomato and Zucchini 58
Chicken Wraps in Bacon with Spinach 56
Chili Baked Zucchini Sticks with Aioli 131
Chili Beef Stew with Cauliflower Grits 30
Chili Broccoli & Pancetta Roast 128
Chili Pulled Chicken with Avocado 53
Chili Turnip Fries 127
Chili Vegetables & Pasta Bake 108
Chimichurri Shrimp 98
Chives & Green Beans Ham Rolls 129
Choco-Coffee Cake 147
Chocolate Cake with Raspberry Frosting 149
Chocolate Chip Bar 155
Chocolate Crunch Bars 150
Chocolate Mocha Ice Bombs 145
Chocolate Mug Cakes 147
Chocolate Peppermint Mousse 122
Chocolate Snowball Cookies 149
Chorizo in Cabbage Sauce with Pine Nuts 76
Chorizo Smoky Pizza 94
Chorizo, Goat Cheese & Eggs 16
Cinnamon Faux Rice Pudding 17
Cinnamon Macadamia Bars 155

Classic Beef Ragu with Veggie Pasta 72
Classic Swedish Coconut Meatballs 73
Classic Zucchini Cake 149
Coconut Butter Ice Cream 145
Coconut Cake 148
Coconut Cake with Raspberries 142
Coconut Chocolate Fudge 125
Coconut Crab Cakes 103
Coconut Turkey Chili 28
Coffee Balls 147
Coffee-Flavored Muffins 16
Colby Cauliflower Soup with Pancetta Chips 28
Cowboy Cookies 151
Crab Cakes 101
Cranberry Cheesecake Bars 155
Cranberry Coconut Parfait 126
Cranberry Glazed Chicken with Onions 62
Cream Cheese & Caramelized Onion Dip 25
Cream Cheese & Turkey Tortilla Rolls 61
Cream Cheese Cookies 152
Creamy Brussels Sprouts Bake 43
Creamy Chicken Thighs 60
Creamy Chicken with Broccoli & Prosciutto 55
Creamy Ham & Parsnip Puree 130
Creamy Mustard Chicken with Shirataki 55
Creamy Salmon with Lemon 103
Creamy Sesame Bread 11
Creamy Strawberry Mousse 143
Creamy Turkey & Broccoli Bake 64
Crispy & Cheesy Salami 134
Crispy Baked Cheese Asparagus 130
Crispy Pancetta & Butternut Squash Roast 131
Crunchy Rutabaga Puffs 131
Cucumber Salsa Topped Turkey Patties 62
Cucumber-Turkey Canapes 61
Cumin Pork Chops 97
Curried Homemade Shrimp 99
Curried Tofu with Buttery Cabbage 40
Curry Cauli Rice with Mushrooms 48

D

Danish Butter Cookies 151
Dark Chocolate Cake 122
Dark Chocolate Cookies 151
Dark Chocolate Fudge 123
Delicious Pancetta Strawberries 128
Delicious Veggies & Chicken Casserole 51
Dijon Pork Loin Roast 82

E

Easy Bacon & Cheese Balls 127
Easy Beef Burger Bake 65
Easy Cheesy Green Pizza 119
Easy Coconut Cocktail Crab Balls 99
Easy No-Bake Cookies 152
Effortless Chicken Chili 28
Egg Cauli Fried Rice with Grilled Cheese 116
Eggplant & Goat Cheese Pizza 114
Eggplant Chicken Gratin With Swiss Cheese 58
Eggplant Fries with Chili Aioli & Beet Salad 42
Enchilada Vegetarian Pasta 110

F

Fake Mushroom Risotto 113
Feta Cheese Choux Buns 26
Fish & Cauliflower Parmesan Gratin 105
Fish Fritters 106
Flan with Whipped Cream 144
Flavorful Chipotle-Coffee Pork Chops 84
Florentine-Style Pizza with Bacon 81
Fried Artichoke Hearts 134
Fried Mac & Cheese 109

G

Garam Masala Traybake 118
Garlic & Parsley Shrimp 102
Garlic-Lime Shrimp Pasta 101
Ginger Cookies 152
Gingerbread Cheesecake 148
Goat Cheese Stuffed Peppers 133
Golden Pork Chops with Mushrooms 96
Grandma's Cauliflower Salad with Peanuts 22
Granny Smith Apple Tart 144
Greek Salad 21
Greek-Style Pizza 40
Greek-Style Pork Packets with Halloumi 88
Green Bean & Mozzarella Roast with Bacon 129
Green Bean Creamy Pork with Fettuccine 92
Grilled BBQ Pork Chops 93
Grilled Chicken Kebabs with Curry & Yogurt 58
Grilled Garlic Chicken with Cauliflower 62
Grilled Zucchini with Spinach Avocado Pesto 39
Ground Pork & Scrambled Eggs with Cabbage 83
Gruyere & Ham Waffle Sandwiches 135
Gruyere Beef Burgers with Sweet Onion 75
Gruyere Breakfast Soufflés 15

H

Haddock in Garlic Butter Sauce 102
Hawaiian Pork Loco Moco 76
Hazelnut & Cheese Stuffed Zucchinis 34
Hazelnut Cod Fillets 104
Hazelnut-Crusted Salmon 105
Heart-Shaped Red Velvet Cakes 150
Hemp Seed Zucchini Chips 140
Herbed Bolognese Sauce 73
Herby Chicken Meatloaf 58
Herby Chicken Stew 32
Herby Mushroom Pizza 112
Herby Mushrooms Stroganoff 34
Homemade Pasta with Meatballs 69
Homemade Philly Cheesesteak in Omelet 68
Hot Chicken Meatball Tray 64
Hot Pork Chops with Satay Sauce 89
Hot Pork Stir-Fry with Walnuts 84
Hot Tex-Mex Pork Casserole 77

I

Indian Pork Masala 87
Italian Chicken-Basil Pizza 61
Italian Pork with Capers 79

J

Jalapeño Nacho Wings 127

Jerk Chicken Drumsticks 60
Jerk Pork Pot Roast 96
Juicy Pork Chops with Parmesan 85

K

Kale & Mushroom Pierogis 38
Kentucky Cauliflower with Mashed Parsnips 47
Keto Brownies 120
Keto Caramel Cake 147
Keto Caramel Shortbread Cookies 152
Keto Deviled Eggs 135
Keto Snickerdoodle Muffins 156
Key Lime Truffles 123
Korean Braised Beef with Kelp Noodles 68

L

Lemon Glazed Cookies 153
Lemon Muffins 18
Lemon Panna Cotta 142
Lemon Sponge Cake with Cream 123
Lemony Greek Pork Tenderloin 84
Lemon-Yogurt Mousse 144
Lime Avocado Ice Cream 121
Louisiana Chicken Fettuccine 57
Lovely Pulled Chicken Egg Bites 54

M

Magic Bars 153
Maple Jalapeño Beef Plate 66
Maple Lemon Cake 144
Maple Pork with Spaghetti Squash 94
Maple Scallion Pork Bites 96
Margherita Pizza with Broccoli Crust 34
Mascarpone and Kale Asian Casserole 117
Mascarpone Ice Bombs 147
Mashed Broccoli with Roasted Garlic 137
Matcha Fat Bombs 146
Meatless Florentine Pizza 34
Mediterranean Deviled Eggs 138
Mediterranean Pasta 114
Mediterranean Roasted Turnip Bites 24
Mediterranean Tilapia 100
Mini Ricotta Cakes 24
Mint Chocolate Cheesecake 122
Mint Ice Cream 114
Minty Coconut Bars 156
Mixed Berry Yogurt Ice Pops 120
Mixed Seed Crackers 139
Mom's Cheesy Pizza 119
Mom's Walnut Cookies 146
Monterey Jack & Sausage-Pepper Pizza 94
Morning Beef Bowl 67
Mozzarella Baked Pork 85
Mushroom & Broccoli Pizza 117
Mushroom & Pork Casserole 86
Mushroom Broccoli Faux Risotto 138
Mushroom Chicken Cheeseburgers 57
Mushroom Lettuce Wraps 41
Mushroom Pizza Bowls with Avocado 37
Mushroom Pork Meatballs with Parsnips 85
Mushroom White Pizza 118
Mustard Beef Collard Rolls 69

Mustard Chicken Cordon Blue Casserole 52

N

No Bake Cheesy Walnut Balls 136
No-Bake & Egg Balls 136
No-Bread Avocado Sandwich 11
Nori Shrimp Rolls 105
Nutty Sea Bass 100

O

Olive & Pesto Beef Casserole with Goat Cheese 66
One-Pot Spicy Brussel Sprouts with Carrots 115
One-Skillet Green Pasta 110
Onion Rings & Kale Dip 137

P

Paleo Coconut Flour Chicken Nuggets 59
Pancake Muffins 157
Pancetta & Egg Plate with Cherry Tomatoes 76
Paprika & Dill Deviled Eggs 133
Paprika Chicken & Bacon Stew 31
Paprika Roasted Nuts 138
Parmesan & Pimiento Pork Meatballs 78
Parmesan Chicken & Broccoli Casserole 49
Parmesan Green Bean Crisps 132
Parmesan Meatballs 46
Parmesan Pork Stuffed Mushrooms 81
Parmesan Pork with Green Pasta 93
Parsley Beef Carbonara 71
Parsley Chicken & Cauliflower Stir-Fry 51
Parsley Sausage Stew 32
Parsley Steak Bites with Shirataki Fettucine 70
Parsnip & Bacon Chicken Bake 51
Party Smoked Salmon Balls 99
Pasta & Cheese Pulled Pork 91
Peanut Butter & Chocolate Ice Cream Bars 143
Peanut Butter Bars 154
Pecan Cookies 17
Pecorino Romano Kohlrabi with Sausage 93
Pepperoni Fat Head Pizza 46
Pesto Caprese Salad Stacks with Anchovies 20
Pesto Mushroom Pinwheels 140
Pesto Tofu Zoodles 37
Pillowy Chocolate Donuts 157
Pistachio Heart Biscuits 121
Pomodoro Zoodles with Sardines 100
Pork & Bacon Parcels 88
Pork & Pecan in Camembert Bake 81
Pork & Pumpkin Stew with Peanuts 31
Pork Bake with Cottage Cheese & Olives 78
Pork Belly with Creamy Coconut Kale 84
Pork Medallions with & Morels 85
Pork Medallions with Pancetta 96
Pork Sausage Omelet with Mushrooms 76
Prosciutto Appetizer with Blackberries 137
Provolone & Prosciutto Chicken Wraps 134
Provolone Chicken Spinach Bake 61
Pulled Pork Tenderloin with Avocado 95
Pumpkin Cookies 153
Pumpkin Donuts 15

Q

Quick Grilled Cheddar Cheese 109
Quick Pork Lo Mein 90
Quick Protein Bars 14

R

Raspberries Turmeric Panna Cotta 122
Raspberry & Red Wine Crumble 125
Raspberry Coconut Cheesecake 143
Red Berries Fat Bombs 121
Rich Veggie Pasta Primavera 111
Roasted Asparagus with Goat Cheese 22
Roasted Bell Pepper Salad with Olives 21
Roasted Broccoli & Cauliflower Steaks 135
Roasted Butternut Squash with Chimichurri 45
Roasted Chicken with Yogurt Scallions Sauce 50
Roasted Chorizo & Mixed Greens 39
Roasted Ham with Radishes 129
Rosemary Beef Meatza 67
Rosemary Cheese Chips with Guacamole 132
Rosemary Turkey Brussels Sprouts Cakes 60
Rustic Lamb Stew with Root Veggies 30

S

Saffron & Cardamom Coconut Bars 145
Saffron Coconut Bars 146
Sage Beef Meatloaf with Pecans 65
Salami & Cheddar Skewers 129
Salami Cauliflower Pizza 36
Salisbury Steak 71
Salmon Caesar Salad with Poached Eggs 106
Samoa Cookie Bars 154
Saucy Salmon in Tarragon Sauce 101
Saucy Thai Pork Medallions 82
Sautéed Thai Beef Shirataki 70
Savory Cheesy Chicken 50
Savory Chicken Wings with Chimichurri 53
Savory Gruyere & Bacon Cake 22
Savory Jalapeño Pork Meatballs 88
Savory Lime Fried Artichokes 132
Savory Pan-Fried Cauliflower & Bacon 129
Savory Pork Tacos 80
Scallion & Saffron Chicken with Pasta 54
Scottish Beef Stew 29
Seeds Breakfast Loaf 12
Seitan Cakes with Broccoli Mash 40
Seitan Cauliflower Gratin 46
Sesame Cauliflower Dip 35
Sesame Pork Meatballs 83
Shakshuka 15
Shallot Mussel with Shirataki 104
Shitake Butter Steak 74
Shortbread Lemon Bar 155
Simple Stuffed Eggs with Mayonnaise 132
Smoked Bacon & Poached Egg Cups 136
Smoked Chicken Tart with Baby Kale 49
Smoked Paprika Grilled Ribs 74
Smoked Paprika-Coconut Tenderloin 86
Smoked Tempeh with Broccoli Fritters 35
South-American Shrimp Stew 33
Soy Chorizo Stuffed Cabbage Rolls 139
Spaghetti Bolognese with Tofu 107

Spanish Paella "Keto-Style" 35
Speedy Beef Carpaccio 22
Speedy Blueberry Sorbet 142
Speedy Custard Tart 120
Speedy Fish Tacos 99
Spicy Cheese with Tofu Balls 44
Spicy Grilled Pork Spareribs 95
Spicy Pistachio Dip 137
Spicy Smoked Mackerel Cakes 103
Spicy Veggie Steaks with Green Salad 39
Spinach Cheesy Puff Balls 134
Spinach Chips with Guacamole Hummus 138
Spinach-Olive Pizza 113
Spiralized Zucchini with Chicken & Pine Nuts 54
Sticky Maple Cinnamon Cake 150
Strawberry & Ricotta Parfait 142
Strawberry Blackberry Pie 125
Strawberry Chocolate Mousse 144
Strawberry Faux Oats 116
Strawberry Scones 157
Stuffed Avocado with Yogurt & Crabmeat 104
Stuffed Peppers with Chicken & Broccoli 57
Stuffed Portobello Mushrooms 113
Sweet & Spicy Brussel Sprout Stir-Fry 44
Sweet Mustard Mini Sausages 128
Sweet Onion & Goat Cheese Pizza 115
Sweet Pork Chops with Brie Cheese 83
Sweet Pork Chops with Hoisin Sauce 89
Sweet Tahini Twists 25
Swiss Pork Patties with Salad 96

T

Tangy Cabbage & Beef Bowl with Creamy Blue Cheese 65
Tangy Lemon Pork Steaks with Mushrooms 86
Tangy Nutty Brussel Sprout Salad 20
Tasty Chicken Pot Pie with Vegetables 53
Tasty Curried Chicken Meatballs 63
Tasty Keto Snickerdoodles 141
Tasty Pork Chops with Cauliflower Steaks 79
Tasty Sambal Pork Noodles 90
Tasty Shrimp in Creamy Butter Sauce 98
Tempeh Coconut Curry Bake 43
Tempeh Garam Masala Bake 42
Tempeh Taco Cups 111
Tender Pork Chops with Basil & Beet Greens 83
Thyme and Collard Green Waffles 113
Thyme Pork Roast with Brussels Sprouts 77
Thyme Tomato Soup 27
Thyme Zucchini & Chicken Chunks Skillet 50
Toast Sticks with Yogurt Berry Bowls 14
Tofu & Bok Choy Stir-Fry 36
Tofu & Spinach Lasagna with Red Sauce 36
Tofu Eggplant Pizza 45
Tofu Jalapeño Peppers 25
Tofu Loaf with Walnuts 36

Tofu Meatballs with Cauli Mash 107
Tofu Nuggets with Cilantro Dip 116
Tofu Pops 23
Tofu Radish Bowls 117
Tofu Stuffed Peppers 139
Tomato & Mozzarella Caprese Bake 115
Tomato Artichoke Pizza 45
Tomato Basil Stuffed Chicken Breasts 61
Tomato Soup with Parmesan Croutons 27
Traditional Salmon Panzanella 102
Tuna & Zucchini Traybake 102
Tuna Salad Pickle Boats 100
Tuna Stuffed Avocado 100
Tuna Topped Pickles 135
Turkey Bolognese Veggie Pasta 62
Turkey Stew with Tomatillo Salsa 31
Turkey with Avocado Sauce 63
Turnip Pork Pie 89
Tuscan Pork Tenderloin with Cauli Rice 87

U

Ultra Flaxy Cookies 15

V

Vanilla & Blackberries Sherbet 142
Vanilla Berry Mug Cakes 148
Vanilla Buttermilk Pancakes 13
Veal Chops with Raspberry Sauce 37
Veal Stew 30
Vegan BBQ Tofu Kabobs with Green Dip 115
Vegan Cheesecake with Blueberries 121
Vegan Cordon Bleu Casserole 46
Vegan Olive and Avocado Zoodles 110
Vegetable Stew 29
Vegetarian Ketogenic Burgers 113

W

Walnut Chocolate Squares 118
Walnut Stuffed Mushrooms 47
Warm Mushroom & Yellow Pepper Salad 23
White Chocolate Chip Cookies 151
White Egg Tex Mex Pizza 108
White Pizza with Mixed Mushrooms 45
White Wine Salmon Shirataki Fettucine 103
Wine Shrimp Scampi Pizza 104
Wrapped Halloumi in Bacon 127

Y

Yellow Squash Duck Breast Stew 32
Yogurt Strawberry Pie with Basil 18
Yummy Chicken Squash Lasagna 52
Yummy Spareribs in Béarnaise Sauce 80

Z

Zoodle Bolognese 43
Zucchini & Dill Bowls with Goat-Feta Cheese 21
Zucchini & Tomato Pork Omelet 79
Zucchini Boats with Vegan Cheese 44
Zucchini Cake Slices 124
Zucchini Muffins 17
Zucchini-Cranberry Cake Squares 116

CPSIA information can be obtained
at www.ICGtesting.com
Printed in the USA
BVHW052106211221
624591BV00003B/631